A TEXT BOOK OF

COMPUTER GRAPHICS

For

Semester - II

SECOND YEAR DEGREE COURSE IN COMPUTER ENGINEERING

As Per New Revised Syllabus of
North Maharashtra University, Jalgaon,
June 2013-2014

Mrs. PINKY JAIN
B.E. (Comp.)
Eminent and Experience Professor
Computer Engineering,
Pune.

N3100

COMPUTER GRAPHICS

ISBN 978-93-83971-05-3

First Edition : January 2014

© : Author

The text of this publication, or any part thereof, should not be reproduced or transmitted in any form or stored in any computer storage system or device for distribution including photocopy, recording, taping or information retrieval system or reproduced on any disc, tape, perforated media or other information storage device etc., without the written permission of Authors with whom the rights are reserved. Breach of this condition is liable for legal action.

Every effort has been made to avoid errors or omissions in this publication. In spite of this, errors may have crept in. Any mistake, error or discrepancy so noted and shall be brought to our notice shall be taken care of in the next edition. It is notified that neither the publisher nor the authors or seller shall be responsible for any damage or loss of action to any one, of any kind, in any manner, therefrom.

Published By :
NIRALI PRAKASHAN
Abhyudaya Pragati, 1312, Shivaji Nagar,
Off J.M. Road, PUNE – 411005
Tel - (020) 25512336/37/39, Fax - (020) 25511379
Email : niralipune@pragationline.com

Printed at
Repro Knowledgecast Limited
India

DISTRIBUTION CENTRES

PUNE
Nirali Prakashan
119, Budhwar Peth, Jogeshwari Mandir Lane
Pune 411002, Maharashtra
Tel : (020) 2445 2044, 66022708
Fax : (020) 2445 1538
Email : niralilocal@pragationline.com

MUMBAI
Nirali Prakashan
385, S.V.P. Road, Rasdhara Co-op. Hsg. Society Ltd.,
Girgaum, Mumbai 400004, Maharashtra
Tel : (022) 2385 6339 / 2386 9976,
Fax : (022) 2386 9976
Email : bookorder@pragationline.com

DISTRIBUTION BRANCHES

NAGPUR
Pratibha Book Distributors
Above Maratha Mandir, Shop No. 3, First Floor,
Rani Jhanshi Square, Sitabuldi, Nagpur 440012,
Maharashtra, Tel : (0712) 254 7129

JALGAON
Nirali Prakashan
34, V. V. Golani Market, Navi Peth, Jalgaon 425001,
Maharashtra, Tel : (0257) 222 0395
Mob : 94234 91860

BENGALURU
Pragati Book House
House No. 1, Sanjeevappa Lane, Avenue Road Cross,
Opp. Rice Church, Bengaluru – 560002.
Tel : (080) 64513344, 64513355,
Mob : 9880582331, 9845021552
Email: bharatsavla@yahoo.com

KOLHAPUR
Nirali Prakashan
New Mahadvar Road,
Kedar Plaza, 1st Floor Opp. IDBI Bank
Kolhapur 416 012, Maharashtra. Mob : 9855046155

CHENNAI
Pragati Books
9/1, Montieth Road, Behind Taas Mahal, Egmore,
Chennai 600008 Tamil Nadu, Tel : (044) 6518 3535,
Mob : 94440 01782 / 98450 21552 / 98805 82331
Email : bharatsavla@yahoo.com

RETAIL OUTLETS
PUNE

Pragati Book Centre
157, Budhwar Peth, Opp. Ratan Talkies,
Pune 411002, Maharashtra
Tel : (020) 2445 8887 / 6602 2707, Fax : (020) 2445 8887

Pragati Book Centre
Amber Chamber, 28/A, Budhwar Peth,
Appa Balwant Chowk, Pune : 411002, Maharashtra,
Tel : (020) 20240335 / 66281669
Email : pbcpune@pragationline.com

Pragati Book Centre
676/B, Budhwar Peth, Opp. Jogeshwari Mandir,
Pune 411002, Maharashtra
Tel : (020) 6601 7784 / 6602 0855

PBC Book Sellers & Stationers
152, Budhwar Peth, Pune 411002, Maharashtra
Tel : (020) 2445 2254 / 6609 2463

MUMBAI
Pragati Book Corner
Indira Niwas, 111 - A, Bhavani Shankar Road, Dadar (W), Mumbai 400028, Maharashtra
Tel : (022) 2422 3526 / 6662 5254
Email : pbcmumbai@pragationline.com

Dedicated to
"Our Beloved Students"

... Author

Preface ...

It gives us immense pleasure to present this book on "Computer Graphics".

The book is written mainly for the second year students of Computer Engineering courses of North Maharashtra University for the subject **"Computer Graphics"**. It is written as per the revised syllabus of North Maharashtra University (w.e.f. 2012).

The book includes information about basic concepts of Computer Graphics. Various Concepts of the Computer Graphics are explained in detail. Mathematical treatment of various concepts are given wherever necessary. Number of Solved Problems and Exercises are included in each unit.

Unit I provides the Basic Concepts of Computer Graphics.

Unit II provides the Concepts of Polygon.

Unit III provides the Concepts of 2D and 3D Geometry.

Unit IV provides the Concepts of Windowing and Clipping.

Unit V provides the Concepts of Light, Colour and Shading.

Nirali Prakashan put the book, what we thought into reality. Our sincere thanks to Shri. Dineshbhai Furia, Shri, Jignesh Furia and Shri. M. P. Munde. The books could be completed in time, due to sincere and hard work of Nirali Prakashan's staff namely Mr. Malik Shaikh, Miss Pallavi Kumari and Miss Chaitali Takale. We thanks them all.

Valuable suggestions from our esteemed readers to improve the text will be most welcome and highly appreciated.

January 2014   **Author**
Pune.

Syllabus ...

Unit I : Basic Concepts   (8 Hours, 16 Marks)

- (a) Introduction to Computer Graphics
- (b) Graphics Standards
- (c) Interactive Computer Graphics
- (d) Linear and Circle Generation

Unit II : Polygons   (8 Hours, 16 Marks)

- (a) Polygons
- (b) Types of Polygons
- (c) Polygon Filling
- (d) Scan Conversion Algorithm
- (e) Segments

Unit III : 2D and 3D Geometry   (8 Hours, 16 Marks)

- (a) 2D Transformation Primitives and Concepts
- (b) 3D Transformations
- (c) 3D Viewing Transformation
- (d) Concept of Parallel Perspective Projections
- (e) Viewing Parameters

Unit IV : Windowing and Clipping   (8 Hours, 16 Marks)

- (a) 2D Clipping and 3D Clipping
- (b) Generalized Clipping
- (c) Polygon Clipping
- (d) Hidden Surfaces and Lines

Unit V : Light, Colour and Shading   (8 Hours, 16 Marks)

- (a) Shading Algorithm
- (b) Colour Models - RGB, HVS, CYM
- (c) Graphical User Interface
- (d) Graphics Standard
- (e) Graphical Applications

***

Contents ...

Unit I : Basic Concepts   1.1 - 1.64

Unit II : Polygons   2.1 - 2.26

Unit III : 2D and 3D Geometry   3.1 - 3.78

Unit IV : Windowing and Clipping   4.1 - 4.32

Unit V : Light, Colour and Shading   5.1 - 5.32

***

BASIC CONCEPTS

1.1 INTRODUCTION

In 1950, the first computer-driven display attached to MIT's Whirlwind I computer was used to generate simple pictures. This display made use of Cathode-Ray Tube i.e. CRT similar to the one used in TVs. Previously, CRT was used as an information storage device by F. Williams.

During the 1950's interactive computer graphics made few processes since the computer of that period were very unsuited for interactive use. Only towards the end of the decade, with the development of machines like MIT's TX-0 and TX-2 did interactive computing become feasible and interest in computer graphics then began to increase rapidly.

By the mid 1960's, large computer graphics research projects were underway at MIT, General Motor, Bell Telephone Laboratories etc.

The 1960's represent the heavy years of computer graphics research, the 1970's have been the decade in which this research began to bear fruit. Interactive graphics display are now use in many countries and are widely used for educational purposes. The instant appeal of computer graphics to users of all ages has helped it to spread into many applications.

1.1.1 Definition of Computer Graphics

Computer graphics is the creation and manipulation of images/pictures with the aid of computer.
There are two types of computer graphics:
1. **Passive CG:** In this, the observer has no control over the image.
2. **Active CG:** In this, the observer has control over the image.

Computer graphics is a study of techniques to improve communication between human and machine. The major product of computer graphics is a picture. With the help of computer graphics pictures can be represented in 2-D as well as in 3-D space.

1.1.2 Importance of Computer Graphics

The importance of computer graphics in computer science can be understood by the following points:
1. The electronic industry is more dependent on the technology. Engineers can draw the circuit in a much shorter time.
2. It provides tools for producing pictures not only of concrete, "real-world" objects but also of abstract, synthetic objects, such as mathematical surfaces in 3D and of data that have no inherent geometry, such as survey results.

3. It has an ability to show, moving pictures and thus, it is possible to produce animations with computer graphics.
4. With computer graphics, user can also control the animation of adjusting the speed, the portion of the total scene in view, the geometric relationship of the objects in the scene to one another, the amount of detail shown and so on.
5. The use of computer graphics is wide spread. It is used in various areas such as industry, business, government organizations, education, entertainment and most recently the home.

1.2 FRAME BUFFER

In a raster scan system, for drawing a picture on screen, the electron beam is swept across the screen one row at a time from top to bottom. When the electron beam sweeps across each row, the beam intensity is turned ON and OFF to create a pattern of illuminated spots. The information about these spots is stored in a memory area known as **'Frame Buffer'**. The frame buffer holds the set of intensity values for all the screen points. The intensity values stored in a frame buffer are then retrieved and pointed on a screen one row at a time. This row is called as **scan line**. Each point on a screen is called as **pixel**. The pixel stands for picture element.

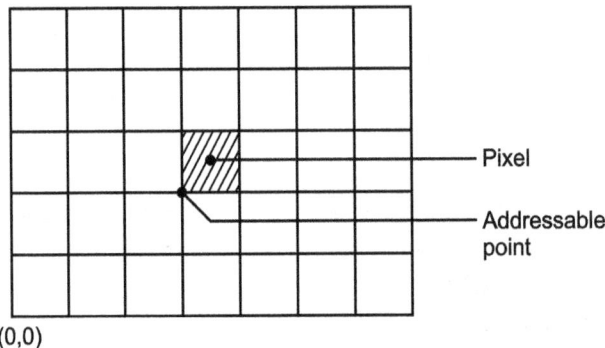

Fig. 1.1

A pixel is addressed or identified by its lower left corner. The pixel occupies a finite area to the right and above this point. The addressing always starts at (0, 0).

The pixel can be defined as the smallest addressable screen element. Every pixel possess a name or address. It is the smallest piece of display screen under control. The name of each pixel corresponds to the co-ordinates, which identify the points. By setting the intensity and colour of pixels, which composes screen, graphic images can be made. Line segments can be drawn by setting the intensities. The display screen can be thought of as a grid or array of pixels or matrix of discrete cells. For drawing a picture on the screen, the intensity values of pixels are placed in an array in the memory. This array is nothing but a frame buffer. Then the display devices access this frame buffer array for determining the intensity of each pixel, which is to be displayed.

In graphic programming using 'C' languages, the put pixels function is used to plot or display a pixel.

Example: Put pixel (100, 200, 5).

In the above example, X-co-ordinate is 100, Y co-ordinate is 200 and third number i.e. 5 denotes the colour number. The put pixel function converts within the raster and stores intensity values at the corresponding positions in the frame buffer array.

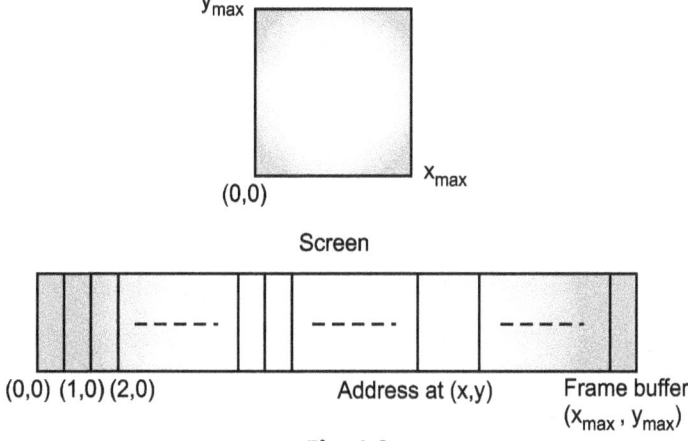

Fig. 1.2

On a black and white system with one bit per pixel the frame buffer is commonly called as bitmap. For system with multiple bits per pixel, the frame buffer is often referred to as pixmap.

1.2.1 Black and White Frame Buffer

If the frame buffer stores one bit pixel information then the size of each element of the frame buffer array is one bit. Hence, it is referred as bit plane. A single bit plane can be store only two values 0 and 1, thus it can yield black and white display. A single bit plane, black and white frame buffer, raster CRT graphic device is shown below in Fig. 1.3.

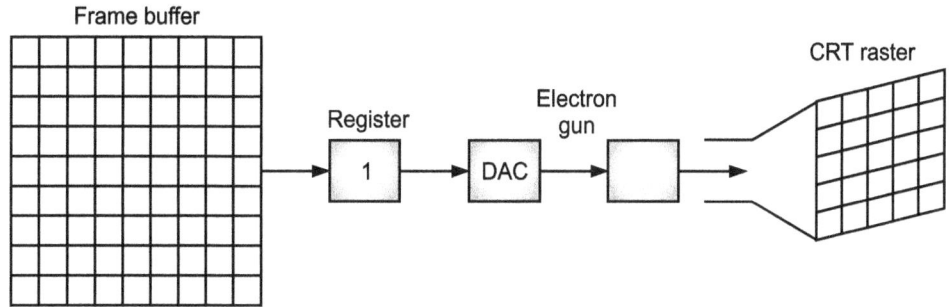

Fig. 1.3

1.2.2 N-Bit Plane Gray Level Frame Buffer

The below figure 1.4 shows an N-bit plane gray level frame buffer. The colour of gray levels are incorporated in the screen of frame buffer raster graphics device using additional bit planes, on the CRT the intensity of each pixel is controlled by a corresponding pixel location in each of the N-bit planes. The binary value i.e. 0 or 1 frame each of the N-bit plane is stored in the register, which is interpreted as an intensity level between 0 and 2^N where 0 represents dark and 2^N represents full intensity. This is then converted into analog voltage by using DAC i.e. Digital to Analog Converter. Thus, total 2^N intensity levels are possible.

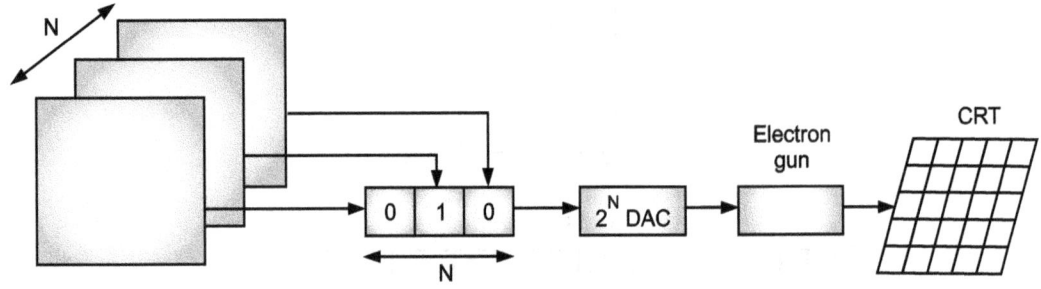

Fig. 1.4

Look-up Table and N-Bit Plane:

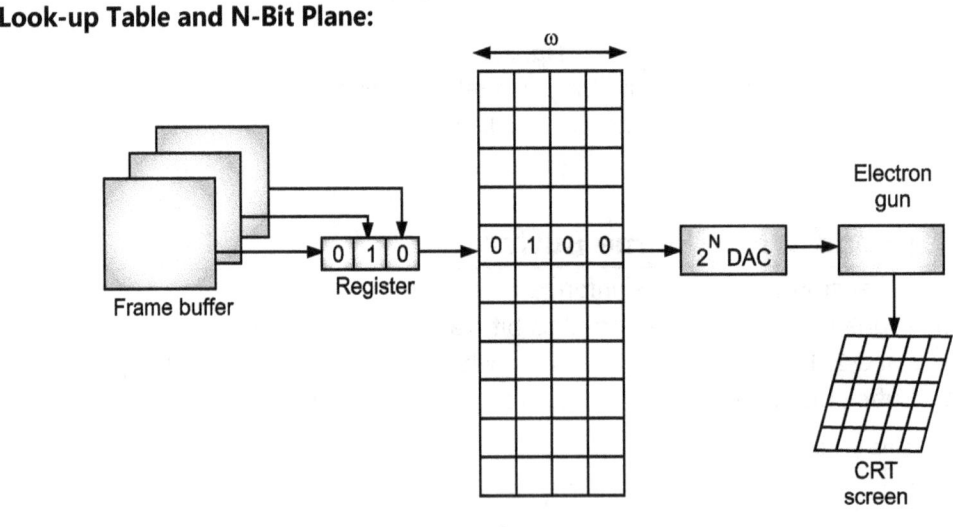

Fig. 1.5

By using look-up table the number of available intensity levels are increased for achieving the modest increase in the memory. After reading the bit planes in the frame buffer, the resulting number is used as an order into the look-up table. The look-up table has 2^N entries, each of which is w-bit wide. The look-up table can be changed or reloaded to get additional intensities.

1.2.3 Colour and 3-Bit Planes

As shown in below figure 1.6, there are three primary colours. Thus, a simple colour frame buffer is implemented with 3-bit planes, one for each primary order. The bit plane drives an individual colour gun for each of the three primary colours in colour video. These three colours can produce $2^3 = 8$ different colours.

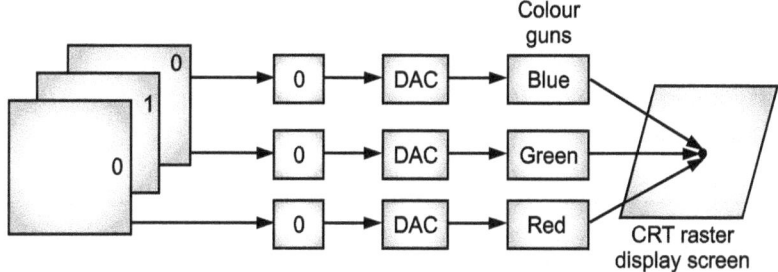

Fig. 1.6

	R	G	B
Black	0	0	0
Red	1	0	0
Green	0	1	0
Blue	0	0	1
Cyan	0	1	1
Yellow	1	1	0
White	1	1	1
Magneta	1	0	1

1.3 VECTORS

Vectors can be defined as a directed line segment which possess magnitude as well as direction.

If two points P_1 and P_2 are given then vector V is defined as the difference between the two point positions.

For 2-Dimension:

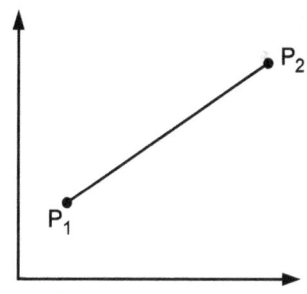

Fig. 1.7

$$V = P_2 - P_1$$
$$= (x_2 - x_1, y_2 - y_1)$$
$$= (V_x, V_y)$$

$V_x, V_y \rightarrow$ Projections of V on x and y axes.

$$|V| = \sqrt{V_x^2 + V_y^2}$$

Thus, when we consider a line segment, it has a fixed position in space. But vector does not have a fixed position in space. The vector does not tell us the starting point. It tells how far to move and in which direction.

1.4 LINE

Two points would represent a line or edge. If the two points used to specify a line are (x_1, y_1) and (x_2, y_2) then the equation for the line is given as,

$$\frac{y - y_1}{x - x_1} = \frac{y_2 - y_1}{x_2 - x_1}$$

$\therefore \quad y = \frac{y_2 - y_1}{x_2 - x_1}(x - x_1) + y_1$

or $\quad y = mx + h$

where, $\quad m = \frac{y_2 - y_1}{x_2 - x_1}$

and $\quad b = V_1 - mx_1$

The above equation is called the slope intercept form of the line. The slope m is the change in height $(y_2 - y_1)$ divided by the change in width $(x_2 - x_1)$ for two points on the line. The intercept b is the height at which the line crosses the y-axis.

1.5 SOME IMPORTANT TERMS

(i) **Persistence:** It is defined as the time taken by the emitted light from the screen to decay to one-tenth of its original intensity.

(ii) **Raster Scan Display:** In this, the beam is moved all over the screen one scan line at a time, from top to bottom and then back to top.

(iii) **Aspect Ratio:** It is the ratio of vertical resolution to horizontal resolution. An aspect ratio of 4/5 means that a vertical line plotted with four points has the same length as a horizontal line plotted with five points.

(iv) **Resolution:** Resolution indicates the maximum number of points that can be displayed without overlap on the CRT. It is defined as the number of points per centimeter that can be plotted horizontally and vertically.

(v) Horizontal sweep frequency: It is related to the number of scan lines per second. It gives the information about how much time is needed to scan one line.

(vi) Vertical sweep frequency: It is related to the number of frames covered by the electron beam in one second.

(vii) Horizontal scan line: It is the time duration of frequency of electron beam to move from left corner to right corner of screen or scan line.

(viii) Vertical scan line: It is the time duration of an electron beam to move from upper left corner to bottom right corner.

(ix) Fluorescence: The glow given off by the phosphor during the excitation period of the electron beam is called as fluorescence.

(x) Phosphorescene: The glow given off by the phosphor after the electron beam is removed. In other words the phosphorescence is time of fluorescence.

(xi) Horizontal refresh rate: It is the time duration of electron beam to come from the right end of the scan line to the left end of another scan line.

(xii) Vertical refresh rate: It is the time required for the electron beam to move from bottom right corner of scan line to the starting left corner of scan line.

1.6 CHARACTER GENERATION

Along with lines and points, strings of characters are often displayed to label, draw and to give instructions and information to the user. Characters are always built into the graphics display device usually as hardware but sometimes through software.

There are three primary methods for character generation:
1. Stroke method
2. Bitmap or Dot-matrix method
3. Starbust method

1. Stroke Method:

This method uses small line segments to generate a character. The small series of line segments are drawn like the strokes of a pen to form a character as shown in diagram.

We can build our own stroke method character generator by calls to the line drawing algorithm. Here, it is necessary to decide which line segments are needed for each character and then drawing these segments using line drawing algorithm we can draw characters on the display. The stroke method supports scaling of the character. It does this by changing the length of line segments used for character drawing.

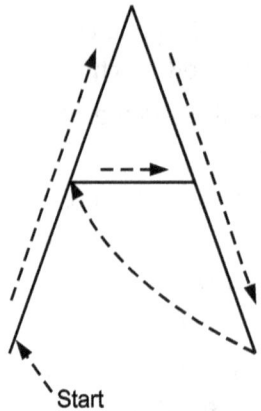

Fig. 1.8: Stroke Method

2. Bitmap/Dot-matrix Method:

This method is used for character generation. It is also called the dot-matrix form.

As shown in figure 1.9, a two dimensional array having columns and rows. A 5 × 8 array is commonly used to represent character shown in a diagram.

However, 7 × 9 and 3 × 13 array are also used. Higher resolution devices such as inkjet printer or lazer printer may use character arrays over 100 × 100.

Each dot in the matrix is a pixel. The character is placed on the screen by copying pixel values from the character array into some portion of the screen's frame buffer. The value of the pixel, controls the intensity of the pixel.

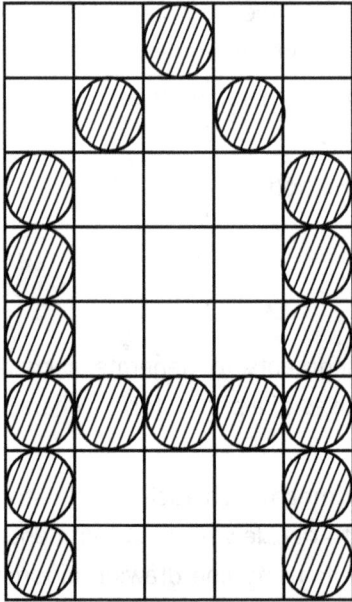

Fig. 1.9: Character A in 5 × 8 Dot Matrix Format

3. Starbust Method:

In this method, a fixed pattern of line segments is used to generate characters. As shown in the figure 1.10 there are 24 line segments. Out of these 24 line segments, the segments required to display a particular character are highlighted.

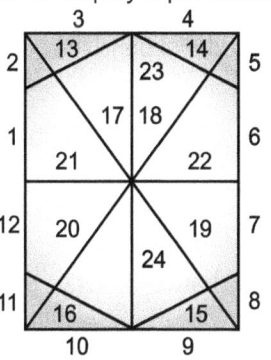 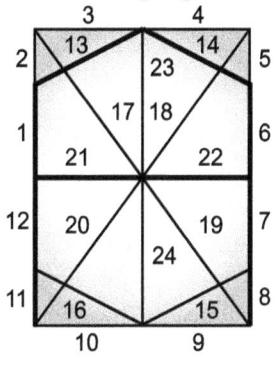 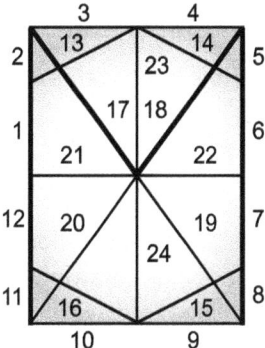

Fig. 1.10

1.7 DISPLAY DEVICES

The display devices used in graphics are based on CRT technology. The various display devices are:

1. DVST.
2. Raster Refresh Graphic Display.
3. Calligraphic Refresh Graphic Display.
4. Plasma Panel Display.
5. Colour CRT Monitors.
6. Flat Panel Display.
7. Liquid Crystal Monitors.
8. Vector Scan Display.

1.7.1 DVST (Direct View Storage Tube)

Conceptually, the DVST is the simplest of all CRT displays. These types of displays are no longer manufactured. The DVST contains long-persistence phosphor. The DVST can also be referred as bistable storage tube. Since the long-persistence phosphor is used hence the line or character remains visible for longer period i.e. upto one hour until erased. The electron beam intensity is increased for drawing a character or line on the display. As the intensity increases the phosphor assume its bright storage state. By flooding the entire tube with a specific voltage, the display is erased. Erase takes approximately half second. The electron beam is intensified to a point, which is just below the threshold that will cause the permanent storage and is also sufficient to brighten the phosphor.

The features of DVST are as follows:
1. The DVST is easy to program.
2. It has flat screen.
3. The display is flicker free.
4. Refreshing is not required.
5. The hard copy produced by DVST is relatively easy, fast and inexpensive.
6. It is not suitable for animation and dynamic motion.

1.7.2 Raster Refresh Graphics Display

The most common graphics display employing CRT is the raster scan display which is based on the television technology. Both the storage tube CRT display and the random scan refresh display are line drawing devices. The straight lines can be drawn directly from one addressable point to other addressable point. This device is a matrix of discrete cells in which each of the cells can be made bright. Thus, it is a point plotting device. Only in some several cases, it is possible to draw a straight line.

The features of Raster refresh graphic display are:
1. Cost is low.
2. It has ability to display areas filled with solid colours.
3. Refresh process is independent of the complexity of image.
4. It controls the intensity of each dot and pixel in a rectangular matrix.

1.7.3 Calligraphic Refresh Graphic Display

A calligraphic refresh CRT display makes the use of a very short persistence phosphor. Due to this the picture painted on the CRT must be repainted or refreshed many times in one second. The refresh rate is atleast 30 times each second with a recommended rate of 40-50 times each second. The image gets flickered due to lower refresh rate.

The features of Calligraphic refresh graphic display are:
1. The speed of communication is slow.
2. Image gets flickered.
3. The instruction pertaining to image are stored in buffer, thus selective modification is possible.
4. Generation of solid figure is difficult.
5. The calligraphic display needs two elements in addition to the Cathode Ray Tube (CRT). They are display buffer and display controller.

1.7.4 Plasma Panel Display

A display device which stores the image but allows selective erasing is the plasma panel. It contains a gas at low pressure sandwiched between horizontal and vertical grid of fine wires.

A large voltage difference between a horizontal and vertical wire will cause the gas to glow as it does in a neon street sign. A lower voltage will not start a glow but will maintain a glow once started. To set a pixel, the voltage is increased momentarily on the wires that intersect the desired point. To extinguish a pixel, the voltage on the corresponding wire is reduced until the glow cannot be maintained.

The features of plasma panel display are:
1. They are very durable.
2. They have been used in PLATO educational system.
3. Less bulky than CRT.
4. Refreshing is not required.
5. Often used in military application.
6. Produces a very steady image, totally flicker free.

Liquid Crystal Monitor: It is a very economical device. It is a flat panel display technology, hence less bulky than CRTs. In liquid crystal display, light is either transmitted or blocked, depending upon the orientation of molecules in the liquid crystal. An electrical signal can be used to change the molecular orientation, turning a pixel on or off. The material is sandwiched between horizontal and vertical grids of electrodes which are used to select the pixel.

The features of liquid crystal displays are:
1. It is economical.
2. Less bulky than CRTs.
3. It is portable, because of its low voltage and power requirements.
4. Liquid crystal televisions are also available.

1.7.5 Vector Refresh Display

The vector refresh display stores the image in the computer's memory, but in a more efficient manner than raster display. It stores the commands necessary for drawing the line segments. The input to the vector generator is saved, instead of the output. These commands are saved in a display file. The lines are drawn using a vector-generating algorithm. This is done on a normal cathode ray tube, so the image quickly fades. In order to present a steady image, the display must be drawn repeatedly. The vector generator must be applied to all the lines in an image fast enough to draw the entire image flicker free.

The features of vector refresh display are:
1. Scan conversion is not required.
2. Draws continuous and smooth lines.

Flat Panel Display: The term flat-panel display refers to a class of video devices that have reduced volume, weight and power requirements as compared to CRT. The important features of flat-panel display is that they are thinner than CRTs. There are two types of flat panel displays, emissive displays and non-emissive displays.

Emissive Displays: They convert electrical energy into light energy. Plasma panels, thin-film electro luminescent displays and light emitting diodes are examples of emissive displays.

Non-emissive Displays: They use optical effects to convert sunlight or light from some other source into graphics patterns. Liquid crystal display is an example of non-emissive flat panel display.

1.8 DISPLAY FILE INTERPRETER

The display file contains information necessary to construct the picture. This information is in the form of commands. The process to convert these instructions into a actual images is performed by a processor called as display file interpreter.

In some graphical system the task of display file interpreter is performed by using a separate computer or CPU. Hence, it acts as an interface between the graphics user program and a display service, which is known as **display processor**.

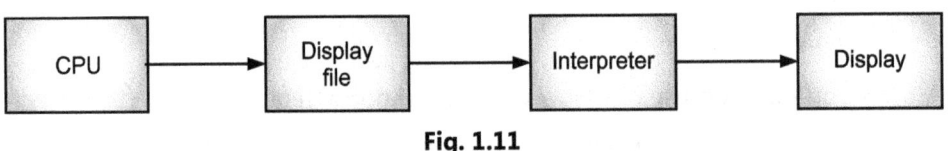

Fig. 1.11

Every instruction possess a MOVE, LINE or PLOT commands. As shown in above figure 1.13 the interpreter executes the instruction and the output will be a visual image.

A graphic program written from a particular display device will not run on different display device. Hence, the program is not possible. On the other hand, if a program has been written, generates display code then only an interpreter is needed for each device, which converts the standard display instruction into the actions of a particular device. Thus, the display device and its interpreter can be thought of as a machine on which any standard program can run. The display file instructions are actually saved in a file for later display or for transfer to another machine. Such files are called as **metafiles**.

The advantage of using interpreter is that saving raw image takes much less storage than saving the picture itself.

1.9 DISPLAY PROCESSOR

Opcode	Command
1	Move
2	Line

As operand is having both x and y parameters we have to separate them. We will store the x co-ordinate in x operand and y co-ordinate in y operand.

In some graphics system, a separate computer is used to interprete the commands in the display file. Such computer is called as a **display processor**. Display processor access display file and it cycles through each command in the display file once during every refresh cycle. Fig. 1.12 shows the vector scan system with display processor.

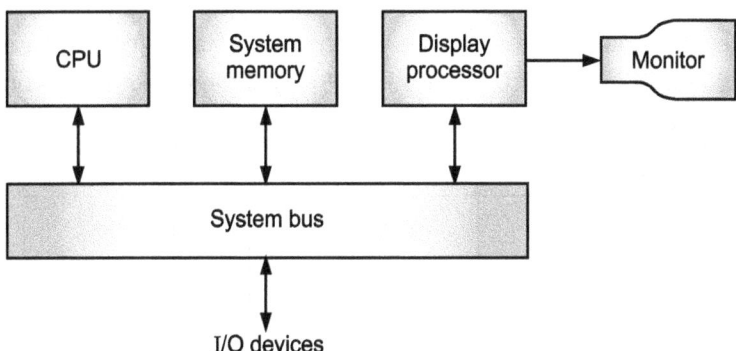

Fig. 1.12: Vector Scan System

In the raster scan display systems, the purpose of display processor is to free the CPU from the graphics routine task. Here, display processor is provided with separate memory. The main task of display processor is to digitize a picture definition given in an application program into a set of pixel intensity values for storage in the frame buffer. This digitization process is known as **scan conversion**.

1.10 DISPLAY FILE STRUCTURE

Every command of display file consists of two parts:
   (i)   Operation code (OPCODE).
   (ii) Operands.

Operation code indicates which type of command it is i.e. either LINE or MOVE.

Operands are the co-ordinate of a point (x, y).

The display file is nothing but a series of above two instructions. Three separate arrays are used for storing these instructions which are as under:

(a) One array for the operation code i.e. DF – OP.

(b) Second array for the x co-ordinate i.e. DF – X.

(c) Third array for the Y co-ordinate i.e. DF – Y.

Before processing, it is very necessary to assign meaning to the possible operation codes. Let us consider two possible instructions MOVE and LINE. Let us define an opcode of 2 to a MOVE command and an opcode of 3 to a LINE command. Then command to MOVE to position x = 0.5 and y = 0.6 would be 2, 0.5, 0.6.

DF – OP [4] ← 2

DF – X [4] ← 0.5

DF – Y [4] ← 0.6

The above statement would be stored in the fourth display file position. Suppose the value of DF – OP [5] is 3 and DF – X [5] = 0.7 and DF – Y[5] = 0.8 then the display would show a line segment from (0.5, 0.6) to (0.7, 0.8) as shown below.

DF – OP	DF – X	DF – Y
1		
2		
3		
4	0.5	0.6
5	0.7	0.8

Instruction of display file.

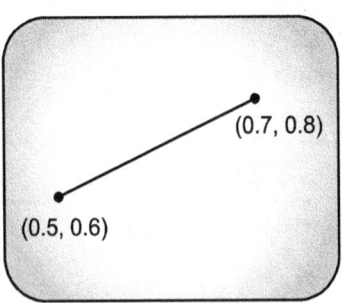

Fig. 1.13

1.11 GRAPHIC STANDARDS

1.11.1 Need for Standards

Graphics is well recognized as an effective means of communication. Some studies indicate that a graphic message is consciously recognized more than twice as fast as a text message. However, for years the use of graphics was limited to sophisticated mainframe systems because of the expense involved.

Complex graphic images require both extensive processing power and vast amounts of memory. Graphics quickly, moved into the: microcomputer environment when the size of processors and the price of memory decreased significantly.

However, this implementation of computer graphics was not widely spread because of incompatible devices and non-communicating software. Currently, graphics implementations are either written as a program for a specific device or custom installed for each graphics device.

Despite of these difficulties, graphics for use with personal computers became popular and users were in need of graphics. Certainly there is user demand for graphics, from simple menu pictorial symbols or icons, to elaborate window systems for concurrent display of data from different processes. But before personal computer graphics can really become widespread, a. standard architecture is needed for writing graphics applications and having them communicate with the huge diversity of available hardware.

From this background, it can be seen
1. Why better graphics has not been available for personal computers?
2. Why stronger efforts have not been made to standardize the production of graphics programs?

To assist in solving these problems, the American National Standards Institute (ANSI) has formed a technical committee to develop computer graphics standards.
Thus finally,
Graphics standards are provided for easy transfer of the graphics from one platform to another as there are many variations in display devices, software packages and even the graphical languages. Due to this reason the standards are developed which provides the portability.

The first standard to be accepted was the Graphical Kernel System (GKS), adopted in October 1984 and previously adopted by the International Standards Organization. GKS defines graphics functions at the programmer level with specification of how those functions are assessed through high-level programming languages.

Other major graphics standards available are:
1. CORE
2. Programmer's Hierarchical Interactive Graphical Standard (PHIGS)
3. Initial Graphics Exchange Standard (IGES)
4. Computer Graphics Metafile Standard (CGM)
5. Virtual Device Metafile (VDM)
6. Virtual Device Interface (VDI)

Let's see these standards in short.

1.11.2 Graphical Kernel System (GKS)

The Graphical Kernel System (GKS) is a second standard also called as 2D version of CORE, it is also influenced by CORE.

The Graphical Kernel System (GKS) defines a common interface to interactive computer graphics for creating, manipulating and displaying or printing computer graphics on different types of computer graphics output devices

The Graphical Kernel System (GKS) was the first ISO standard for low-level computer graphics, introduced in 1977. GKS provides a set of drawing features for two-dimensional vector graphics suitable for charting and similar duties. The calls are designed to be portable across different programming languages, graphics devices and hardware, so that applications written to use GKS will be readily portable to many platforms and devices.

The Graphical Kernel System (GKS) is a document produced by the International Standards Organisation (ISO) which defines a common interface to interactive computer graphics for application programs. GKS has been designed by a group of experts representing the national standards institutions of most major industrialized countries. The full standard provides functional specifications for some 200 subroutines which perform graphics input and output in a device independent way. Application programs can thus move freely between different graphics devices and different host computers. For the first time, graphics programs have become genuinely portable.

However, one should point out that GKS itself is not portable. Individual GKS implementations will vary substantially as they have to support different graphics devices on different computers. Moreover, GKS is a kernel system, and thus does not include an arbitrary collection of functions to produce histograms or contour plots etc.

In order to allow particular applications to choose a graphics package with the appropriate capability, GKS has been defined to have different levels. The level structure has two dimensions, one for output (0, 1 or 2) and one for input (a, b or c). Higher levels include the capabilities of lower levels. In the United States, ANSI has defined also a level 'm', for very simple applications, which sits below output level '0'. Most implementations provide all output (level '2') and intermediate input (level 'b'). The reason input level 'c' is not usually supported is that it requires asynchronous input facilities not found in all operating systems.

The GKS functions have been defined independently from a specific programming language, and bindings to individual languages are subject to separate standard efforts which have been undertaken for all the major languages.

The Graphical Kernel System for two dimensional graphics was adopted as an ISO standard in 1985, and since that date work has been in progress to define a three dimensional super-set which was accepted as an International Standard during 1988. The FORTRAN binding to GKS-3D has also been published as a Draft International Standard

The GKS functions are separated into those which pass values to GKS for control, setting or output, and those which inquire about status information. There are 8 distinct classes:
1. Control functions
2. Output attributes
3. Output primitives
4. Segment functions
5. Transformations
6. Input functions
7. Metafile functions
8. Inquiry functions

GKS-3D: A Three-Dimensional Extension to the Graphical Kernel System:

GKS-3D is nothing but a machine, language, operating system and device independent specification of a set of services for displaying and interacting with 2D and 3D pictures.

The three-dimensional Graphical Kernel System is designed to provide a basic set of 3D function with incorporating hidden-line/hidden-surface removal. Every attempt has been made to ensure full compatibility with GKS so that programs can run unmodified in the GKS-3D environment. For effective operation in a 3D environment.

The purpose of GKS-3D standards are:
1. For providing the portability of graphics application programs.
2. To assist in understanding of graphics method by application program

1.11.3 Core

CORE provides the standardized set of commands which controls the construction and display of graphics image. These commands are device independent that means "device which is used to create or display the graphics image and independent of the language in which the graphics programs were written." It provides a devices-independent viewing package that would other, more application-specific packages including modeling packages to be build on top. And hence the term "Core".

1.11.4 Programmer's Hierarchical Interactive Graphics System (PHIGS)

PHIGS - the Programmer's Hierarchical Interactive Graphics System is a programming library for 3D graphics. It is devised and maintained by the International Organisation for Standardisation (ISO), it is most commonly used on the X Window System and commonly available from several workstation venders. The PHIGS high-level graphics library contains over 400 functions ranging from simple line drawing to lighting and shading. Fully one-half of them let you determine the state of an output device or recall settings made earlier in a program. It provides to a graphics application a standard interface to display devices of any manufacturer that supports the PHIGS standard.

Before displaying a picture, the application first stores all its graphics information in the PHIGS graphics database. Thus, PHIGS is referred to as a "display list" system. The application then appears on one or more display devices and then passes the list to them. Because of its display list system structure, PHIGS is well-suited to applications that create a graphics model and then edit portions of it frequently or view it in different ways.

This basic version of PHIGS included the following major features:
- A editable hierarchical organization of graphics data called the structure store.
- A powerful logical input model in support of interaction devices.
- A workstation mechanism to allow support of multiple simultaneous input and output devices.
- 3D graphics primitives which could be specified using either 2D or 3D functions.
- Separate attributes based on primitive type.

Limitations of PHIGS:

PHIGS does not do many things necessary for photorealistic and advanced animation purposes.
- It does not do ray tracing.
- It doesn't compute shadows.
- It doesn't provide texture mapping.
- It limits the number of light sources.
- It deson't do depth cueing.

Thus, PHIGS is very appropriate for most engineering and industrial applications but may not be adequate for more advanced visualization.

1.11.5 Initial Graphics Exchange Standard (IGES)

Initial Graphics Exchange Standard has been a British standard since 1988. It is useful for exchanging data between different CAD/CAM systems. The difference between IGES (and similar standards) and CGM is that a CAD design incorporates the geometric modelling information plus information on materials, weights, costs etc. and all these are easily stored in an IGES file but not as easily in a CGM file. Like many other standards, the reality of importing IGES files does not match up to the dream and work has been done by ISO to develop STEP which has become an international standard. STEP (Standard for the exchange of product model data) includes conformance testing and it is being backed by the US government and all the major car and aerospace manufacturers and all national standards bodies.

IGES successfully met a critical need. The IGES Publication establishes information structures to be used for the digital representation and communication of product definition data. The specification is concerned with the data required to describe and communicate the essential engineering characteristics of physical objects such as manufactured products.

The Initial Graphics Exchange Specification is the U.S. national standard for the exchange of data between dissimilar CAD systems. The IGES standard, now in its sixth revision, has been expanded to include most concepts used in major CAD systems. All major and most minor non-PC-based CAD systems support some version of the IGES standard.

Applications:
1. The IGES file format can be used to transfer engineering models between Powershape and PATRAN.
2. Using IGES, a CAD user can exchange product data models in the form of circuit diagrams, wire frame, freeform surface or solid modeling representations.
3. Applications supported by IGES include traditional engineering drawings, models for analysis, and other manufacturing functions.

1.11.6 The Computer Graphics Metafile Standard (CGM)

The Computer Graphics Metafile standard was adopted by ISO in 1987 to enable transfer of pictures between various graphics packages or between different machines. For example, UNIRAS on the SUN systems could be used to create one picture and Cerel Draw on the PC could be used to create another picture. The two pictures could be combined and dressed up in GSHARP to produce another picture, which is then imported into Microsoft Word. Unfortunately, not all implementations of CGM incorporate all the variations available under the standard and so there are often difficulties in interpreting CGM files produced by different packages. Please ask for advice at the Helpdesk who will contact the Graphics Section for you.

CGM files contain snapshots, i.e. there is no information about the structure of the picture and there is no standard way of holding other data besides the picture data. This means that CAD packages often do not use CGM files to store designs or drawings for retrieval by other CAD packages. However, this standard for supporting storage of 2D graphical data has become popular and is important in the University community.

There are different requirements for the storage and retrieval of pictures. These are:
    (a) minimal file size,
    (b) ease of transfer across computer networks,
    (c) speed at which file can be generated and interpreted,
    (d) human readability of stored files.

To address these requirements, three encodings are defined in the CGM standard. These are:
- character encoding
- binary encoding
- clear text encoding

1.11.7 Virtual Device Interface (VDI)

It defines the standard way for a program to drive a graphics device. It is a standard developed by ANSI. It's main purpose is to provide a device independent way to control hardware. It is a lower level standard.

The role of the VDI is to provide device independence by creating a logical graphics device interface. Such an interface allows an application to control any graphics peripheral, regardless of individual peculiarities. For input devices, the VDI specifies the kinds of actions, such as pointing or string input, which an input device should be capable of performing. Similarly for output devices, the VDI specifies conceptual capabilities, such as the drawing of lines and polygons. The VDI developed by Graphic Software Systems provides for device independence through the following capabilities

- Device driver management.
- Co-ordinate transformation.
- Text models.
- Character I/O.
- Emulation of certain graphics primitives.
- Device inquiry.
- Error reporting.

1.11.8 Virtual Device Metafile (VDM)

It is a data format used to record pictures on disk files. A metafile is a means of permanent picture storage. It is also a graphics standard used to communicate graphical data between program or between computers. For example a graphics produced by one program may be read by other program.

1.12 ADVANTAGES OF GRAPHICS STANDARDS

Any ideal graphics software standard has a perfect device independence which allows it to operate all graphical input and output devices. Therefore advantages of such standard are as follows:

- The user can select any graphics hardware to upgrade graphics display.
- Being device independent, graphics generated based on these standards is economical for developer and user.
- Reuse of code in terms of ready routines is possible, and hence standard software packages can be used for developing other packages.
- It facilitates transport of application program from one computer to another.
- It also facilitates programmer portability.

1.13 HAZARDS OF GRAPHICS STANDARDS

Practically 100% ideal standard does not exist, and hence there are some of it's hazards, which are as follows:

- The given application may not run equally well on wide variety of devices.
- Poor definition of standard may create problems to the user.
- Standards once defined may create difficulties in accommodating new needs.
- The methods of the standard are treated as only suitable methods for solving problems, though there can be other suitable ones.

1.14 INTERACTIVE DEVICES/INPUT DEVICES

Input device allows to communicate with computer. Using this one can feed in the information.

Most commonly used input devices are:

(i) Mouse, (ii) Trackball, (iii) Touch panel, (iv) Light pen, (v) Joystick, (vi) Tablets, (vii) Keyboard etc.

1.14.1 Mouse

A mouse is a palm-sized box used to position the screen cursor. It consists of ball on the bottom connected to wheels or rollers to provide the amount and direction of move. One, two or three buttons are usually provided on the top of the mouse for signaling the execution of some operation. Now-a-days, mouse consists of one more wheel on the top to scroll the screen pages.

A different type of mouse is optical mouse. Here, the ball is replaced by two apertures, one for optical source and other for receiving the optical ray reflected from the metallic mouse-base plate.

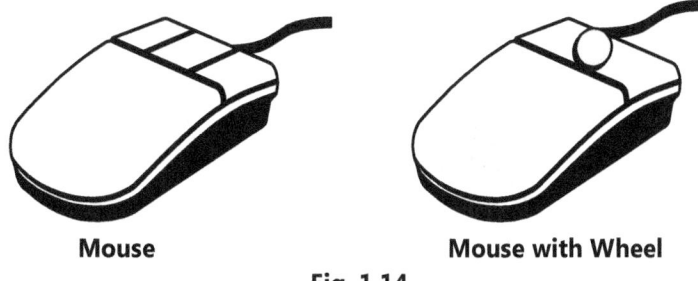

Mouse   **Mouse with Wheel**

Fig. 1.14

Trackball: Trackball can be seen as an inverted mouse where the ball is held inside a rectangular box. As the name implies, a trackball is a ball that can be rotated with the fingers or palm of the hand to produce screen cursor movement. The potentiometers attached to the trackball are used to measure the amount and direction of rotation.

The trackball is a two dimensional positioning device whereas spaceball provides six degree of freedom. It does not actually move. It consists of strain gauges which measures the amount of pressure applied to the space ball to provide input for spatial positioning and orientation as the ball is pushed or pulled in various directions. It is usually used in three-dimensional positioning and selecting operations in virtual-reality systems.

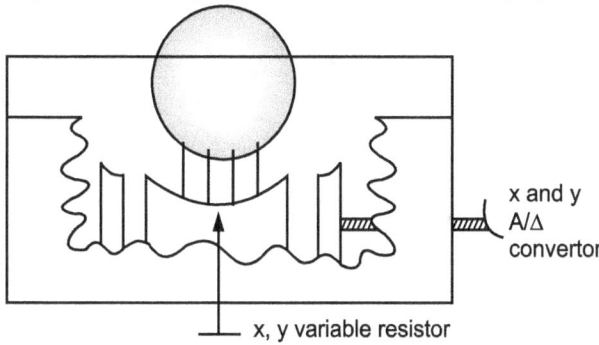

Fig. 1.15

1.14.2 Touch Panel

Touch panels allow display objects or screen positions to be selected with a touch of finger. It is used in the selection of processing options that are represented with a graphical icons. Touch panels are of various types:
- Optical touch panel
- Electrical touch panel
- Acoustical touch panel

- Optical touch panels consists of a line of infrared light-emitting diodes (LEDs) along one vertical edge and along one horizontal edge of the frame. The opposite vertical and horizontal edge contains light detectors. These detectors are used to record which beams are interrupted when the panel is touched.
- An electrical touch panel is constructed with two transparent plates separated by a small distance. When the outer plate is touched, it is forced into contact with the inner plate. This contact creates a voltage drop across the resistive plate that is converted into the co-ordinate values of the selected screen position.
- Acoustical touch panels, uses high frequency sound waves to determine the point of contact.

Light Pen: A light pen is a pointing device shaped like a pen acts as a computer input device. The tip of the light pen contains a light sensitive element which, when placed against the screen, detects the light from the screening enabling the computer to identify the reaction of the pen on the screen.

Light pen wave the advantage of 'drawing' directly onto the screen. It allows the user to point to displayed objects, or drawn on the screen, in a similar way to a touch screen.

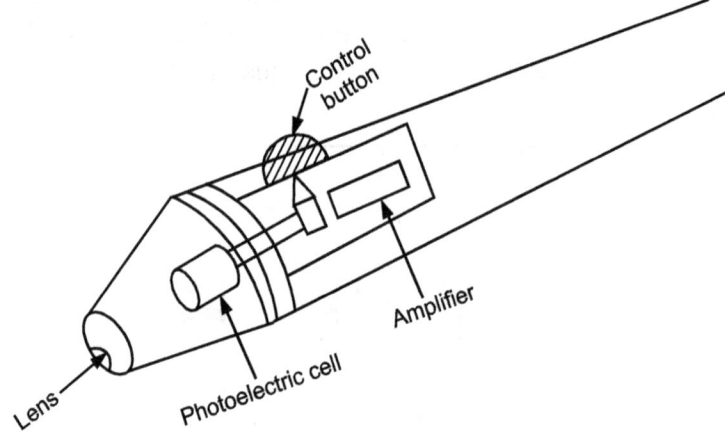

Fig. 1.16

It allows the user but with greater positional accuracy. A light pen can work with any CRT-based monitor, but not with LCD screens, projectors or other display devices.

The light pen consist of a photoelectric cell housed in a pen like case. It works by sensing the sudden small change in brightness of a point on the screen when the electron gun refreshes that spot.

By noting exactly where the scanning has reached at that moment, the x, y position of the pen can be resolved.

For slow displays transistor type photo-cells such as diodes are used.

1.14.3 Joystick

A joystick has a small vertical lever (called the stick) mounted on the base and used to steer the screen cursor around. It consists of two potentiometers attached to a single lever. Moving the lever changes the settings on the potentiometer. The left or right movement is indicated by one potentiometer and forward or back movement is indicated by other potentiometer. Thus, with a joystick both x and y co-ordinate positions can be simultaneously altered by the motion of a single lever as shown below.

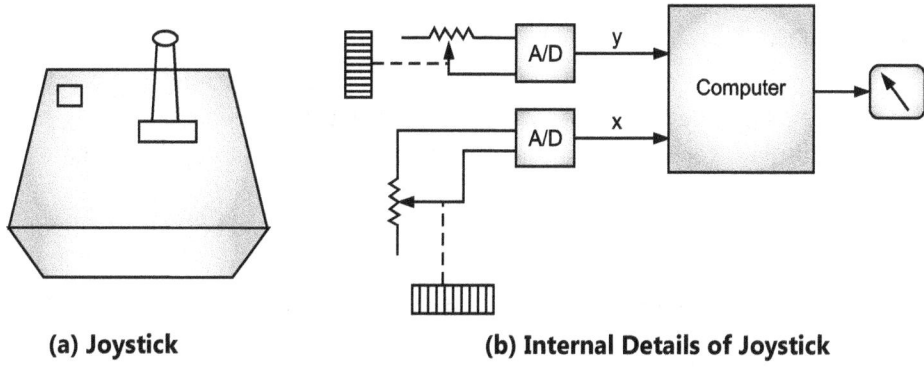

(a) Joystick   (b) Internal Details of Joystick

Fig. 1.17

Some joystick may return to their zero (center) position when released. Joystick are inexpensive and are quite commonly used where only rough positioning is needed.

1.14.4 Tablet

For applications, such as tracing we need a device called a digitizer or a graphical tablet. It consists of a flat surface ranging in size from about 6 by 6 inches upto 48 by 72 inches or more which can detect the position of movable styles.

The Fig. 1.18 below shows a small tablet with pen like stylus.

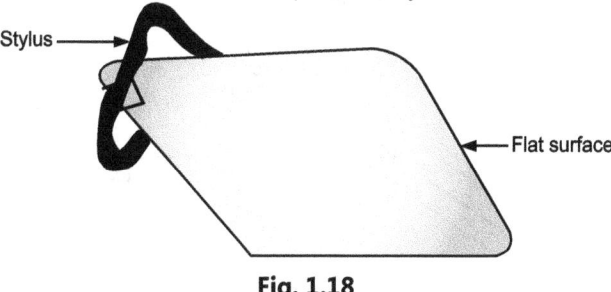

Fig. 1.18

Different graphics tablets use different techniques for measuring position, but they all resolve the position into a horizontal and a vertical direction, which corresponds to the axes of the display.

Most graphics tablets use an electrical sensing mechanism to determine the position of the stylus. In one such arrangement a grid of wire on 1/4 to 1/2 inches centers is embedded in the tablet surface. Electromagnetic signals generated by electrical pulses applied in sequence to the wires in the grid induce an electrical signal in a wire coil in the stylus.

The signal strength is also used to determine roughly how far the stylus or cursor is from the graphical tablet.

Every time user may not wish to enter stylus position into the computer. In such cases user can lift the stylus or make the tablet off by pressing a switch provided on the stylus.

1.14.5 Keyboard

An alphanumeric keyboard on a graphics system is a primary device used for entering text strings. It is an effective device for inputting non-graphic data as picture labels associated with a graphic display. Keyboards can also be provided with features to facilitate entry of screen co-ordinates, menu selections or graphic functions.

General purpose keyboards contain cursor-control keys and function keys. Cursor-control keys can be used to select displayed objects or co-ordinate positions by positioning the screen cursor. The function keys are used to enter frequently used operations in a single keystroke. Numeric keypad is also present for inputting the numeric data.

1.14.6 Scanner

The scanner is a device, which can be used to store graphs, photos or text available in printed form for computer processing.

The scanners use the optical scanning mechanism to scan the information. The scanner records the gradation of gray scales or colour and stores them in the array.

Finally, it stores the image information in a specific file format such as JPEG, GIF, TIFF, BMP and soon.

Once the image is scanned, it can be processed or we can apply transformations to rotate, scale or crop the image using image processing softwares such as photo-shop or photo-paint. Scanners are available in variety of sizes and capabilities.

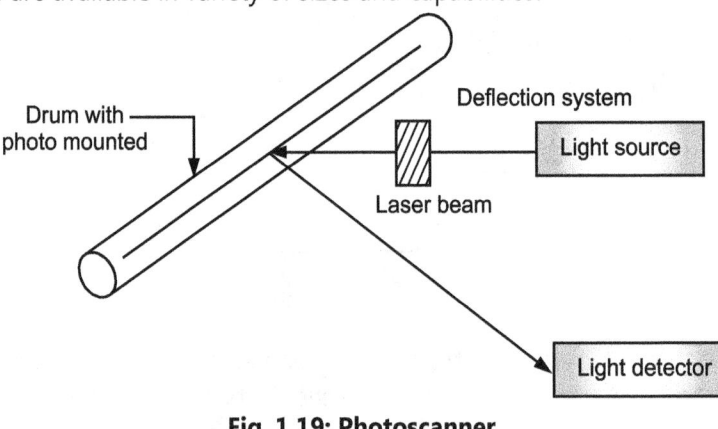

Fig. 1.19: Photoscanner

Previous figure 1.19 shows the working of photoscanner.

For coloured photographs, multiple passes are made, using filters in front of the photocell to separate out various colours.

Other type of scanners are electro-optical devices that use arrays of light sensitive charge coupled devices (CCDs) to turn light reflected from, or transmitted through artwork, photographs, slides etc. into a usable digital fire composed of pixel information.

The optical resolution and colour depth are the two important specifications of the scanner. The photoscanners have the resolution upto 2000 units per inch. Resolution of the CCD array is 200 to 1000 units per inch which is less than the photoscanner. The colour depth is expressed in bits. It specifies the number of colours a scanner can capture.

The scanners can also be classified into following types as per construction:
1. Flat-bed Scanner
2. Drum Scanner
3. Sheet-fed Scanner
4. Handheld Scanner.

1.15 TEXT AND LINE STYLE

1.15.1 TEXT

Text output is a primitive operation which has a large number of options and attributes. For example, style or font of the characters such as Roman, Helvetia, Clarinda etc. their appearance i.e. Roman, Bold, Italic, Underlined etc. their size which is typically measured in points, widths, the intercharacter spacing, the spacing between consecutive lines, the angle at which characters are drawn such as horizontal, vertical or at a specified angle etc. Therefore, it is always complex in a graphics package to specify and implement a text drawing.

In simple hardware and software all characters occupy the same width and the spacing between them is constant. On the other hand, the special softwares supports the proportional spacing. In which both the width of characters and the spacing between them varies to make the text as legible and aesthetically pleasing as possible. All Desk Top Publishing (DTP) packages use proportional spacing. SRGP provides in between functionality: Text is horizontally aligned, character width vary, but spacing between characters is constant.

1.15.2 Line-Style

It is a type of primitive. Many display devices offer a selection of line styles. Lines may be continuous, or they may be dashed or dotted. The user is also able to select the colour of the line or its intensity or thickness. Sometimes, it is desirable to change the line style in the middle of the display process. Thus, a display file command is used to change the line style.

When the interpreter encounters such a command, the line style is changed and all subsequent lines are drawn in this new style. The display-file commands are composed of three-parts, the opcode and the two operands for the x and y co-ordinates. A special opcode is used to indicate the change of line style (colour or intensity).

1.16 LINES

A point can be specified with an ordered pair of numbers (x, y), where x is the horizontal distance from the origin and y is the vertical distance. Two points will specify a line. Consider two points of a line as (x_1, y_1) and (x_2, y_2) then the equation for the line will be,

$$\frac{y - y_1}{x - x_1} = \frac{y_2 - y_1}{x_2 - x_1}$$

Solving the above equation, we get,

$$y = \frac{y_2 - y_1}{x_2 - x_1}(x - x_1) + y_1$$

or

$$y = mx + b$$

where,

$$m = \frac{y_2 - y_1}{x_2 - x_1}$$

and

$$b = y_1 - mx_1$$

This is called as slope intercept form of line where m is the slope and b is the intercept.

1.16.1 Vector Generation

The process of "turning on" the pixels for a line segment is called **vector generation**. Suppose the end points of the segment are known, then how to decide which pixels intensity should be changed. There are two approaches to this problem.
1. DDA i.e. Digital Differential Analyzer.
2. Bresenham's Algorithm.

The major problem in vector generation is to select pixels which is near to the line segment. It is not easy to determine the pixels which passes through the line segment and since vector generation may be performed especially for animated displays and complex image, it must be very efficient. Another problem is that the apparent thickness of the line would change with slope and position. An alternative approach is to step along the columns of the pixels and for each column ask which row is closest to the line. Then turn on the pixel in that row and column. But this approach will work for lines with slopes between −1 and 1. For steeply rising or falling lines this approach will not work.

To overcome all the above problems algorithm is used called as DDA.

1.16.2 DDA i.e. Digital Differential Analyzer

This is the simplest algorithm of line drawing. This algorithm makes the use of differential equation of line to obtain recursion relation defining the co-ordinate of next point in terms of co-ordinate of current point. This recursive relation is then used to select pixel position.

If Δx and Δy are incremented in x and y direction then for straight line, equation will be,

$$\frac{\Delta y}{\Delta x} = \frac{y_2 - y_1}{x_2 - x_1}$$

x_1, x_2, y_1, y_2 are co-ordinates of end points.

The recursion relation thus obtained will be,

$$y_{i+1} = y_1 + \Delta y$$
$$x_{i+1} = x_1 + \Delta x$$

where, x_{i+1} and y_{i+1} are the co-ordinates of next point. x_1 and y_1 are the co-ordinates of current point.

Thus, it is positive to incrementally go on selecting the pixel position by starting with one of the end point and by making the use of Δx and Δy till the other end point has been reached.

(a) Algorithm:

Step 1: Approximate the line length. If abs $(x_2 - x_1) \geq$ abs $(y_2 - y_1)$.
    then length = abs $(x_2 - x_1)$
    else length = abs $(y_2 - y_1)$

Step 2: Initialize Δx or Δy to be equal to one raster unit.

$$\Delta x = (x_2 - x_1)/length$$
$$\Delta y = (y_2 - y_1)/length$$

Step 3: Round the values rather than truncate. Sign function is used to make the algorithm work on all quadrants.

$$x = x_1 + 0.5 \, sign(\Delta x)$$
$$y = y_1 + 0.5 \, sign(\Delta y)$$

Step 4: Main loop
    Initialise i = 1
    while (i≤length)
    plot (integer (x), integer (y))
        x = x + Δx
        y = y + Δy
        i = i + 1
    end while
    end

Note:
1. (x_1, y_1) (x_2, y_2) are to end points of a line which are assumed not equal.
2. The sign function is used which return 1, 0 −1 for the argument as greater than zero, equal to zero and less than zero respectively.
3. Floor integer function is used.
   For example,   1.5 = 1
   −1.5 = −2

(b) Advantages of DDA:
1. The logic is very simple to understand.
2. The integer arithmetic is involved.
3. It is the simplest algorithm and does not require special skills for implementation.
4. It is a faster method for calculating pixel position.

Disadvantages of DDA:
1. Floating point arithmetic is needed thus, it is very time consuming.
2. Division logic is needed, which switches it towards hardware logic.
3. Floor integer values are used in place of normal integer values, which may give different values.
4. The line is orientation dependent, i.e. line which is drawn in IInd and IVth quadrant tend to slightly diverted from the actual path of the line, sometimes extra pixels get activated which deteriorate the accuracy of end point.

(c) Numericals:

Example 1.1:

Consider the line from (1, 1) to (5, 6). Use DDA line drawing algorithm to rasterize the line.

Solution: The end points of line are (1, 1) and (5, 6).

$$\text{So, } x_1 = 1 \quad y_1 = 1$$
$$x_2 = 5 \quad y_2 = 6$$
$$\text{Length} = \text{abs}(y_2 - y_1)$$
$$= \text{abs}(6 - 1)$$
$$= 5$$
$$\therefore \quad \text{Length} = 5$$

Now,
$$\Delta x = (x_2 - x_1)/\text{length}$$
$$= \frac{5-1}{5} = 0.8$$
$$\Delta y = (y_2 - y_1)/\text{length}$$

$$= \frac{(6-1)}{5} = 1$$

$$\Sigma x = x_1 + 0.5 \text{ sign}(\Delta x)$$
$$= 1 + 0.5 \text{ sign}(0.8)$$
$$= 1.5$$
$$y = y_1 + 0.5 \text{ sign}(\Delta y)$$
$$= 1 + 0.5 \text{ sign}(1)$$
$$= 1.5$$

Tabulating the result of each iteration, we get,

i	Plot	x	y
1	(1, 1)	1.5	1.5
2	(2, 2)	2.3	2.5
3	(3, 3)	3.1	3.5
4	(3, 4)	3.9	4.5
5	(4, 5)	4.7	5.5
6	(5, 6)	5.5	6.5
7	(6, 7)	6.3	7.5

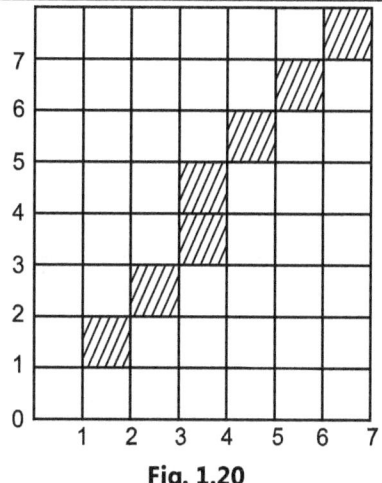

Fig. 1.20

Example 1.2:

Using DDA algorithm draw a line from (1, 1) to (5, 3).

Solution: The end points of line are (1, 1) and (5, 3).

So, $x_1 = 1$, $x_2 = 5$
$y_1 = 1$, $y_2 = 3$

∴ Length = abs $(x_2 - x_1)$
= abs $(5 - 1)$
= 4

Now,

$$\Delta x = (x_2 - x_1)/\text{length}$$
$$= (5 - 1)/4$$
$$= 4/4$$
$$= 1$$
$$\Delta y = (y_2 - y_1)/\text{length}$$
$$= (3 - 1)/4$$
$$= 2/4 = 0.5$$
$$x = x_1 + 0.5 \text{ sign } (\Delta x)$$
$$= 1 + 0.5 \text{ sign } (1)$$
$$= 1.5$$
$$y = y_1 + 0.5 \text{ sign } (\Delta y)$$
$$= 1 + 0.5 \text{ sign } (0.5) (2)$$
$$= 1 + 0.5$$
$$= 1.5$$

Tabulating the result of each iteration.

i	Plot	x	y
1	(1, 1)	1.5	1.5
2	(2, 2)	2.5	2
3	(3, 2)	3.5	2.5
4	(4, 3)	4.5	3
5	(5, 3)	5.5	3.5

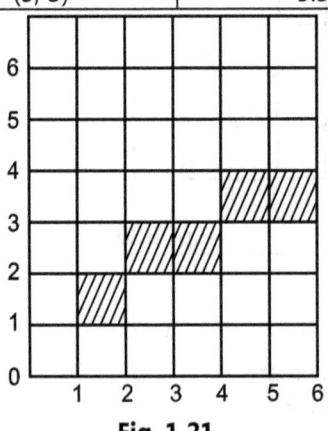

Fig. 1.21

Example 1.3:
Rasterize the line from (6, 0) to (−8, −4) using simple DDA algorithm.
Solution: $x_1 = 0, y_1 = 0$

$x_2 = -8, y_2 = -4$

abs $(x_2 - x_1)$ = abs $(-8 - 0) = 8$
abs $(y_2 - y_1)$ = abs $(-4 - 0) = 4$

∴ Length = 8

$\Delta x = (x_2 - x_1)/\text{length}$
$= -8/8$
$= -1$

$\Delta y = (y_2 - y_1)/\text{length}$
$= -4/8$
$= -0.5$

$x = x_1 + 0.5 \text{ sign}(\Delta x)$
$= 0 + 0.5 (-1)$
$= -0.5$

$y = y_1 + 0.5 \text{ sign}(\Delta y)$
$= 0 + 0.5 \text{ sign}(-0.5)$
$y = -0.5$

i	Plot	x	y
1	(−1, −1)	− 0.5	− 0.5
2	(−2, −1)	− 1.5	− 1
3	(−3, −2)	− 2.5	− 1.5
4	(−4, −2)	− 3.5	− 2
5	(−5, −3)	− 4.5	− 2.5
6	(−6, −3)	− 5.5	− 3
7	(−7, −4)	− 6.5	− 3.5
8	(−8, −4)	− 7.5	− 4

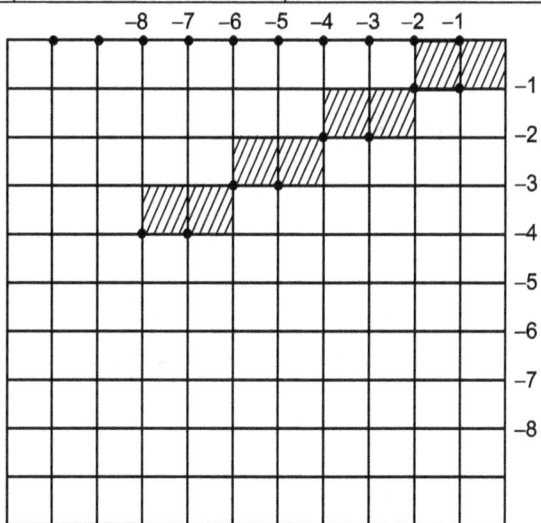

Fig. 1.22

Example 1.4:

Rasterize a line from (0, 0) to (8, −4).

Solution: $x_1 = 0, y_1 = 0$
$x_2 = 8, y_2 = -4$

$abs(x_2 - x_1) = abs(8 - 0) = 8$
$abs(y_2 - y_1) = abs(-4 - 0) = 4$

∴ Length = 8

$\Delta x = x_2 - x_1 / length$
$= 8/8$

$\Delta y = y_2 - y_1 / length$
$= -4/8 = -0.5$

$x = x_1 + 0.5\ sign(\Delta x)$
$= 0 + 0.5\ (1)$
$= 0.5$

$y = y_1 + 0.5\ sign(\Delta y)$
$= 0 + 0.5\ (-1)$
$= -0.5$

i	Plot	x	y
1	(0, −1)	0.5	− 0.5
2	(1, −1)	1.5	− 1
3	(2, −2)	2.5	− 1.5
4	(3, −2)	3.5	− 2
5	(4, −3)	4.5	− 2.5
6	(5, −3)	5.5	− 3
7	(6, −4)	6.5	− 3.5
8	(7, −4)	7.5	− 4

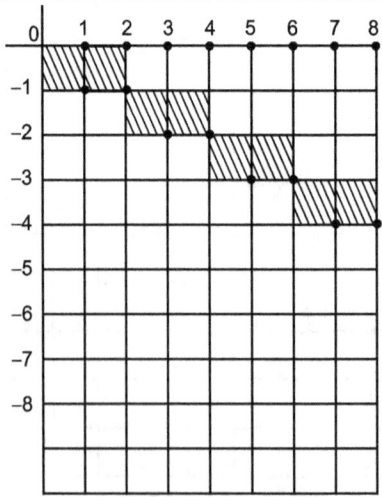

Fig. 1.23

COMPUTER GRAPHICS

BASIC CONCEPTS

Example 1.5:

Rasterize the line y = 2x + 10.

Solution:

$$y = 2x + 10$$

Put $x = 0$, $y = 10$

Put $y = 0$, $x = -5$

∴ The end points of line are (0, 10) to (−5, 0).

∴ $x_1 = 0$, $x_2 = -5$

$y_1 = 10$, $y_2 = 0$

$$\text{abs}(x_2 - x_1) = \text{abs}(-5 - 0) = 5$$
$$\text{abs}(y_2 - y_1) = \text{abs}(10 - 0) = 10$$

∴ Length = 10

$$\Delta x = x_2 - x_1/\text{length}$$
$$= -0.5$$
$$\Delta y = y_2 - y_1/\text{length}$$
$$= -1$$
$$x = x_1 + 0.5 \text{ sign}(\Delta x)$$
$$= 0 + 0.5 \text{ sign}(-0.5)$$
$$= -0.5$$
$$y = y_1 + 0.5 \text{ sign}(\Delta y)$$
$$= 10 + 0.5 \text{ sign}(-1)$$
$$= 9.5$$

i	Plot	x	y
1	(−1, 9)	−0.5	9.5
2	(−1, 8)	−1	8.5
3	(−2, 7)	−1.5	7.
4	(−2, 6)	−2	6.5
5	(−3, 5)	−2.5	5.5
6	(−3, 4)	−3	4.5
7	(−4, 3)	−3.5	3.5
8	(−4, 2)	−4	2.5
9	(−5, 1)	−4.5	1.5
10	(−5, 0)	−5	0.5

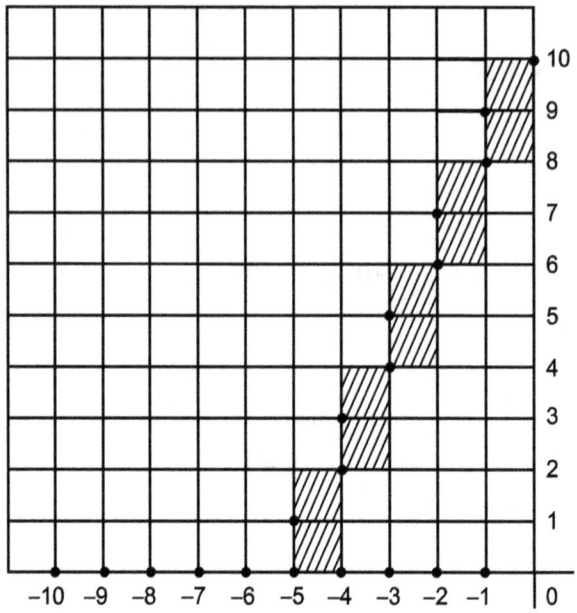

Fig. 1.24

Example 1.6:

Rasterize a line from (−3, −3) to (5, 2).

Solution: $x_1 = -3, x_2 = 5$

$y_1 = -3, y_2 = 2$

abs $(x_2 - x_1)$ = abs $(5 - (-3))$ = 8

abs $(y_2 - y_1)$ = abs $(2 - (-3))$

= abs (5)

= 5

∴   Length = 8

Δx = $x_2 - x_1$/length

= 8/8

= 1

Δy = $y_2 - y_1$/length

= 5/8

= 0.625

x = x_1 + 0.5 sign (Δx)

= −3 + 0.5 sign (1)

= −2.5

COMPUTER GRAPHICS
BASIC CONCEPTS

i	Plot	x	y
1	(−3, −3)	−2.5	−2.5
2	(−2, −2)	−1.5	−1.875
3	(−1, −1)	−0.5	−1.25
4	(0, −1)	0.5	−0.625
5	(1, 0)	1.5	0
6	(2, 1)	2.5	0.625
7	(3, 1)	3.5	1.25
8	(4, 2)	4.5	1.875

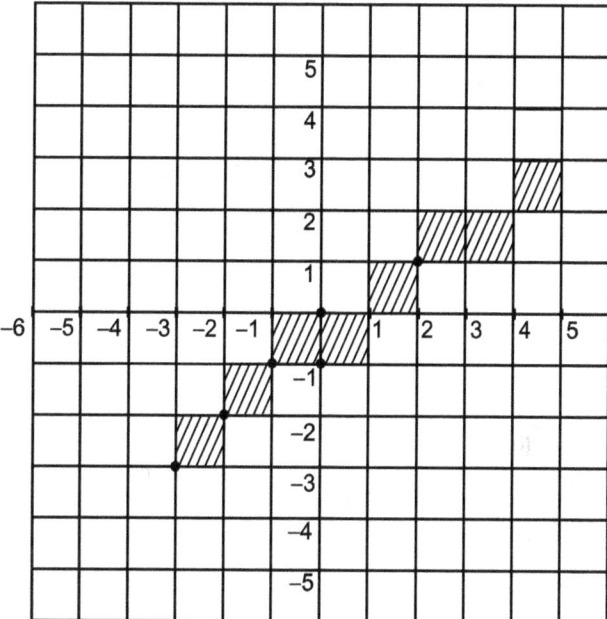

Fig. 1.25

1.16.3 Bresenham's Algorithm

This algorithm selects the optimal raster location and either increments x or y depending on the slope of the line. It always performs the increment in one of the direction by one unit while the increment of other variable is done by checking 'decision variable' or 'error term'.

(a) Error Term/Decision Variable:

This can be defined as a distance between actual line location and the nearest grid location. An error term is maintained to decide which pixel is closer to line. The selection of next pixel location is done according to the value of error term, the sign of error term need not to be checked.

Consider the line in first quadrant. If the slope of a line through (0, 0) is greater than 1/2, then its intercept with the line x = 1 will be closer to the line y = 1 as compared to that of line y = 0. Thus, the raster point at (1, 1) will better represent the path of line i.e. y is incremented. In the similar manner, if slope of line is less than 1/2 then its intercept with line x = 1 will be closer to line y = 0, than to line y = 1. Thus, raster point at (1, 0) will be better represent the path of line.

$$\frac{1}{2} \le \frac{\Delta y}{\Delta x} \le 1 \quad (\text{error} \ge 0)$$

and then pixel selected is (1, 1).

$$0 \le \frac{\Delta y}{\Delta x} \le \frac{1}{2} \quad (\text{error} < 0) \text{ and the pixel selected is (1, 0).}$$

the pixel selected is (1, 0).

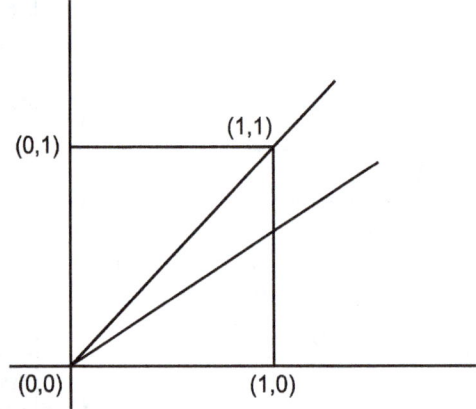

Fig. 1.26

Most of the line do not pass precisely through raster location exactly hence the error term will be initialized to $-\frac{1}{2}$.

The value of error term or decision parameter 'e' for the next raster location will be,

$$e = e + m$$

If e + m is negative then m is less than 0.5 hence line (1, 0) will better represent the path of line.

If e + m is positive then line (1, 1) will better represent the path of line.

Thus, by maintaining error term as explained above and by initializing it to −1/2 and also updating it by adding slope of line at next pixel position, the selection of next pixel which is more closer to line can be easily done. This is what is done in Bresenham's algorithm.

(b) Bresenham's Algorithm for the line whose slope is between 0 to 45°:

Step (i): Initialise variable

$x = x_1, y = y_1$

$\Delta x = x_2 - x_1$

$\Delta y = y_2 - y_1$

Step (ii): Initialise $\bar{e}$ to compensate for non-zero intercept.

$$\bar{e} = -\frac{1}{2} \qquad \bar{e} = 2e\,\Delta x$$

$$\frac{\bar{e}}{2\Delta x} = -\frac{1}{2} \qquad \therefore \bar{e} = -\Delta x$$

Step (iii): For i = 1 to Δx

    Plot (x, y)

$$x = x + 1$$

$$\bar{e} = \bar{e} + 2\Delta y$$

  if ($\bar{e} \geq 0$) then

    $y = y + 1$

    $\bar{e} = \bar{e} - 2\Delta x$

  next i

finish

where,
1. x, y, Δx, Δy are assumed to be integers.
2. e is real.
3. end points (x_1, y_1) (x_2, y_2) are assumed not equal.
4. Normal integer functions are used.

In above algorithm if slope is greater than 1 then this indicates that Δy is greater than Δx. Thus, increment in y is always by one unit where as increment in x is either 0 or 1 which depend upon the sign of error term.

This can be notified further by taking absolute value of x_1, x_2, y_1, y_2 and Δx and Δy respectively and also by using return value of sign function for incrementing x and y respectively to make the algorithm work in all quadrants. Thus, the general integer Breseham's algorithm is used which works in all quadrants.

(c) General Integer Bresenham's Algorithm:

Comments:

(a) All variables are integer.

(b) Line end points are assumed integers as not equal.

(c) Sign function is used which returns −1, 0, 1 which take arguments as less than 0, equal to 0 and greater than 0 respectively.

Algorithm:

Step (i): Initialise the variable

$x = x_1, y = y_1$

$\Delta x = abs(x_2 - x_1)$
$\Delta y = abs(y_2 - y_1)$
$s_1 = sign(x_2 - x_1)$
$s_2 = sign(y_2 - y_1)$

Step (ii): Interchange Δy or Δx depending on the slope of line.

If $\Delta y > \Delta x$ then
    temp = Δx
    $\Delta x = \Delta y$
    Δy = temp
    flag = 1
else flag = 0
end if

Step (iii): Initialise the error term

$\bar{e} = -\Delta x$

Step (iv): Main loop

For i = 1 to Δx
Plot (x, y)
If flag = 1 then
y = y + s_2
else
x = x + s_1
end if

$\bar{e} = \bar{e} + 2\Delta y$

while ($\bar{e} \geq 0$)
If flag = 1 then
x = x + s_1
else y = y + s_2
end if

$\bar{e} = \bar{e} - 2\Delta x$

end while

next i

finish

(d) Numericals:

Example 1.7:

Rasterize a line (1, 1) to (4, 5) using a general Bresenham's algorithm.

Solution:

Step (i): Initialise the variables

$x_1 = 1, y_1 = 1$
$x_2 = 4, y_2 = 5$
$x = x_1 = 1, y = y_1 = 1$

$$\Delta x = abs(x_2 - x_1)$$
$$= abs(4 - 1)$$
$$= 3$$
$$\Delta y = abs(y_2 - y_1)$$
$$= abs(5 - 1)$$
$$= 4$$
$$s_1 = sign(x_2 - x_1)$$
$$= sign(3)$$
$$= 1$$
$$s_2 = sign(y_2 - y_1)$$
$$= sign(4)$$
$$= 1$$

Step (ii): Interchange Δy or Δx depending on the slope of line.

$\Delta y > \Delta x$
$4 > 3$ yes
$\therefore$ Flag = 1
$\Delta y = 3, \Delta x = 4$

Step (iii): Initialize error term.

$\therefore \quad \bar{e} = -\Delta x$
$\bar{e} = -4$

Step (iv):

i	Plot	$\bar{e}$	x	y
1	(1, 1)	-4	1	1
		2	2	2
		-6		
2	(2, 2)	0	3	3
		-8		
3	(3, 3)	-2	3	4
4	(3, 4)	4	4	5

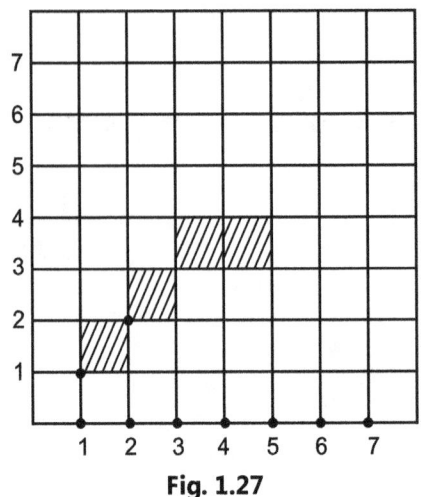

Fig. 1.27

Example 1.8:

Rasterize a line from (−3, 3) to (6, −4).

Solution: Initialise the variable

$x_1 = -3, y_1 = 3$
$x_2 = 6, y_2 = -4$

$$x = x_1 = -3$$
$$y = y_1 = 3$$
$$\Delta x = abs(x_2 - x_1)$$
$$= abs(6 - (-3))$$
$$= 9$$
$$\Delta y = abs(y_2 - y_1)$$
$$= abs(-4 - 3)$$
$$= 7$$
$$s_1 = sign(x_2 - x_1)$$
$$= 1$$
$$s_2 = sign(y_2 - y_1)$$
$$= 1$$

Step (ii): Interchange Δy or Δx depending

$\Delta y > \Delta x$
$7 > 9 \Rightarrow NO$
∴   Flag = 0
$\Delta x = 9$
$\Delta y = 7$

COMPUTER GRAPHICS — BASIC CONCEPTS

Step (iii): Initialize the error term.

$$\bar{e} = -\Delta x$$
$$= -9$$

Step (iv): Main loop.

i	Plot	$\bar{e}$	x	y
1	(−3, 3)	−9	−3	3
		5	−2	2
		−13		
2	(−2, 2)	1	−1	1
		−17		
3	(−1, 1)	−3	0	1
		11	1	0
4	(0, 1)	−7		
5	(1, 0)	7	2	−1
		−11		
6	(2, −11)	3	3	−2
		−15		
7	(3, −2)	−1	4	−3
8	(4, −3)	13	5	−4
		−5		

Example 1.9:

Rasterize a line from (0, 0) to (−8, −4).

Solution:

Step (i): Initialize the variable

$x_1 = 0$, $x_2 = -8$
$y_1 = 0$, $y_2 = -4$

$$x = x_1 = 0$$
$$y = y_1 = 0$$
$$\Delta x = 8$$
$$\Delta y = 4$$
$$s_1 = \text{sign}(x_2 - x_1)$$
$$= 1$$
$$s_2 = \text{sign}(y_2 - y_1)$$
$$= 1$$

Step (ii): Interchange Δy or Δx depending upon slope of line.

Δy > Δx
4 > 8 NO
∴   Flag = 0
Δx = 8
Δy = 4

Step (iii): Initialise the error term:

$$\bar{e} = -\Delta x$$

∴ $\bar{e} = -8$

Step (iv): Main loop

i	Plot	$\bar{e}$	x	y
1	(0, 0)	−8	0	0
2	(−1, −1)	0	−1	−1
		−16		
3	(−2, −1)	−8	−2	−1
4	(−3, −2)	0	−3	−2
		−16		
5	(−4, −2)	−8	−4	−2
6	(−5, −3)	0	−5	−3
		−16	−6	−3
7	(−6, −3)	−8	−7	−4
8	(−7, −4)	0	−8	−4

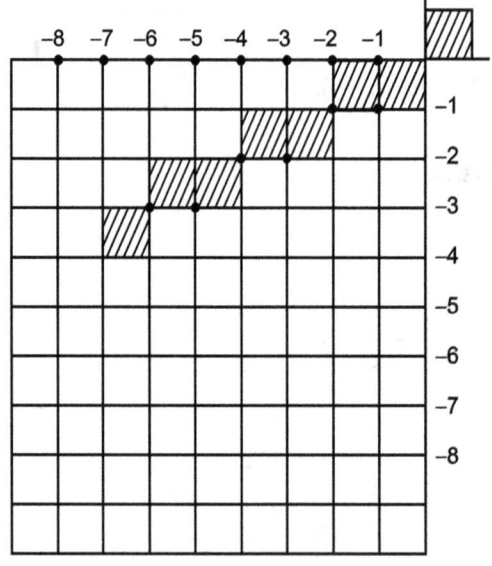

Fig. 1.28

COMPUTER GRAPHICS   BASIC CONCEPTS

Example 1.10:

Generate a line y = 2x + 10. Using Bresenham's line generation algorithm.

Solution:

Step (i): Initialize the variables

$$y = 2x + 10$$

Put x = 0, y = 10
Put y = 0, x = −5
Thus, the end points of line are,
     (0, 10) to (−5, 0)
     $x_1 = 0$, $x_2 = -5$
     $y_1 = 10$, $y_2 = 0$
     $x = x_1 = 0$, $y = y_1 = 10$

$$\Delta x = abs(x_2 - x_1) = 5$$
$$\Delta y = abs(y_2 - y_1) = 10$$

$s_1 = -1, s_2 = -1$

Step (iii): Initialise the error term

$$\bar{e} = -\Delta x = -5$$

Step (iv): Main loop

i	Plot	$\bar{e}$	x	y
1	(0, 10)	−5	0	10
2	(−1, 9)	0	−1	9
		−20		
3	(−1, 8)	−10	−1	8
		0	−2	7
4	(−2, 7)	−20		
5	(−2, 6)	−10	−2	6
6	(−3, 5)	0	−3	5
		−20		
7	(−3, 4)	−10	−3	4
8	(−4, 3)	0	−4	3
		−20		
9	(−4, 1)	−10	−4	2
10	(−5, 1)	0	−5	1
		−20		
		−10	−5	0

Chp 1 | 1.45

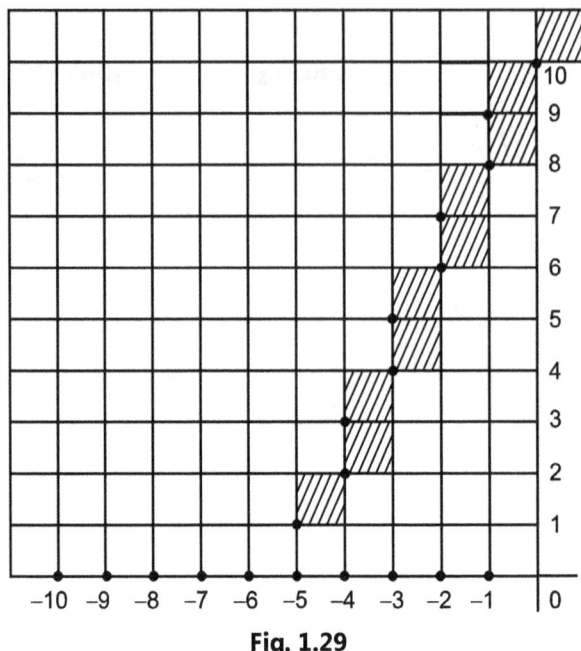

Fig. 1.29

Example 1.11:

Consider the line from (2, 7) to (5, 5) use Bresenham's line drawing algorithm to rasterize this line.

Solution:

Step (i): Initialize the variables.

$x_1 = 2, y_1 = 7$

$x_2 = 5, y_2 = 5$

$x = x_1 = 2$

$y = y_1 = 7$

$$\Delta x = abs(x_2 - x_1)$$
$$= 3$$
$$\Delta y = abs(y_2 - y_1)$$
$$= 2$$
$$s_1 = 1$$
$$s_2 = -1$$

Step (ii): Interchange Δy or Δx depending upon slope of line.

$\Delta y > \Delta x$

2 > 3 NO

∴ Flag = 0

$\Delta x = 3$

$\Delta y = 2$

COMPUTER GRAPHICS — BASIC CONCEPTS

Step (iii): Initialise error term.

$$\bar{e} = -\Delta x$$
$$= -3$$

Step (iv): Main loop

i	Plot	$\bar{e}$	x	y
		1	2	7
1	(2, 7)	−1	3	6
2	(3, 6)	3	4	6
3	(4, 6)	2	5	5

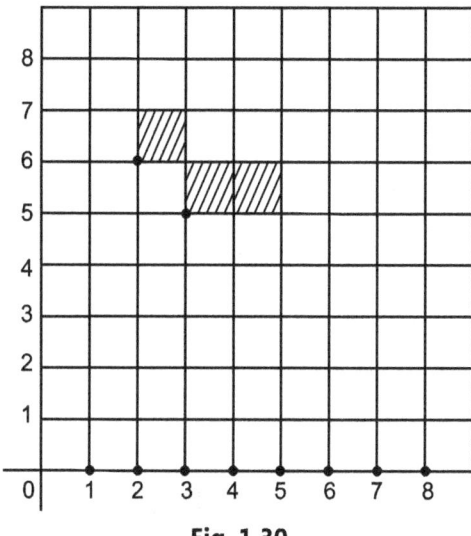

Fig. 1.30

Example 1.12:

Consider the line from (4, 9) to (7, 7). Draw a line using Bresenham's line drawing algorithm.

Solution:

Step: Initialize the variables

$x_1 = 4, x_2 = 7$
$y_1 = 9, y_2 = 7$
$x = 4, y = 9$

$$\Delta x = abs(x_2 - x_1)$$
$$= abs(7 - 4)$$
$$= 3$$
$$\Delta y = abs(y_1 - y_1)$$
$$= abs(7 - 9)$$
$$= 2$$

Chp 1 | 1.47

$$s_1 = \text{sign}(x_2 - x_1)$$
$$= 1$$
$$s_2 = \text{sign}(y_2 - y_1)$$
$$= -1$$

Step (ii): Interchange Δy or Δx depending upon the slope.

$$\text{Is } \Delta y > \Delta x$$
$$2 > 3 \text{ NO}$$
$$\therefore \quad \text{Flag} = 0$$
$$\Delta x = 3$$
$$\Delta y = 2$$

Step (iii): Initialise the error term.

$$\bar{e} = -\Delta x$$
$$= -3$$

Step (iv): Main loop

i	Plot	$\bar{e}$	x	y
1	(4, 9)	−3	4	9
2	(5, 8)	1	5	8
3	(6, 8)	−5	6	8
4	(7, 7)	3	7	7

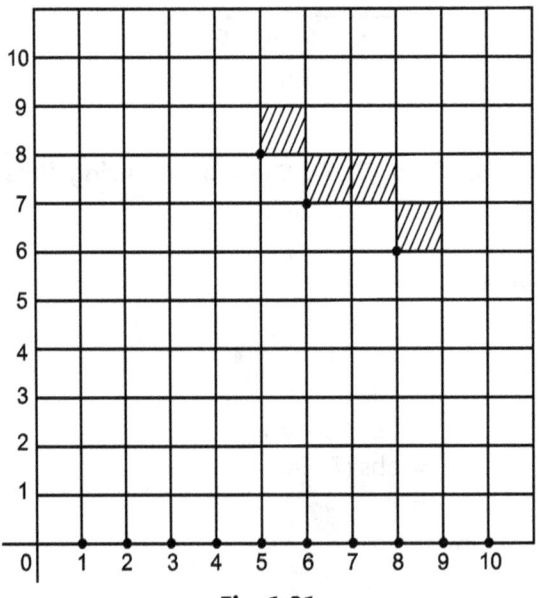

Fig. 1.31

Example 1.13:

Using Bresenham's line algorithm draw line from (1, 1) to (5, 3).

Solution:

Step (i): Initialise the variables

$x_1 = 1$, $x_2 = 5$

$y_1 = 1$, $y_2 = 3$

$x = x_1 = 1$

$y = y_1 = 1$

$$\Delta x = abs(x_2 - x_1)$$
$$= 4$$
$$\Delta y = abs(y_2 - y_1)$$
$$= 2$$
$$s_1 = 1$$
$$s_2 = 1$$

Step (ii): Interchange Δy or Δx depending upon slope of line.

$$\text{Is } \Delta y > \Delta x$$
$$2 > 4 \text{ No}$$

∴
$$\text{Flag} = 0$$
$$\Delta x = 4$$
$$\Delta y = 2$$

Step (iii): Initialise the error term.

$$\bar{e} = -\Delta x$$
$$= -4$$

Step (iv): Main loop.

i	Plot	$\bar{e}$	x	y
		−4	1	1
1	(1, 1)	0	2	2
		−8		
2	(2, 2)		3	2
3	(3, 2)			
			4	3
		−8		
4	(4, 3)	−4	5	3

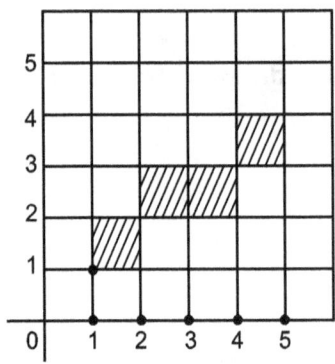

Fig. 1.32

(e) Comparison between DDA and Bresenham's:

DDA Algorithm:

1. It is orientation dependent hence the end point accuracy deteriorates.
2. Floating point arithmetic is used which is time consuming.
3. Floor integer functions are used thus the result obtained are different from those obtained using normal integers.

Bresenham's Algorithm:

1. Normal integer functions are used.
2. All variables are assumed integers.
3. Sign of error term is considered.
4. Sign function is used.

(f) Gentle Slope and Sharp Cases:

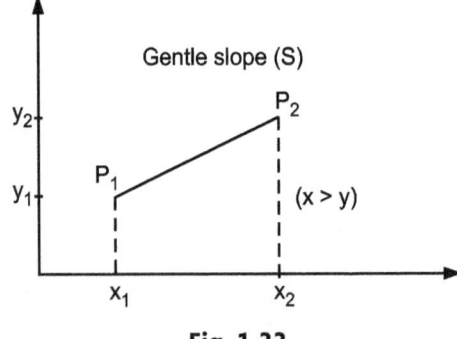

Fig. 1.33

For gentle slope ($-1 < m < 1$) there are more column than rows ($x > y$). These lines segments where the length of x component $\Delta x = (x_b - x_a)$ is longer than length of y component $D_y = (y_b - y_a)$ that is ($D_x > D_y$). For gentle cases we step across the column and solve for rows.

1.16.4 Comparison between Vector Generation Algorithm and Bresenham's Algorithm

Vector Generation Algorithm	Bresenham's Line Algorithm
1. It uses floating point arithmetic	1. It uses only integer addition, subtraction and multiplication by 2.
2. Less efficient.	2. More efficient.
3. Due to floating point arithmetic it takes more time.	3. It is comparatively quicker.
4. Where speed is important this algorithm needs to be implemented in hardware.	4. Hardware implementation is not required.

1.16.5 Thick Line Segment

The raster displays allows the display of lines having thickness greater than one pixel. For producing thick line segment the two vector generation algorithms must run in parallel to find the pixels along the line edges. While moving along the line finding successive edges pixels, the pixels which lie between the boundaries must be turned on.

For a gentle sloping line between (x_a, y_a) and (x_b, y_b) with thickness w, the top boundary between the points $(x_a, y_a + w_y)$, and $(x_b, y_b + w_y)$ and the bottom boundary between $(x_a, y_a - w_y)$ and $(x_b, y_b - w_y)$.

where w_y is given by equation –

$$w_y = \frac{(w-1)\left[(x_b - x_a)^2 + (y_b - y_a)^2\right]^{1/2}}{|x_b - y_a|}$$

This w_y is the amount by which the boundary lines are moved from the center of line. The $(w - 1)$ factor is the width. This factor is divided by 2 since only half of thickness will be used to offset the top boundary and the other half is used to move bottom boundary. The x and y values are used to find the amount to shift up and down in order to achieve the proper width w.

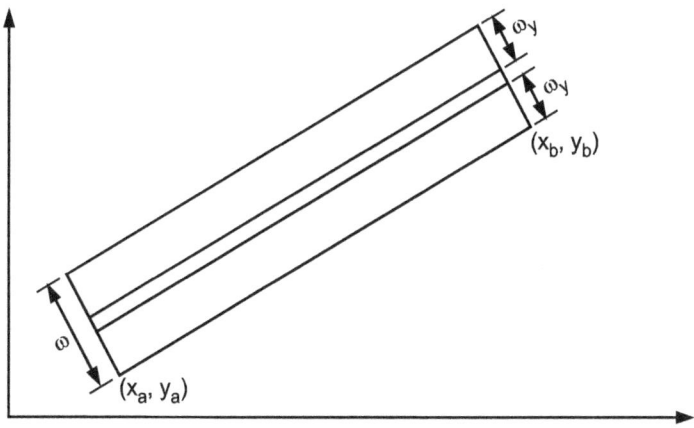

Fig. 1.34: Construction of Thick Line

1.16.6 Desirable and Essential Characteristics of Line Drawing Algorithm

The desirable and essential characteristics of line drawing algorithm are:

   1. Line Should Appear Straight: Point plotting technique are admirably suited to the generation of lines parallel or at 45° to the x and y axes. Other line causes a problem. A line segment through it starts and finished at addressable point may happen to pass through no addressable point in between. In these cases, we must approximate the line by choosing addressable point close to it. If we choose properly, then the line will appear straight. If not then we will get crooked lines.

   2. Lines Should Terminate Accurately: Unless lines are plotted properly they may terminate at wrong place. The effect is often seen as a small gap between the end points of one line and the starting point of the next line or as a cumulative error.

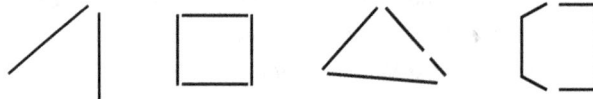

Fig. 1.35

   3. Lines Should Have Constant Density: With bright line plotted on dark background line density is observed on brighten when the line is black and background is light, it is seen as blackness. In either cases, line density is proportional to the number of dots displayed by the length of line. To maintain constant density, dots should be equally spaced. This can be achieved only in lines which are parallel or at 45° to the axes. In other cases, we must attempt to achieve as even spacing as possible. Bunching of dots will otherwise be visible as particular bright or dark regions on the line.

Fig. 1.36

   4. Lines Density Should be Independent of the Line Length and Angle: This is a difficult requirement to satisfy. As we have just seen that, to achieve constant line density we must maintain a constant number of dots per unit length. Before plotting the line, we must therefore determine the exact length, which involves computing a square root. Also we must be able to control the rate in terms of distance travelled at which dots are plotted. None of the above approach can be easily done. Normally, the best we can do is to compute an approximate line length estimate and to use a line generation algorithm that keeps line density constant within the accuracy of this estimate.

5. Lines should be Drawn Rapidly: In interactive application, we would like lines to appear rapidly on the screen. This implies using the minimum of computation to draw the line.

1.16.7 Aliasing and Antialiasing

The images which are different but posses same graphical representation are called as **alias** and phenomenon is referred as **aliasing**.

The main cause of aliasing is the finite size of pixel. If the size of pixel get reduced then the effect of aliasing will also be reduced. The size of pixel depends upon hardware resolution. Thus, for the reduction of aliasing effect and for the improvement of visual resolution the software method is used, which is referred as **antialiasing**.

For effective antialiasing, it is necessary to understand the reason of aliasing. The appearance of aliasing effect is due to the lines, polygon edges, and colour boundaries etc. which are continuous while a raster device is discrete. For plotting line, polygon edge etc. on the raster display device, it must be sampled at discrete locations. This will have a very unexpected result.

The two important antialiasing techniques are:
1. Super sampling or post filtering or averaging.
2. Area sampling or prefiltering.

1. Super Sampling/Post Filtering/Averaging:

The method of sampling object characteristics at high resolution and at the same time displaying the results at low resolution is referred to as super sampling or post filtering or averaging method.

This is a straight forward technique to increase the sampling rate by treating the screen as if it were covered with time grid then is actually available. The multiple sample points can be used across this timer grid for determination of an appropriate intensity level for each screen pixel.

This technique can be implemented in two ways:
 (a) Uniform averaging.
 (b) Averaging using weights.

2. Area Sampling/Prefiltering:

In polygon filling and line rasterization algorithms, the intensity or colour of a pixel is identified according to the intensity or colour of a single point within the pixel area. In this method, it is assumed that the pixel is a mathematical point rather than a finite area. In area, antialiasing method, the pixel is treated as a finite area.

In an ideal primitive the line should have zero width, but here the line has non-zero width. Hence, the line can be thought of as a rectangle of a desired thickness, which covers a portion of grid as shown in Fig. 1.37.

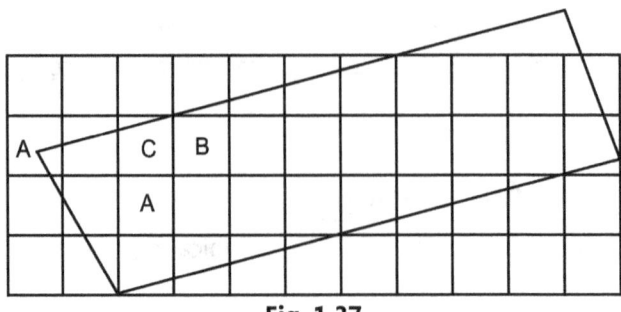

Fig. 1.37

As shown in above figure, consider pixel A. The overlapping of line and the pixel A is 100%. Thus, the intensity of pixel is maximum.

The pixel B is overlapped 80%. Hence, the intensity of pixel would be 80% of maximum intensity. In similar manner the overlapping region of pixel C and D is 50% and 10% respectively. Thus, their intensities should be 50% and 10% of maximum intensity respectively. Antialiasing by computing overlap area is referred as Area sampling or prefiltering.

Q. 1 Explain how aliasing effect can be removed in vector generation algorithm.

Ans. The aliasing effect can be minimized by increasing resolution of the raster display. By increasing resolution and making it twice the original one, the line passes through twice as many column of pixels and therefore has twice as many jags, but each jag is half as large in x and in y direction.

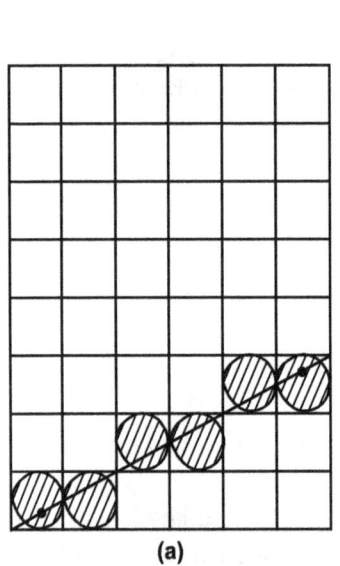
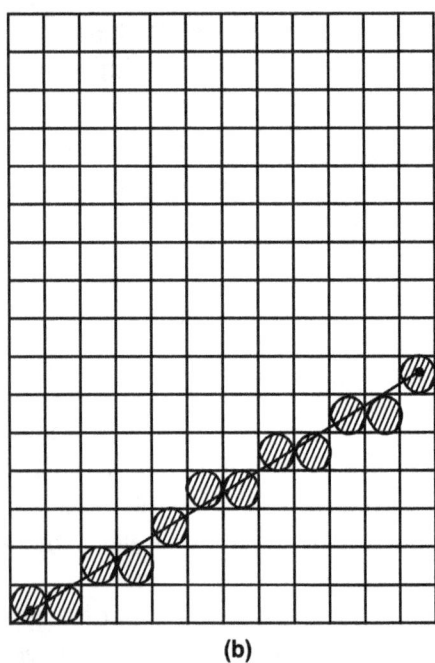

(a)　　　　　　　　　　　　　　(b)

Fig. 1.38: Effect of Aliasing with Increasing in Resolution

As shown in Fig. 1.40, line looks better in twice resolution, but this improvement comes at the price of quadrupling the cost of memory, bandwidth of memory scan-conversion time. Thus, increasing resolution is an expensive method for reducing aliasing effect.

With raster systems that are capable of displaying more than two intensity levels (colour or gray scale), we can apply antialiasing methods to modify pixel intensity. By appropriately varying the intensities of pixels along the line or object boundaries, we can smooth the edges to lessen the stair-step or jagged appearance.

1.17 CIRCLE GENERATING ALGORITHMS

Before knowing circle generating algorithms let's see the symmetry of circle. Very first of all circle is a symmetrical figure. The shape of circle is similar in each quadrant. After that circle is also symmetrical between octants. Thus, circle has eight way symmetry i.e. symmetrical in all octants. Once one point in one octant is calculated, it can be mapped into other seven circle points in other octants.

Following Fig. 1.39 shows symmetry of a circle where point (x, y) in first octant gives circle points in other seven octants.

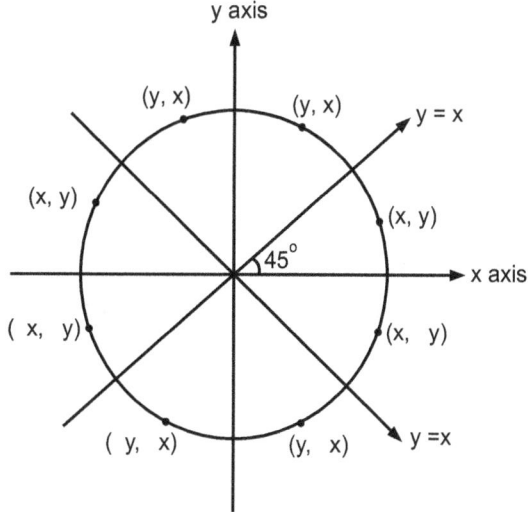

Fig. 1.39: Symmetry of Circle

Now, we will see the actual circle generating algorithms as
1. DDA Algorithm
2. Bresenham Algorithm
3. Mid-point Algorithm

1.17.1 DDA Circle Generating Algorithms

The differential equation of a circle with center as origin is

$$\frac{dy}{dx} = \frac{-x}{y}$$

From above equation we can construct a circle by using x and y incremental values Δx and Δy as,

$\Delta x = \varepsilon y$ and

$\Delta y = -\varepsilon x$

Where,

$\varepsilon = 2^{-n}$

$2^{n-1} \le r \le 2^n$ and r is radius of circle.

Thus, we can get next pixel by using following equation

$x_{n+1} = x_n + \varepsilon\, y_n$

$y_{n+1} = y_n - \varepsilon\, x_n$

Unfortunately above equations gives a spiral shape instead of a circle. To make it a circle we need to do correction in above equation as,

$x_{n+1} = x_n + \varepsilon\, y_n$

$y_{n+1} = y_n - \varepsilon\, x_{n+1}$

Merits of DDA Algorithm:
1. It is well suited to hardware implementation.
   This algorithm is summarized as below:

Algorithm 4: DDA circle Drawing Algorithm:
   Step 1: Read radius of circle (r) and calculate value of ε (epsilon).
   Step 2: x = 0
             y = r
   Step 3: $x_1 = x$
             $y_1 = y$
   Step 4: While (($y_1 - y$) < ε || ($x - x_1$) > ε)
             {
             $x_1 = x_1 + \varepsilon\, y_1$
             $y_1 = y_1 + \varepsilon\, x_1$
             plot (int (x_1), int (y_1))
             }
   Step 5: Stop.

1.17.2 Bresenham's Circle Generating Algorithm

This algorithm uses the symmetry of circle as seen before.
Here Bresenham's line generating algorithm is adopted for generating circle, where at each sampling step decision parameter decides the closest pixel to the circumference of circle.
We will firstly see one octant from 90° to 45°.

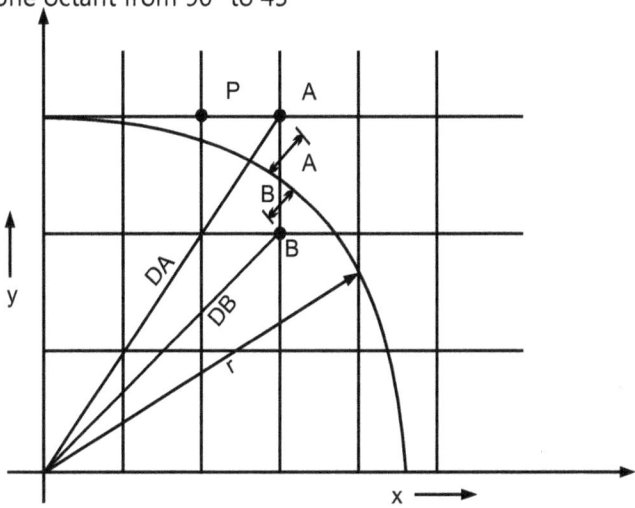

Fig. 1.40

Referring to Fig. 1.40 P is the latest scan converted pixel. Now, the decision parameter P_k decides which next pixel select for plotting, either A or B. The distances of pixels A and B from origin are given as,

$$D_A = \sqrt{(x_i+1)^2+(y_i)^2} \quad \ldots (1.1)$$

and $\quad D_B = \sqrt{(x_i+1)^2+(y_i-1)^2} \quad \ldots (1.2)$

Distances of A and B from true circle path are given as
$$\Delta A = D_A^2 - r^2 \quad \ldots (1.3)$$
$$\Delta B = D_B^2 - r^2 \quad \ldots (1.4)$$

The decision factor P_i is
$$P_i = \Delta A + \Delta B \quad \ldots (1.5)$$

From Fig. 2.6 ΔA is always positive and ΔB is always negative.

∴ for $P_i < 0$, $x_{i+1} = x_i + 1$ and
for $P_i \geq 0$, $x_{i+1} = x_i + 1$ and
$$y_{i+1} = y_i - 1$$

As we know
$$P_i = \Delta A + \Delta B$$

From equation (1.3) and (1.4)
$$P_i = DA^2 - r^2 + DB^2 - r^2$$
From equation (1.1) and (1.2)
$$P_i = (x_i + 1)^2 + (y_i)^2 - r^2 + (x_i + 1)^2 + (y_i - 1)^2 - r^2$$
To find out initial value of decision parameter, at starting point, $x_i = 0$ and $y_i = r$.
Putting these values in above equation
$$P_i = (0 + 1)^2 + (r)^2 - (r)^2 + (0 + 1)^2 + (r - 1)^2 - r^2$$
$$P_i = 1 + 1 + r^2 - 2r^2 + 1 - r^2$$
$$P_i = 3 - 2r \qquad \ldots (1.6)$$

The derivation of P_{i+1} will be,
 For $P_i < 0$, $P_{i+1} = P_i + 4x_i + 6$ and
 For $P_i \geq 0$, $P_{i+1} = P_i + 4(x_i - y_i) + 10$
Now we summarize the algorithm in following Algorithm 5

Algorithm 4: Bresenham Circle Generating Algorithm.

Step 1: Read radius (r) of circle.

Step 2: Calculate initial decision variable P_i.

Step 3: $x = 0$ and $y = r$

Step 4: if ($P_i < 0$)
```
          {
            x = x + 1
            P_i = P_i + 4x + 6
          }
        else if (P_i ≥ 0)
          {
            x = x + 1
            y = y - 1
            P_i = P_i + 4 (x - y) + 10
          }
```

Step 5: Plot pixels in all octants as
 Plot (x, y)   (∵ Referring to Fig. 1.39)
 Plot (y, x)
 Plot (-y, x)
 Plot (-x, y)
 Plot (-x, -y)
 Plot (-y, -x)
 Plot (y, -x)
 Plot (x, -y)

Step 6: Stop

1.17.3 Mid-point Circle Generating Algorithm

Mid-point algorithm follows the following circle equation

i.e. $r^2 = x^2 + y^2$ ... (1.7)

Therefore circle function $f(x,y) = x^2 + y^2 - r^2$ ... (1.8)

Where,

r is radius of circle

x, y are co-ordinates of a point

Any point (x, y), if it is exactly on the boundary of circle with ridus r, then it satisfies the circle function i.e. f(x, y) = 0.

Depending on position of the point (x, y), sign of circle function would change i.e.

Case 1: f (x, y) < 0 (i.e. f (x, y) is negative), if point (x, y) is inside circle boundary.

Case 2: f (x, y) > 0 (i.e. f (x, y) is positive), if point (x, y) is outside circle boundary.

Case 3: f (x, y) = 0, if (x, y) is on circle boundary.

We have taken a decision parameter in line drawing algorithm, similarly here in mid-point algorithm, we take this circle function as decision parameter. Once one (first) known point is plotted on circle boundary, algorithm should detect next point near to circle boundary and should plot it. This is explained through following Fig. 1.41.

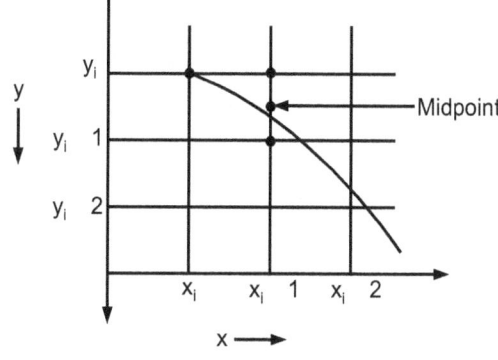

Fig. 1.41

From above Fig. 1.41 point (pixel) at (x_i, y_i) is plotted (known point is plotted). Now next, algorithm determines whether the pixel at position(x_i + 1, y_i) or pixel at (x_i + 1, y_i – 1) is near to circle boundary is plot pixel whichever is near. So the task and to find out which pixel is near to circle boundary. For this decision parameter (i.e. here circle function) is evaluated at the mid-point of these two pixels. From Fig. 1.41 co-ordinates of this mid-point are (x_i + 1, $y_i - \frac{1}{2}$).

Decision parameter (P_i) is circle function.

∴ $P_i = f(x, y)$

Putting values of mid-point in circle function i.e. equation (1.8)

$$P_i = (x_i + 1)^2 + (y_i - \frac{1}{2})^2 - r^2 \qquad \ldots (1.9)$$

From above three cases which we have seen,

1. if $P_i < 0$, then mid-point is inside circle boundary, and it means that circle passes through above mid-point. Therefore point $(x_i + 1, y_i)$ is closer to circle boundary and is selected for plotting.

2. else, if $P_i > 0$ then mid-point is outside circle boundary and it means that circle pass through, below mid-point. Therefore point $(x_i + 1, y_i - 1)$ is closer to circle boundary and is selected for plotting.

To find out next successive decision parameter $(P_i + 1)$, put co-ordinates of next point on circle in equation of decision parameter. i.e. equation (1.9) where, co-ordinate of next point are

$x_i = x_{i+1}$

$y_i = y_{i+1}$ OR $y_i = y_i + 1$

Therefore put $x_i = x_i + 1$ and $y_i = y_i + 1$ in equation (1.9) we get,

$$P_{i+1} = ((x_{i+1}) + 1) + ((y_{i+1}) - \frac{1}{2})^2 - r^2$$

∴ $P_{i+1} = P_i + 2(x_{i+1}) + (y_{i+1}^2 - y_i^2) - (y_{i+1} - y_i) + 1$ ... (1.10)

as said, depending on sign of P_i next y co-ordinate i.e. y_{i+1} can be either y_i or $y_i - 1$

Therefore if $P_i < 0$, then put $y_{i+1} = y_i - 1$ in equation (1.10).

∴ $P_{i+1} = P_i + 2(x_i + 1) + 1$ ... (1.11)

else, if $P_i > 0$ then put $y_{i+1} = y_i - 1$ in equation (1.10)

∴ $P_{i+1} = P_i + 2(x_i + 1) + 1 - 2(y_i + 1)$ ... (1.12)

To find out initial decision parameter, put co-ordinates of starting point of circle in equation (1.9) (decision parameter equation).

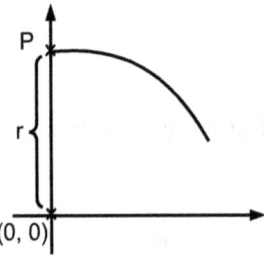

Fig. 1.42: 0-45° quadrant

From Fig. 1.42 co-ordinates of strat point P can be (0, r) where r is radius of circle. Therefore put (0, r) in equation (2.19).

∴ $P_0 = (0+1)^2 + (r - \frac{1}{2})^2 - r^2$

∴ $P_0 = \frac{5}{4} - r$ ... (1.13)

As algorithm does all increments as integers and even r is also considered as integer. Therefore above equation (1.13) can be rounded to,

$P_0 = 1 - r$ ... (1.14)

Now, we summarize these derivations of algorithm in following algorithm.

Algorithm 5: Mid-point circle generating Algorithm.

Step 1: Read radius (r) of circle.
Step 2: obtain first point on circle boundary as $(x_0, y_0) = (0, r)$
Step 3: Calculate initial decision parameter as $P_0 = 1 - r$
Step 4: if ($P_i < 0$)
{
  $x_i = x_i + 1$
  $y_i = y_i$
  $P_{i+1} = P_i + 2(x_{i+1}) + 1$
}
else if ($P_i > 0$)
{
  $x_i = x_i + 1$
  $y_i = y_i - 1$
  $P_{i+1} = P_i + 2(x_{i+1}) + 1 - 2y_{i+1}$
}

Step 5: Plot pixel (x_i, y_i) and also plot pixels in rest all seven octants as,
  Plot (y, x)   (∵ Referring to Fig. 1.42)
  Plot (-y, x)
  Plot (-x, y)
  Plot (-x, -y)
  Plot (-y, -x)
  Plot (y, -x)
  Plot (x, -y)

Step 6: Repeat step 4 and 5 until $x_i \geq y_i$
Step 7: Stop

Note: Above algorithm assumes that circle is centred at origin. If one wants to draw a circle at some other centre position above algorithm is modified to accept center co-ordinates (x_c, y_c) in step 1.

COMPUTER GRAPHICS — BASIC CONCEPTS

At the end of step 4, where next point (x_i, y_i) is calculated, shift this (x_i, y_i) to new position on circle boundary of centre (x_c, y_c) by following equation.

$x_i = x_i + x_c$

$y_i = y_i + y_c$

Following example shows problem to demonstrate mid-point circle drawing algorithm.

Example 1.14: Given radius of circle r = 8 with center at origin.

Solution:

Note: Here origin is centre of circle and we will demonstrate algorithm execution for determining points along circle boundary only in first quadrant from x = 0 and x = y.

Now, following are the steps of algorithm.

Step 1: r = 8

Step 2: $(x_0, y_0) = (0, 8)$

Step 3: $P_0 = 1 - r$

$\therefore P_0 = 1 - 8 = -7$

Step 4: Following table shows iterative execution of this step to calculate each next x_i, y_i (i.e. x_{i+1}, y_{i+1}) till $x_i \geq y_i$.

i	P_i	(x_{i+1}, y_{i+1})	P_{i+1} if $(P_i < 0)$	P_{i+1} if $(P_i > 0)$
0	−7	(1, 7)	−3	−
1	−3	(2, 7)	+2	−
2	2	(3, 6)	−	−3
3	−3	(4, 6)	6	−
4	6	(5, 5)	−	7

Step 5: For each value of i in step 4. Plot (x_{i+1}, y_{i+1}) and also plot all symmetric points in all rest octants.

Step 6: Note: Actually step 4 and 5 are executed in iteration for each values of i step 4 followed by step 5 is executed.

Step 7: Stop.

Note: Above algorithm assumes that circle is centred at origin. If one wants to draw a circle at some other centre position above algorithm is modified to accept center co-ordinates (x_c, y_c) in step 1.

At the end of step 4, where next point (x_i, y_i) is calculated, shift this (x_i, y_i) to new position on circle boundary of centre (x_c, y_c) by following equation.

$x_i = x_i + x_c$

$y_i = y_i + y_c$

Following example shows problem to demonstrate mid-point circle drawing algorithm.

Example 1.14: Given radius of circle r = 8 with center at origin.

Solution:

Note: Here origin is centre of circle and we will demonstrate algorithm execution for determining points along circle boundary only in first quadrant from x = 0 and x = y.

Now, following are the steps of algorithm.

Step 1: r = 8

Step 2: $(x_0, y_0) = (0, 8)$

Step 3: $P_0 = 1 - r$

$\therefore P_0 = 1 - 8 = -7$

Step 4: Following table shows iterative execution of this step to calculate each next x_i, y_i (i.e. x_{i+1}, y_{i+1}) till $x_i \geq y_i$.

i	P_i	(x_{i+1}, y_{i+1})	P_{i+1} if $(P_i < 0)$	P_{i+1} if $(P_i > 0)$
0	-7	(1, 7)	-3	-
1	-3	(2, 7)	+2	-
2	2	(3, 6)	-	-3
3	-3	(4, 6)	6	-
4	6	(5, 5)	-	7

Step 5: For each value of i in step 4. Plot (x_{i+1}, y_{i+1}) and also plot all symmetric points in all rest octants.

Step 6: Note : Actually step 4 and 5 are executed in iteration for each values of i step 4 followed by step 5 is executed.

Step 7: Stop.

EXERCISE

1. What is pixel? What is the importance of using frame buffer? Is it dynamic storage structure?
2. What is antialiasing? How aliasing effect is removed in vector generator method.
3. Differentiate Bresenham's and vector generation algorithm for line.
4. State different display devices. Define resolution of display devices. What is aspect ratio?
5. State and explain different methods of character generation.
6. What is vector generation? Explain vector generation algorithm for circle.

7. Explain DDA algorithm for line. Discuss its advantages and disadvantages.
8. Draw and explain the following input devices :
   (i) Trackball, (ii) Joystick, (iii) Mouse, (iv) Light Pen System, (v) Frame Buffer.
9. What is aliasing? Explain any two anti-aliasing techniques.
10. Derive the expression for decision parameter used in Bresenham's circle algorithm. Also explain Bresenham's circle algorithm.
11. Explain the features of various display devices.
12. What are the steps required to plot the line whose slope is between 0 to 45° using Bresenham's method?
13. Explain the concept of Display file structure.
14. Explain mid-point circle drawing algorithm.
15. Explain the following graphic primitives :
    (i) Tablets, (ii) Touch Panels, (iii) Light
16. Explain what is Stroke method and bitmap method.
17. Describe Bresenham's algorithm for line drawing. Explain gentle slope and sharp slope cases.
18. Define : Pixels, Vectors, Line, Frame buffers.
19. Describe Bresenham's algorithm for line drawing.
20. What is aliasing? Discuss situation in which these artifacts matter and those in which they do not. Discuss various ways to minimize the effects of jaggies and explain what the costs of these remedies might be.
21. Explain display file interpreter and display processor.
22. Write a short note on "text and line style"
23. Give differences between Bresenhams and DDA line drawing algorithm.
24. What do you mean by graphics standard?
25. List any five graphics standards. State features of any one?
26. List any two disadvantages of graphics standards?

POLYGONS

2.1 INTRODUCTION

So far we have discussed about the line and circle. The earlier display devices such as plotters, DVSTs, vector refresh displays were line – drawing devices. However the raster displays can display solid objects and patterns too. Thus, we must know the fundamental aspects of graphics primitives. The basic surface primitive is polygon. The polygon is a figure with many sides. A polygon can be represented as a group of connected edges, which forms a closed figure. The line segments which form the boundary of polygon are called as edges or sides. The end point of the edges or sides of the polygon are called as vertices.

Example: Triangle – It is a polygon having three edges and three vertices.

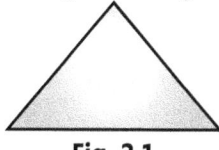

Fig. 2.1

However, polygon must be any shape as shown below in Fig. 2.2.

 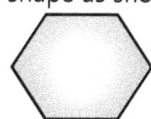 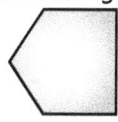 

Fig. 2.2

2.2 POLYGON

A polygon is a chain of connected line segments. It is specified by giving the vertices (nodes), $P_0, P_1, P_2, \ldots$ and so on. The first vertex is called the initial or starting point and the last vertex is called the final or terminal point as shown below. When starting point of any polyline is same i.e. when polyline is closed, then it is called polygon.

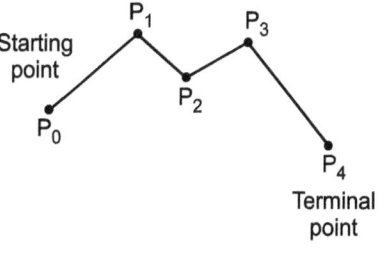 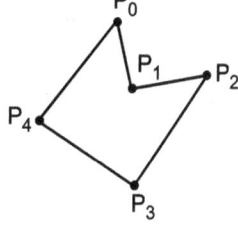

Fig. 2.3

2.2.1 Types of Polygon

There are two types of polygon:
1. Convex Polygon
2. Concave Polygon

A polygon is said to be convex, if the line joining any two interior points of the polygon lies completely inside the polygon.

Example: Triangle, Square, Rectangle etc.

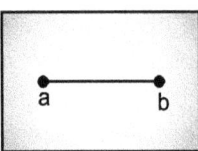 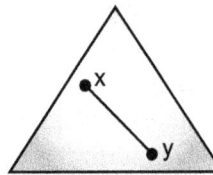 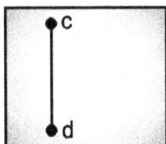

Fig. 2.4

A polygon is said to be concave if the line joining any two interior points of the polygon does not lie completely within the polygon.

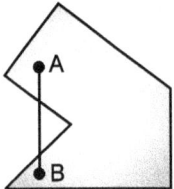 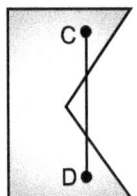 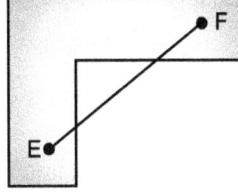

Fig. 2.5

A normal convention of writing the polygon as P vertices $P_1, P_2, ..., P_N$.

A polygon is said to be positively oriented if visiting of all the vertices in the given order produces a counter clockwise circuit, otherwise it is said to be negatively oriented.

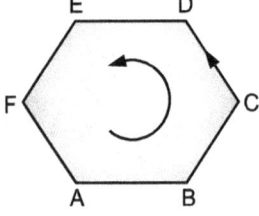 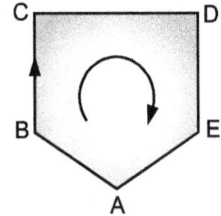

Positive Orientation   **Negative Orientation**

Fig. 2.6

2.2.2 Methods of Testing Pixel Inside the Polygon

(a) Even-Odd Method OR (An Inside Test):
1. Once the polygon is entered in the display file, we can draw the outline of the polygon. To show polygon as a solid object we have to set the pixels inside the polygon as well as pixels on the boundary of it.

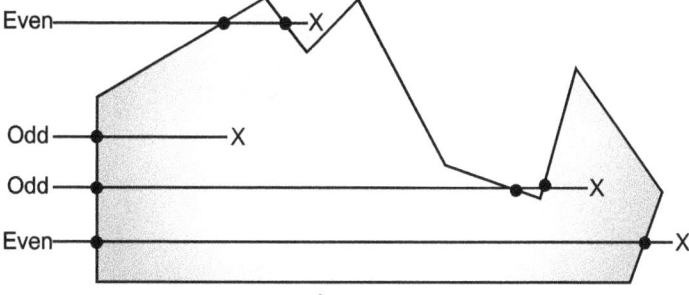

Fig. 2.7

2. Now the question is how to determine whether or not a point is inside of a polygon.
3. A simple method is to construct a line segment between the point in question and a point.
4. Now count how many intersections of the line segment with the polygon boundary occur. If there are an odd number of intersections, then the point in question is inside; otherwise it is outside.
5. This method is called the even-odd method of determining polygon inside points.

(b) Winding Number Method:
Another method for defining a polygon's interior point is called the winding number. Consider a piece of elastic between point of question (A) and a point on polygon boundary, in figure 2.8 below. Treat that elastic is tied to point of question firmly and other end of elastic is sliding along the boundary of the polygon until it has made one complete circuit.

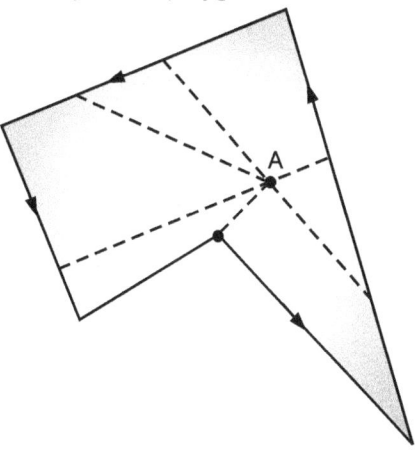

Fig. 2.8

Then, we check how many times the elastic has been wound around the point of question (A). If it is wound at least once then the point is inside. If no net winding then point is outside.

To explain in more simple words, we begin with even-odd method. We draw a line between point of question and outside point, as shown below.

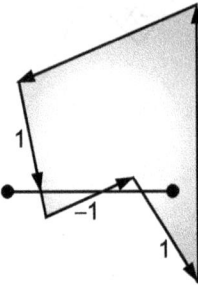

Fig. 2.9

Then, consider the edge or sides of polygons where this line crosses. In even-odd method, we just count the number of intersections. But in winding number method we give direction number to each boundary line which is crossed by this line and we sum these direction numbers. Direction number indicates the direction in which polygon edges are drawn.

The side which starts above the drawn line and crosses line and then ends below the line, we give −1 to direction number. Then find the sum of these numbers. If it is non-zero, then the point is inside. If sum is zero, the point is outside.

2.3 REGIONS

The regions are mainly divided into two types:
1. Interior defined
2. Boundary defined

1. Interior Defined Region:

In interior defined region, every pixel inside the region has unique intensity value as compared to the pixel, which is outside the region.

The interior defined region can be either four connected or eight connected. In case of four connected interior defined region, every pixel inside the region can be accessed with the help of four moves i.e. left, right, top and bottom.

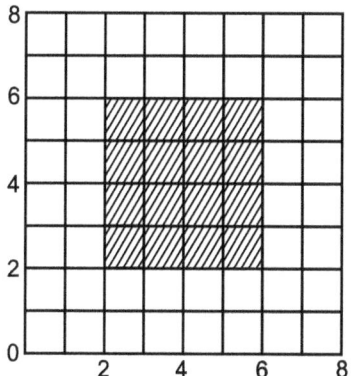
Fig. 2.10: The Interior Defined Region

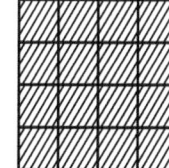
Fig. 2.11: 4-Connected Interior Defined Region

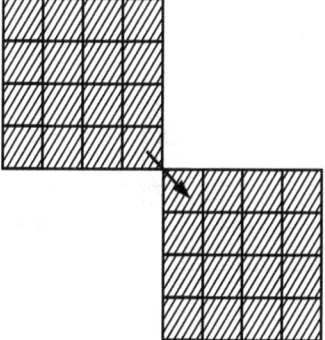
Fig. 2.12: 8-Connected Interior Defined Region

2. Boundary Defined Region:

In a boundary defined region, all the pixels on the boundary region have unique colour and unique intensity value. None of the pixels, which are interior to the region, have this unique colour and intensity value. Thus, every pixel, which is inside the region, has unqiue intensity value, as compared to that of the boundary and outside the region.

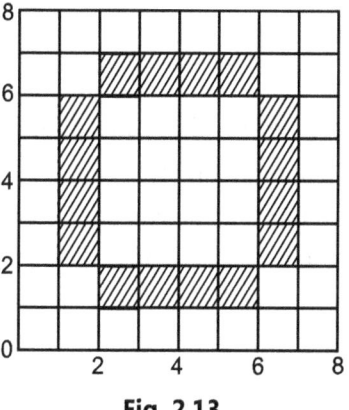
Fig. 2.13

These regions can be either four connected of eight connected.

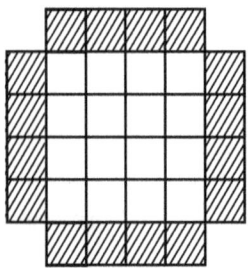

Fig. 2.14: 4-Connected Boundary Defined Region

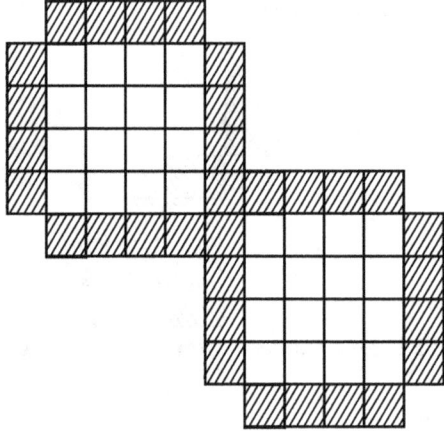

Fig. 2.15: 8-Connected Boundary Defined Region

- The algorithm that fill interior defined regions are referred as flood fill algorithm and those that fill boundary defined region are referred as boundary fill algorithm.
- The interior or boundary defined region may be either four connected or eight connected.
- In a four connected region every pixel can be reached by combination of moves in only four directions i.e. left, right, up and down.
- In an eight connected region, every pixel can be reached by combination of moves in only two horizontal, two vertical and four diagonal directions.
- Algorithm for filling 8-connected region can be used to fill 4-connected region, but an algorithm for filling 4-connected region cannot be used to fill 8-connected region unless 8-connected region is divided into 4-connected region and then fill each of the 4-connected region separately.

2.4 POLYGON FILLING

The processes of colouring the area of polygon is called as polygon filling. It is also referred as scan conversion or contour filling. The techniques which are used to fill a polygon are generally divided into two categories:

1. Scan Conversion Technique.
2. Seed Fill Technique.

2.4.1 Scan Conversion Technique

The scan conversion technique determines in the scan line order whether a point is inside a polygon or not. While using a scan conversion technique for filling a polygon rather than testing for every pixel for whether or not it lies inside, the advantage of the fact is taken that adjacent pixels on a scan line are likely to have same characteristics. This property is called as **scan line coherence**.

When polygon edge intersects the scan line, then the characteristics of pixel on a given scan line changes. Thus, if the intersections of polygon edges with a given scan line are computed, the scan lines are divided into regions. If these intersections are exterior and considered in pairs then the intervals or regions formed by pair of intersection are outside the polygon otherwise the pair of intersection is interior to the polygon. In this way, by considering these intersections in pairs, it is very easy to decide which pixels are to be activated.

When the intersection occurs at a vertex of a polygon and at the same time, if the vertex is at local minima or local maxima then consider the intersection at vertex as two intersections otherwise consider it only as one intersection.

Thus, the pixel is addressed by its lower left corner co-ordinates. It is found that the area pixel is more than the actual area.

Consider a polygon having vertices A (1, 1), B (4, 1), C (4, 3) and D (1, 3).

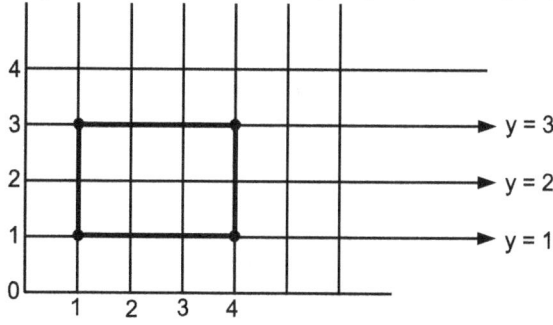

Fig. 2.16

The actual area of the polygon is 6 units. The scan line at y = 3, y = 2 and y = 1 are intersecting the polygon edges at (1, 3) (4, 3), (1, 2) (4, 2) (1, 1) (4, 1) respectively.

Now activate all the pixels starting from (1, 3) upto (4, 3).

As shown in above figure 2.16, it has been observed that the area covered by activated pixel is 12 units, which is much greater than the actual area. To solve this problem, the scan line co-ordinate system and the activation test must be modified. The scan lines are considered to pass through the center of the pixels and thus it is referred as half interval san lines and the pixel will be activated. If the center of pixel is to the right of the point of intersection then it will be considered within the interval and then activated. However, the addressing of pixel is always done by the lower left corner of a co-ordinate.

The scan conversion technique is divided into following types:

1. Simple ordered edge list algorithm
2. Edge Fill Algorithm
3. Fence Fill Algorithm.
4. Edge Flag Algorithm.

(a) Edge Fill Algorithm:

1. This algorithm goes in a scan line order. For each polygon edge it computes the point of intersection of the edge under consideration and the scan line.
2. Then, it compliments all the pixels whose mid-point lies to the right of the point of intersection.
3. Repeat this procedure for every polygon edge. The order in which the polygon edges are considered does not matter.

The algorithm is as follows:

If the point of intersection is,

$\left(x, y + \frac{1}{2}\right)$ then

complement all the pixels whose mid-point or center lies to the right of $\left(x, y + \frac{1}{2}\right)$ i.e.

Complement every pixel (x, y) such that $(x_1 \leq \left(x + \frac{1}{2}\right)$.

Advantages:

(i) The algorithm can be used conveniently with frame buffer.

(ii) The algorithm is easy to implement.

(iii) The algorithm can be considered in any order.

Disadvantages:

(i) The pixels are addressed more than once, thus, the input/output requirement is increased.

(ii) The number of pixels visited can be reduced by introducing a fence suitable vertex location, usually at the center of vertex of figure or polygon. The resulting algorithm is then called as **fence fill algorithm**.

(b) Features of Scan Line Polygon Filing Algorithm:

The various features of scan line polygon filling algorithm are as follows:

(1) The recursive seed fill procedures require stacking of neighbouring points so to avoid this, the other method used is scan line polygon filing algorithm.

(2) Such method fills horizontal pixel spans across scan lines, instead of proceeding to 4-connected or 8-connected neighbouring points. This is achieved by identifying the rightmost and leftmost pixels of the seed pixel and then drawing the horizontal line between these two boundary pixels.

(3) With this efficient method, we have to stack only a beginning position for each horizontal pixel span, instead of stacking all unprocessed neighbouring positions around the current positions.

(4) The figure 2.17 below shows sorted edges of the polygon with active edges.

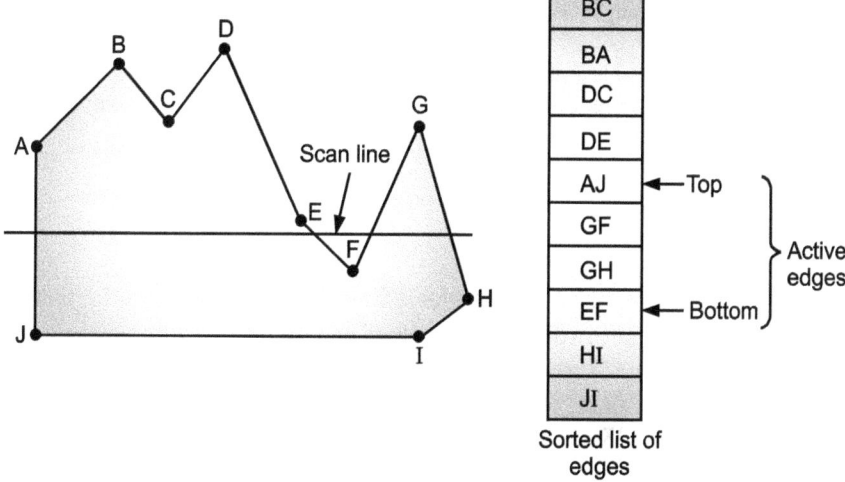

Fig. 2.17: Sorted List of Edges

5. A scan line algorithm for filling polygon begins by ordering the polygon sides on the largest y value. It begins with the largest y value and scans down the polygon.

6. For each y, it determines which sides can be intersected and finds the x values of these intersection points. It then sorts, pairs and passes these x values to a line drawing routine.

(c) Characteristics of Scan Line Polygon Fill Algorithm:

Characteristics:
1. It fills horizontal pixel spans across the line.
2. It avoids the stacking of neighbouring points.
3. It is used in orthogonal projection.
4. It is non-recursive algorithm.
5. Used for filling of polygon.
6. Solved the problem of hidden.

(d) Steps for Filling Polygon in Scan Line Method:
1. Read n, the number of vertices of polygon.
2. Read x and y co-ordinates of all vertices and array x[n] and y[n].
3. Find y_{min} and y_{max}.
4. Store the initial x value (x_1), y values y_1 and y_2 for two end points and x increment Δx from scan line to scan line for each edge in the array edges [n] [4].
   While doing this, check that $y_1 > y_2$, if not interchange y_1 and y_2 and corresponding x_1 and x_2 so that for each edge y_1 represent its maximum y co-ordinate and y_2 represents its minimum y co-ordinate.
5. Sort the rows of array, edges [n] [4] on descending order of y_1, descending order of y_2 and ascending order of x_2.
6. Set $y = y_{max}$.
7. Find the active edges and update active edge list:
   if ($y > y_2$ and $y \leq y_1$)
   [edge is active]
   else
   [edge is not active]
8. Compute the x intersects for all active edges for current y value [initially x-intersect is x_1 and x intersects for successive y values can be given as,
   $x_{i+1} \leftarrow x_i + \Delta x$.
   where, $\Delta x = -\dfrac{1}{m}$ and
   $m = \dfrac{y_2 - y_1}{x_2 - x_1}$ i.e. slope of a line segment.
9. If x intersect is vertex i.e. $x - intersect = x_1$ and $y = y_1$ then apply vertex test to check whether to consider one intersect or two intersects. Store all x intersects in the x-intersect [ ] array.
10. Sort x- intersect [ ] array in the ascending order.
11. Extract pairs of intersects from the sorted x- intersect [ ] array.

12. Pass pairs of x values to line drawing routine to draw corresponding line segments.
13. Set y = y – 1.
14. Repeat steps 7 through 13 until y ≥ y_{min}.
15. Stop.

2.4.2 Seed Fill Technique

The seed fill algorithm requires one of the pixel position inside the polygon or region to be filled. This pixel is inside the region and set to polygon value. This pixels is referred as seed pixel. Then the algorithm tries to find the all other pixels interior to the polygon and subsequently colour them. Then one of the adjacent pixel will become the new seed pixel. Then the algorithm is applied for the new seed pixel. There are two types of seed fill algorithms.

1. Flood Fill Algorithm
2. Boundary Fill Algorithm.

(a) Flood Fill Algorithm:

1. In flood fill algorithm the given initial interior pixel is considered as seed pixel.
2. Starting from this seed, the algorithm inspects all the surrounding eight pixels to check whether these pixels are boundary pixels or they are inside the region.
3. Those pixels which are inside the region are set to polygon value i.e. they are coloured and the boundary pixels are left as it is.
4. This process is repeated till all the interior pixels are inspected.

Example: Consider a polygon ABCD having vertices A (0, 0), B (4, 0), C (0, 4) and D (4, 4). Seed pixel is (2, 2). Now we have to fill this polygon using food fill algorithm.

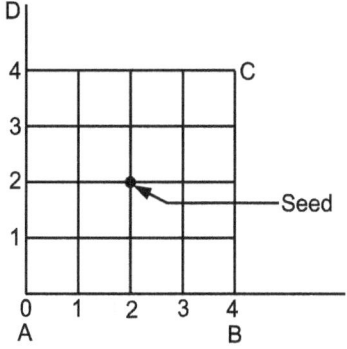

Fig. 2.18

(i)

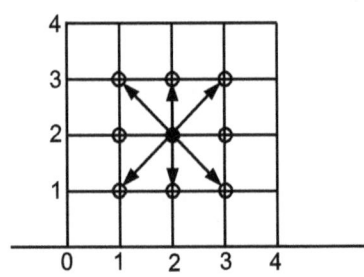

Fig. 2.19

(ii) Adjacent eight pixels to be inspected.

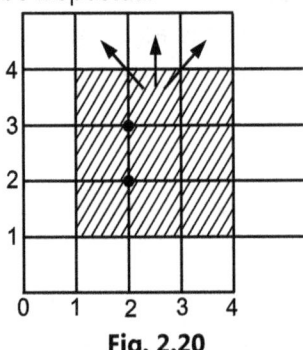

Fig. 2.20

(iii) (2, 3) as new seed pixel.

As shown in Fig. 2.18, the (2, 2) is seed pixel. Now in Fig. 2.19, the algorithm inspects all the eight points surrounding the seed – (1, 1) (1, 2) (1, 3) (2, 3) (3, 3) (3, 2) (3, 1) and (2, 1) since none of the pixels are boundary pixels hence each one will be filled. Now, consider any pixels adjacent to seed (2, 2) as new seed. As shown in Fig. 2.20, pixel (3, 4) is considered as new seed pixel. The algorithm continues in this way until all the points surrounding all the seeds enter the border.

(b) Boundary Fill Algorithm:

1. In boundary fill algorithm, the process begins with a given seed pixel. Then the algorithm inspects the right and left pixels of the seed.
2. If they are inside the region then they are filled.
3. Then the process continues to identify the pixels to right and left to it, till the leftmost and rightmost boundary pixels have been reached.
4. The algorithm then finds the pixels above and below the line just drawn.
5. And repeat the process. This process is repeated till all pixels are taken into account.

The basic requirement of seed fill algorithm is that the pixels of an area must be sorted in the display memory.

Algorithm for Polygon Filling by Seed Fill Algorithm:

Here, stack is used as the main data structure. Simple seed fill algorithm using stack is,

1. Push the seed pixel onto the stack.
2. While (stack not empty) do.
3. Pop the pixel from the stack.
4. Set the pixel to polygon value.
5. For each of the four connected pixels adjacent to the current pixel, check if it is a boundary pixel or it is already set to the polygon value.
6. In either cases ignore it.
7. Otherwise push pixel into the stack.
8. End while.

The procedure is completed when the stack is empty.

Pseudo-C Algorithm for Polygon filling by Seed Fill Algorithm:

Procedure:

```
boundary_fill (x,y,f_colour,b_colour)
{
    if(getpixel(x,y)!=b_colour&&getpixel(x,y)!=f_colour)
    {
        putpixel(x,y,f_colour)
        boundary_fill(x+1,y,f_colour,b_colour);
        boundary_fill(x,y+1,f_colour,b_colour);
        boundary_fill(x-1,y,f_colour,b_colour);
        boundary_fill(x,y-1,f_colour,b_colour);
    }
}
```

Note: 'getpixel' function gives the colour of specified pixel.

'putpixel' function draws the pixel with specified colour.

2.4.3 Comparison between Seed Fill and Edge Fill

Seed Fill Algorithm	Edge Fill Algorithm
1. It works on the principle of a seed pixel.	1. It works on the principle of scan lines.
2. It is time consuming.	2. It is less time taking.
3. It needs a data structure such as stack.	3. There is no need of stack.
4. Starting with the seed pixel, all the adjacent pixels are inspected, if they are inside the polygon they are filled.	4. This algorithm determines in the scan line order whether a point is inside a polygon or not.

2.5 SCAN CONVERSION

Generating a picture on raster refresh display by using video technologies require presenting the information about every pixel position on the screen. The information such as intensity value of a pixel, must be in a scan line order i.e. from top to bottom and also for every scan line from left to right. To get the information about every pixel position presented in scan line order and for every scan line left to right, it is necessary that a picture must be organized into a precise pattern. This process of organisation of picture into a precise pattern according to the requirement is referred as scan conversion. In other words, the process of converting the rasterized picture stored in a frame buffer to a rigid display pattern of video is called as scan conversion.

The process of scan conversion can be accomplished in four ways :
1. Real Time Scan Conversion.
2. Run Length Encoding.
3. Cell Encoding.
4. Using Frame Buffer.

2.5.1 Real Time Scan Conversion

In the real time scan conversion method, the picture is represented in terms of visual and geometric attributes. The visual attributes such as colour, intensity and geometric attributes such as slopes, x, y co-ordinates, text etc. The information about geometric and visual attributes of picture is written in a "display list". The processor scans through the information and for each scan line computes the intensity of every pixel on the screen during the presentation of each frame.

The simplest implementation for real time scan conversion is that it processes the entire display list to get the intersection of each line in the display list, with a particular scan line it is displayed. At video refresh rate of 63.5 microseconds the entire display list is processed each time a scan line is displayed. This short span of time forces to use this method for simplest line drawing display.

Generally, it is not necessary that every edge in the display list will have intersection with every scan line. Thus, if a display processor considers only those edges which are intersecting with the current scan line then the amount of work required to be done can be reduced. Hence, in real time scan conversion, a list of those edges are prepared which have intersection with current scan line and this list is updated when display processor moves to next scan line. There are two ways to maintain the list:
1. Using active edge list.
2. Using y-bucket method.

Advantages:
1. Less memory is required for scan conversion. It is required to hold only the display list and one scan line.
2. Since the picture information is held in a randomly organized display list, it is easier to add or delete information from the list. Thus, real time scan conversion facilitates dynamic picture representation.

Disadvantages:
1. Complexity of picture is limited by speed of the display of processor because it is necessary to process entire display list within one scan line interval. This means that the number of line segments or polygons in the picture, the number of intersections on a scan line, the number of gray scales or colour is limited.
2. The size of display list is limited.

2.5.2 Run Length Encoding

The run length encoding scheme is based on the fact that larger areas of the picture have the pixels having same intensity values. The run length encoding scheme, in its simplest form is denoted by the following format :

Intensity	Run length

Intensity → Intensity of pixel
Run length → Number of pixel with the intensity values

Advantages:
   (i)   The data compression is high.
   (ii) The transmission time is less.
   (iii) The technique is simple to implement.
   (iv) Less memory is required to store picture.
   (v)   Saves storage space for computer generated animated sequence or films.

Disadvantages:
   (i)   There is overhead involved with both encoding and decoding of picture.
   (ii) The addition and deletion of lines or text for the picture is difficult and time consuming.
   (iii) Storage requirement can approach twice that for pixel by pixel for short run.

2.5.3 Cell Encoding

The cell encoding technique represents areas of picture with minimum of information. This simplest alphanumeric CRT terminal makes the use of real encoding for real time operation. The screen area is divided into cells or areas large enough to contain one character.

For example, a 512 × 512 monitor can have 64 × 64 cells and 8 × 8 pixels/cells.

Out of 8 × 8 pixels/cells, 5 × 7 pixels are used to represent the actual characters and other pixels are used for intercharacter spacing. The other configuration for cells are also possible such as 60 × 80 cells for 480 × 640 resolution monitor. All the pixel patterns are stored in ROM.

The combination of these patterns in adjacent cells can be used to construct complete lines.

For a cell having n × n pixels, 2^{n^2} patterns can be generated. This number is too large and it is observed that 108 patterns are enough and the remaining patterns can be obtained by applying transformation on these 108 patterns.

The intersecting patterns can be obtained by ORing or Anding the contents of two cells.

Disadvantage:
The interactivity of such terminal is very low.

2.5.4 Using Frame Buffer

The frame buffer can be implemented using shift register, rotating memory apart from semiconductor RAM. The shift registers can be conceptually considered as a first-in-first-out (FIFO) stack.

If a stack is full, then new data bits are added to the top of the stack and then the first data bits are pushed out of the bottom. The data, which is pushed out of the stack, can be treated as the intensity of a pixel on a scan line. Shift register frame buffer can be implemented using one shift register per pixel on a scan line with each shift register having the length as per the number of scan lines.

In rotating memory, the interactivity is reduced due to disk access time. The screen is required to be refreshed about 30 times per second. This shorter time period does not allow the use of rotating memory for frame buffer.

The configuration of frame buffer is similar to that of line drawing refresh display.

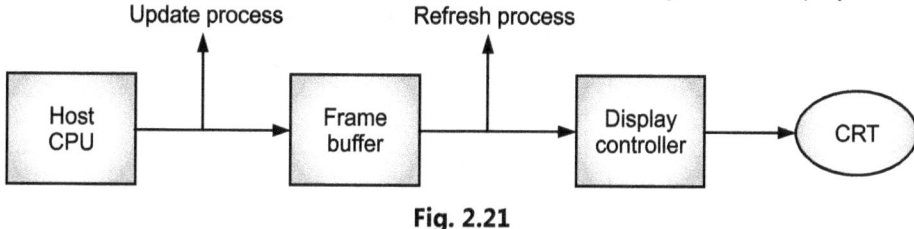

Fig. 2.21

The display controller cycles through the frame buffer in scan line order and transfers the information to the video monitor to refresh the display. The frame buffer can be implemented as a separate memory or as a part of host memory.

2.6 SEGMENTS : INTRODUCTION

In reality the image is made-up of several pictures or items or information. Thus, organizing the image or displaying as a single picture in display file can not reflect this subpicture structure. This does not allow the selective transformation of the portion of the entire scene.

Thus it is very necessary to organize the display file in such a way that it will be divided into several segments, where each segment posses the portion of overall picture. Hence the segment can be defined as a logical unit, in the display file of the screen, not necessarily contiguous. It can be simply viewed as a collection of display file instructions which represents graphic primitives that can be manipulated as a single unit.

The set of attributes are also associated with each segment. One such attribute is visibility, which decides whether the segment is visible or not. By the variation in visibility attribute, a picture setting can be altered. One can make the segments visible or invisible, it is obvious that the visible segments will be displayed and non-visible segments will not be displayed.

Another attributes, which can be associated are scaling, rotation and translation of each segment i.e. transformation, which helps to shift the position of the image. For example, a fan in classroom, if one wants to show it as rotating so set the image transformation attribute for that segment containing fan, appropriately.

Segments Table: The segment table is formed by using arrays. First array holds the segment name, second array holds the starting location for that segment, the third array holds the segment size information while the fourth indicates the visibility and so on. This is illustrated below:

Segment no.	Segment start	Segment size	Scale x	Scale y	Colour	Visibility.........
0						
1						
2						
3						
⋮	⋮	⋮	⋮	⋮	⋮	⋮

For the organization of a display file, it is very necessary to give a unique name to each segment so that it can be specified. This will help to distinguish a segment from all others. With each segment name it is necessary to associate the information about the position of the first instruction corresponding to the segment in a display file.

The information about how many instructions are present in display file and where the display file instructions for the segment begins is also required. In other words the size of the segment measured in terms of number of display file instruction is needed. Each row in the segment table represents information of one segment including name, position, size, attributes and the image transformation parameters.

For example to make the segment 4 visible, the corresponding entry in the array is set 'ON'. The display file interpreter initially checks the start, size and visible attribute of the segments and it interprets only those segments which are to be made visible.

There are other possible schemes for implementing the segment table, many with the substantial advantages over array scheme. But this scheme allows simple accessing, does not require any new data structure and its updating is straight forward.

In case when no segment name is specified, then the instructions must be placed in a special 'unnamed' segment. Thus the information for unnamed segment such as display file starting position, segment size etc. must be stored just as for the named segment. A special entry must be placed in the segment table for the unnamed segment.

An alternative approach is the linked list. The linked list uses the additional field called the link or pointer which gives the location of the segment in the segment table. In case of arrays, maximum numbers of arrays that can be included in the segment table are equal to the length of arrays. But with linked list there is no such limit on the maximum number of segments, the growth of a linked list is dynamic as shown below –

Table 2.1: Segment Table using linked list

Segment number	Segment start	Segment size	Scale x	Scale y	Colour	Visibility	Link
1							4
2							3
3							2
4							5
5							Null

2.7 SEGMENT CREATION

The creation of segment means to make subsequent instruction to be entered in the file to correspond to a new segment. Thus it is necessary to give name of the segment which is to be created.

The procedure is described in the form of an algorithm:

Step 1 : Check, whether some other segment is open, if yes then generate error, 'Error-segment still open' and goto step 9.

Step 2 : Read the name for new segment.

Step 3 : Check the validity of segment name if not valid generate error message and go to step 9.

Step 4 : Confirm that there should not exist a segment under the same name. If yes then generate error 'duplicate segment name' and goto step 9.

Step 5 : Create segment table entry using segment name as index at segment table and by setting start for this entry to be the next free location in the display file.

Step 6 : Set segment size field for this new segment to zero, since any instruction corresponding to this newly created segment is not entered.

Step 7 : Initialize all other parameters attributes to some default values.

Step 8 : Indicate that this new segment is open by setting the value of 'current open' variable to segment name. This indicates that the segment, which is created just now is currently open.

Step 9 : End.

Note: "Current open" is a global variable, which is used to keep track of currently open segment.

Once the segment is opened all operations following it become the members of that segment. To indicate that we are no larger using the segment one needs to close the segment. So for closing the segment simply change the value of indicator, to default value. There is an unnamed segment as zeroth entry, so while closing the segment, one can't set the indicator value to zero. However there should not be two unnamed segment instructions, we need to delete those. But the unnamed segment instruction must be kept in a ready position to receive the instructions in next free display file location.

Closing A Segment: Once the drawing instructions are completed, it is required to close it. To close a currently open segment it is needed to change the value of current open variable. The simplest way is to change the value of current open variable to 0 i.e. unnamed segment. So that if no segment name is specified further then the subsequent instructions will be received as instructions of any other segment. But the problem with this method is that already one unnamed segment is present in the segment table, since two unnamed segments are not desirable. Hence close segment routine should be preferred, which is given below –

Step 1 : Check whether any segment is open i.e. if current – open = 0 if yes then return error that no segment is open and go to step 6.

Step 2 : Delete segment (0).

Step 3 : Initialize start open segment indicators to the original values i.e. segment start as free.

Step 4 : Set segment size as zero.

Step 5 : Initialize open-segment as null.

Step 6 : Stop

Deleting a Segment: When a segment is no longer needed, then the display file storage occupied by its instructions must be emptied.

To delete a segment it is very necessary to check whether the segment to be deleted is a valid segment or not, if valid then whether it is currently open segment or not. Because if the segment is open then it is still in use and deleting an open segment is error. Then check the size of the segment, because if the size of the segment to be deleted is zero, then there are no instructions in the display file corresponding to this segment and hence there is no need to remove any segment from display file. Thus no further processing is necessary otherwise all the instructions will be relocated in the display file which are coming after the last instruction of the segment to be deleted and then by setting the size of segment to be deleted in segment table entry to be zero. For this the algorithm is as follows.

Step 1 : Check the validity of segment name if seg-name is invalid return error.
Step 2 : Check whether the segment is open then return error and goto step 8.
Step 3 : Check size of the segment if seg – size = 0 then return error and goto step 8.
Step 4 : Initialize,
   put = seg – start (seg – name)
   size = seg – size (seg – name)
   Get = put + size
Step 5 : While (Get < free) do
   begin
   Copy instruction from location get to location put in display file.
   put = put + 1
   Get = Get + 1
   End
   Free = put
Step 6 : For I = 0 to number of segment (n) do begin
   If seg – start [i] > seg – start [seg – name]
   Then
   seg – start [i] = seg – start [i] – size
   End
Step 7 : Seg – size [seg – name] = 0
Step 8 : STOP

Note : The variable 'free' in step 5 indicates that there are no instructions. The step 6 is needed for checking the start of a segment, which lies beyond the start of the segment to be deleted. Then its start is to be subtracted by the size of the segment to be deleted.
The actual method for deleting a segment is presented in the form of a flow chart.

2.8 RENAMING A SEGMENT

The renaming of the segment is used to keep a replication of the original segment. In case of a display device having an independent display processor. This display processor continuously reads the display file contents and shows its contents. However in applications involving the animation there is a need to resent the sequence of images, each with slight modifications.

For instance consider an image of a house. In animation as we start a walkthrough, the display must change. One way to do this is by deleting the existing segment and re-creating a new segment with desired modification. But this involves a little bit of delay. Since one may begin working on the next image as soon as the last one is completed, one may infact continually look at actually completed images. In order to avoid this the existing segment should not be deleted until the next requited segment is ready. Thus two segments at a time are needed, in the display file. This can be done by building the new invisible image with temporary name. This method is called as double buffering.

The rename segment algorithm is as follows –

Step 1 : Check for the validity of old name and new name. If not valid then return error and goto step 6.

Step 2 : Check either new-name or old-name is corresponding to any other segment then return error and goto step 6.

Step 3 : Check new segment name does not exist in the display file already. If yes then return error and goto step 6.

Step 4 : Copy segment table entries for old-name into segment table entries for new name.

Step 5 : Set seg_size (old_name) = 0

Step 6 : STOP

VISIBILITY

Every segment is provided with a visibility attribute. The visibility of the segment is stored in an array, which is a part of the segment table. By scanning the array one can determine whether to display the segment or not. The segments visibility can also be changed according to the users view. So that the user can decide to show or not to show the segment.

2.9 IMAGE TRANSFORMATION

Basically transformation means applying some modifications to the object. Image transformation means shifting the whole image to the new location by using translation, or changing the size of the image by scaling, or rotating the image in clockwise/anticlockwise direction. The display file stores the image which is to be displayed on the monitor. So the image transformation is carried out on the contents of the display file.

For image transformation, the values of scaling factors in x and y direction, x and y values for translating image and the rotation angle must be specified. To transform the entire picture of the selected images there should be the provision for transformation of individual segment.

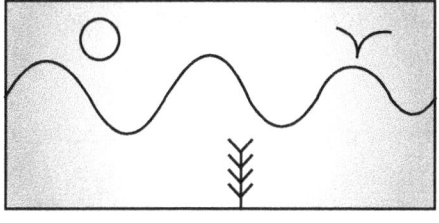
Before Transformation

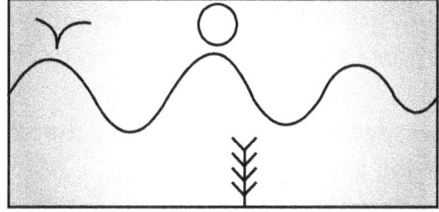
After Transformation

Fig. 2.22

Consider the above figure, the image transformation is clearly shown. In the first part, the bird is at the right side of the sun and in second part the bird is at the left side of the sun i.e. here the transformations are applied only on bird segment. And the transformation is translation i.e. shifting the whole image of the bird.

So in image transformation, additional five attributes for each segment must be provided. The five arrays should be used to store the individual parameters for each of the display file segment. Thus the segment table would become as shown below :

Segment name	Segment start	Segment size	Visibility	Scale X	Scale Y	Translate X	Translate Y	Rotation angle

2.9.1 Algorithm for Image Transformation

The algorithm for image transformation will be –

Step 1 : Read the segment name.

Step 2 : Check the validity of the segment name. If not valid then return error and goto step 8.

Step 3 : Read the translation factor tx and ty.

Step 4 : Read the scaling factor sx, sy.
Step 5 : Read the angle of rotation.
Step 6 : Set the various parameters for the segment.
       i.e.   Translation – X(segment) = tx
                     Translation – Y(segment) = ty
                     Scale – X(segment) = sx
                     Scale – Y(segment) = sy
Step 7 : Check the visibility of the segment. If visible then create a new frame for it.
Step 8 : Stop

Note: Scale – x, Scale – y, Translation – X, Translation – Y are the arrays storing the scaling factors and translation factors respectively. Rotate is an array storing the angle of rotation. Here an array data structure is used for the display file, but other efficient data structures can also be used for the same purpose.

Q. 1 How segmentation be used for the animation purpose ? Explain with a suitable example having at least two segments.

Ans : The animation can be produced by showing a sequence of drawings, each drawing showing the aim at a different position. This is illustrated below.

Fig. 2.23: Animation of arm

When these images are displayed one after another, the arm is perceived as moving through the sequence.

The segmentation allows the modifications in pictures by changing segment attributes. Thus, the animation just discussed can be easily implemented using segmented display file. Each segment will store the attribute of arm corresponding to particular image, when such segments are linked and displayed in a proper sequence the motion of the arm can be seen.

Q. 2 What are the advantages of using segmented display file ? Explain with an example the functions needed to maintain a segmented display file.

Ans. The advantages of using segmented display files are –
1. Segmentation allows to organize display files in subpicture structure.
2. It allows to apply different set of attributes to the different portions of the image.
3. Due to segmentation selective portion of the image can be displayed.

4. Segmentation makes it easier to modify the picture by changing segment attributes or by replacing segments.
5. Segmentation allows application of transformation on selective portion of the image.

The functions which are performed on display file are –
1. Insertion
2. Selection and
3. Deletion.

For the above operations various data structures have been used. The array is the simplest one. While insertion and selection are easy, detection may not be very efficient. To remove an instruction at the beginning of the display file it is needed to move all the succeeding instructions. For large display file, lot of processing is needed to recover only a small amount of storage. Hence another data structure which can be used are, linked list.

In a linked list, instructions are not stored in order. A new field called as link or pointer is added to an instruction. This new field gives the location of the next instruction. The instruction cells, which are still unused are also linked to form a list of available space. To add new instruction to a display file, first of all a cell is obtained from the list of available space then the correct instruction opcode and operands are stored and the cell has been linked to the display file list.

To delete a cell from a liked list, only change the pointer which points to that cell so that it points to succeeding cell as shown below –

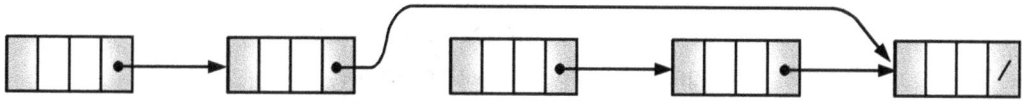

Fig. 2.24: Deleting Display File Instruction from Linked List

Another effective scheme is paging. In this scheme the display file is arranged as a member of small arrays called pages. These pages are linked to form a linked list of pages. Each segment begins at the beginning of the page. In case, if segment ends at some point other than a page boundary then the remainder of that page is not used. In this method to access the instruction within a page the same method is used as used to access the instruction in an array.

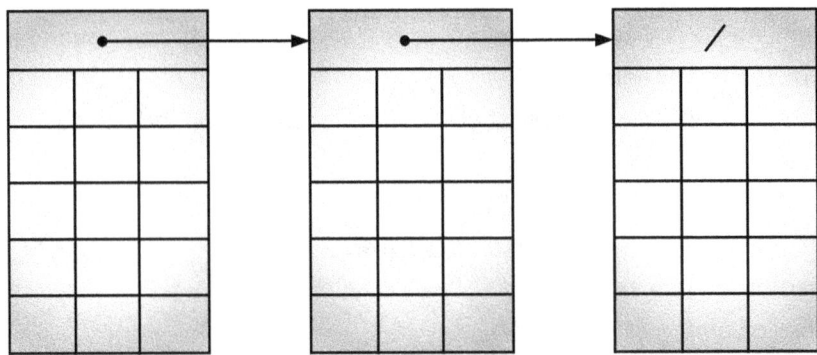

Fig. 2.25: Linked Pages of Display File Instructions

EXERCISE

1. Explain the different methods for testing a pixel inside of polygon.
2. Explain boundary fill algorithm for polygon.
3. Write a pseudo-C algorithm for polygon filling by seed fill polygon.
4. What are the steps involved in filling polygon in scan line method ?
5. With suitable diagram explain concave and convex polygon ?
6. What is window and viewport ? State applications of viewing transformation.
7. Explain and compare seed fill algorithm and edge fill algorithm for polygon.
8. What is polygon ? Explain different types of polygon.
9. Discuss the merits and demerits of real time scan conversion and run length decoding?
10. What is a segment? Explain a segment table and a deletion operation.
11. Describe the pseudo code to create and rename the segment.
12. How segment is implemented using different data structures?
13. Explain segment table and different operations performed on it.
14. Write a short note on image transformation with example.

***

2D AND 3D GEOMETRY

3.1 INTRODUCTION

The process of changing the position of object or performing certain alteration of the picture or may be any combination of these is called as *'Transformation'*.

Transformation allows to uniformly alter the entire picture. This process is very useful in hand drawing techniques, where it is usually easier to change a small portion of a drawing than it is to create an entirely new picture.

For example, suppose the manager wants to alter the scale of the graphs in a report or the architect wants to view a building from a different angle or the animator needs to change the position of a character, all these alterations can be easily performed by using geometric transformations, because the graphic image has been coded as numbers and stored within the computer. The numbers may be modified by mathematical operations referred as Transformations.

3.2 TWO DIMENSIONAL TRANSFORMATIONS

3.2.1 Translation

The process of changing the position of an object is called as **translation**. This is done by adding to each point the amount by which the picture is to be shifted.

For example, consider point P(x, y) where x, y are the co-ordinates.

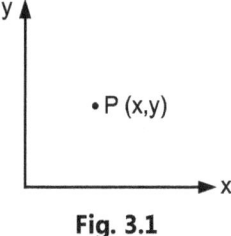

Fig. 3.1

This point P is to be shifted to new position P' (x', y').

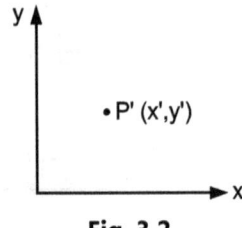

Fig. 3.2

Here the point P has been shifted by some units in X-direction as well as in Y-direction. Let t_x, t_y be the quantities by which the point P has to be shifted in x and y direction respectively.

$$x' = x + t_x$$
$$y' = y + t_y$$

t_x, t_y → Translation factors.

The translation matrix will be,

$$T = \begin{bmatrix} 1 & 0 & 0 \\ 0 & 1 & 0 \\ t_x & t_y & 1 \end{bmatrix}$$

The transformation matrix should only contain the translation factors and no co-ordinate values.

Thus, for the translation of point P(x, y) to P' (x', y') the transformation matrix will be,

$$[x'\ y'\ 1] = [x\ y\ 1] \begin{bmatrix} 1 & 0 & 0 \\ 0 & 1 & 0 \\ t_x & t_y & 1 \end{bmatrix}$$

Or

$$\begin{bmatrix} x' \\ y' \\ 1 \end{bmatrix} = \begin{bmatrix} 1 & 0 & t_x \\ 0 & 1 & t_y \\ 0 & 0 & 1 \end{bmatrix} \begin{bmatrix} x \\ y \\ 1 \end{bmatrix}$$

Example 3.1:

Translate the triangle ABC with co-ordinates A(1, 1) B(1, 3) C(5, 0) by 2 units in X-direction and 3 units in Y-direction.

Solution: The translation factors are $t_x = 2$, $t_y = 3$.

∴ The translation matrix will be,

$$T = \begin{bmatrix} 1 & 0 & 0 \\ 0 & 1 & 0 \\ 2 & 3 & 1 \end{bmatrix}$$

The new point co-ordinates are,

$$A' = A[T]$$

$$= [1\ 1\ 1] \begin{bmatrix} 1 & 0 & 0 \\ 0 & 1 & 0 \\ 2 & 3 & 1 \end{bmatrix}$$

$$= [3\ 4\ 1]$$

B' = B[T]

$$= [1\ 3\ 1] \begin{bmatrix} 1 & 0 & 0 \\ 0 & 1 & 0 \\ 2 & 3 & 1 \end{bmatrix}$$

$$= [3\ 6\ 1]$$

C' = C[T]

$$= [5\ 0\ 1] \begin{bmatrix} 1 & 0 & 0 \\ 0 & 1 & 0 \\ 2 & 3 & 1 \end{bmatrix}$$

$$= [7\ 3\ 1]$$

Thus the co-ordinates of shifted triangle will be A' (3, 4), B' (3, 6), C' (7, 3).

The graphical representation will be,

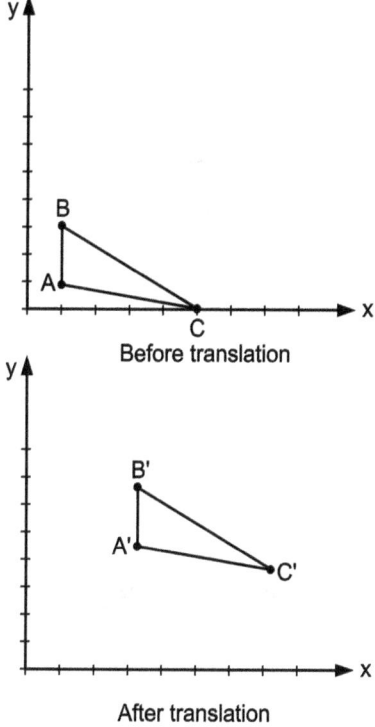

Before translation

After translation

Fig. 3.3

3.2.2 Scaling

This transformation is used to alter the size of an object i.e. either to magnify or reduce the size of an object.

For example, consider an object point P(x, y). This point is to be scaled to P' (x', y'). Then the scaling factors will be S_x and S_y for the x and y co-ordinates respectively.

To obtain the scaled object point the original point co-ordinates is to be multiplied by the scaling factors as –

$$x' = x \cdot S_x$$
$$y' = y \cdot S_y$$

The scaling matrix will be,

$$S = \begin{bmatrix} S_x & 0 & 0 \\ 0 & S_y & 0 \\ 0 & 0 & 1 \end{bmatrix}$$

Thus, for the scaling of point P(x, y) to P'(x', y') transformation matrix will be,

$$[x'\ y'\ 1] = [x\ y\ 1] \begin{bmatrix} S_x & 0 & 0 \\ 0 & S_y & 0 \\ 0 & 0 & 1 \end{bmatrix}$$

The scaling transformation not only scales the object but also shifts it from original point. Suppose the end points are not origin and the object is to be shifted whether right, left, up or down then it depends on the sign and magnitude of S_x and S_y.

If,

$S_x > 0$, Increase in size

$S_x < 0$, Reduction in size

$S_x = 0$, Uniform scaling

Example 3.2:

Magnify the triangle A(0, 0), B(1, 1), C(5, 2) to twice its size.

Solution:

To magnify the triangle the scaling matrix will be needed. The scaling factors will be $S_x = 2$, $S_y = 2$.

The scaling matrix will be,

$$S = \begin{bmatrix} 2 & 0 & 0 \\ 0 & 2 & 0 \\ 0 & 0 & 1 \end{bmatrix}$$

For,
$$A' = A[S]$$
$$= [0\ 0\ 1] \begin{bmatrix} 2 & 0 & 0 \\ 0 & 2 & 0 \\ 0 & 0 & 1 \end{bmatrix}$$
$$= [0\ 0\ 1]$$
$$B' = B[S]$$
$$= [1\ 1\ 1] \begin{bmatrix} 2 & 0 & 0 \\ 0 & 2 & 0 \\ 0 & 0 & 1 \end{bmatrix} = [2\ 2\ 1]$$
$$C' = C[S]$$
$$= [5\ 2\ 1] \begin{bmatrix} 2 & 0 & 0 \\ 0 & 2 & 0 \\ 0 & 0 & 1 \end{bmatrix}$$
$$= [10\ 4\ 1]$$

Thus, the co-ordinates of scaled triangle will be, A'(0, 0) B'(2, 2) C'(10, 4).

3.2.3 Rotation

This type of transformation allows the movement of an object along the circular path. In this case the object can be rotated by a given angle in either clockwise or counterclockwise direction.

Consider point P(x, y). Let the angle of rotation be $\theta°$.

(i) Transformation Matrix for Counterclockwise Direction.

To rotate the P(x, y) in counterclockwise direction by $\theta°$ with respect to origin.

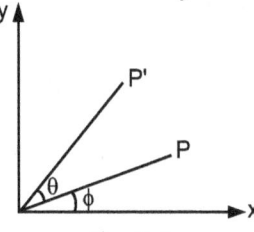

Fig. 3.4

As shown in above Fig. 3.4 when the object is rotated about origin, it gets rotated with fixed radius,

∴
$$x = r \cos \phi$$
$$y = r \sin \phi$$

$\phi \to$ initial angle of P with respect to origin.

$$x' = r \cos (\theta + \phi)$$
$$y' = r \sin (\theta + \phi)$$
$$x' = r \cos (\theta + \phi)$$
$$= r (\cos \theta \cos \phi - \sin \theta \sin \phi)$$

$$= r\cos\theta\cos\phi - r\sin\theta\sin\phi$$
$$= x\cos\theta - y\sin\theta$$
$$(\because r\cos\phi = x$$
$$r\sin\phi = y)$$
$$y' = r\sin(\theta + \phi)$$
$$= r(\sin\theta\cos\phi + \cos\theta\sin\phi)$$
$$= r\cos\phi\sin\theta + r\sin\phi\cos\theta$$
$$= x\sin\theta + y\cos\theta$$

$\therefore$
$$x' = x\cos\theta - y\sin\theta$$
$$y' = x\sin\theta + y\cos\theta$$

In the matrix form it can be represented as –

$$R = \begin{bmatrix} \cos\theta & \sin\theta & 0 \\ -\sin\theta & \cos\theta & 0 \\ 0 & 0 & 1 \end{bmatrix}$$

Thus, for rotation of point P(x, y) to P' (x', y') the transformation matrix will be,

$$[x'\ y'\ 1] = [x\ y\ 1] \begin{bmatrix} \cos\theta & \sin\theta & 0 \\ -\sin\theta & \cos\theta & 0 \\ 0 & 0 & 1 \end{bmatrix}$$

(ii) The Transformation Matrix for Clockwise Direction

To rotate the point P(x, y) in clockwise direction by θ° with respect to origin. The sign of an angle determines the direction of rotation. To rotate the image in a counter clockwise direction, positive angle is used hence, for clockwise direction negative angle will be used. So the rotation matrix will be,

$$R = \begin{bmatrix} \cos(-\theta) & \sin(-\theta) & 0 \\ -\sin(-\theta) & \cos(-\theta) & 0 \\ 0 & 0 & 1 \end{bmatrix}$$

$\because$
$$\cos(-\theta) = \cos\theta$$
$$\sin(-\theta) = -\sin\theta$$

$$R = \begin{bmatrix} \cos\theta & -\sin\theta & 0 \\ \sin\theta & \cos\theta & 0 \\ 0 & 0 & 1 \end{bmatrix}$$

Thus, for rotation of P(x, y) to P'(x', y') in clockwise direction the transformation matrix will be,

$$[x'\ y'\ 1] = [x\ y\ 1] \begin{bmatrix} \cos\theta & -\sin\theta & 0 \\ \sin\theta & \cos\theta & 0 \\ 0 & 0 & 1 \end{bmatrix}$$

Example 3.3:

Rotate the triangle A(1, 1), B(2, 2), C(6, 3) in counter clockwise direction by 90°.

Solution:

To rotate the triangle in counter clockwise direction, the rotation matrix will be,

$$R = \begin{bmatrix} \cos\theta & \sin\theta & 0 \\ -\sin\theta & \cos\theta & 0 \\ 0 & 0 & 1 \end{bmatrix}$$

Put $\theta = 90°$

$\cos 90° = 0$

$\sin 90° = 1$

$$\therefore \quad R = \begin{bmatrix} 0 & 1 & 0 \\ -1 & 0 & 0 \\ 0 & 0 & 1 \end{bmatrix}$$

For

$$A' = A[R]$$

$$= [1\ 1\ 1] \begin{bmatrix} 0 & 1 & 0 \\ -1 & 0 & 0 \\ 0 & 0 & 1 \end{bmatrix}$$

$$= [-1\ 1\ 1]$$

$$B' = B[R]$$

$$= [2\ 2\ 1] \begin{bmatrix} 0 & 1 & 0 \\ -1 & 0 & 0 \\ 0 & 0 & 1 \end{bmatrix}$$

$$= [-2\ 2\ 1]$$

$$C' = C[R]$$

$$= [6\ 3\ 1] \begin{bmatrix} 0 & 1 & 0 \\ -1 & 0 & 0 \\ 0 & 0 & 1 \end{bmatrix}$$

$$= [-3\ 6\ 1]$$

Thus, the co-ordinates of triangle will be A' (−1, 1), B' (−2, 2) and C' (−3, 6).

3.3 HOMOGENEOUS CO-ORDINATE SYSTEM

In order to combine sequence of transformations it is required to eliminate the matrix addition associated with the translation terms in m_1. To achieve this the matrix m should be represented as 3×3 matrix instead of 2×2 by introducing an additional dummy co-ordinate ω. Here, points are specified by three numbers instead of two. This co-ordinate system is called **'homogeneous co-ordinate system'** and it allows to express all transformation equations as matrix multiplication.

In this system every point (x, y) can be expressed as [x y ω]. For 2-D transformation the value of ω is 1 and thus the representation of matrix for (x, y) will be [x, y, 1].

Comparison between Homogeneous and Normalized Co-ordinates.

Homogeneous Co-ordinates	Normalized Co-ordinates
1. Real co-ordinates.	1. Co-ordinates defined in device independent unit.
2. Co-ordinate system designed to combine sequence of transformations.	2. Co-ordinate system designed to display image with unique size on the screen, independent of the display resolution.

Example 3.4:

A triangle defined by the point (0, 2) (2, 0) (3, 2) is enlarged twice in x-direction and thrice in y-direction. The enlarged triangle is reduced 1/3 in x-direction. Find out the combined transformation and resultant points.

Solution:

Scaling matrix is,

$$S = \begin{bmatrix} S_x & 0 & 0 \\ 0 & S_y & 0 \\ 0 & 0 & 1 \end{bmatrix}$$

Now scaling twice in x-direction i.e. $S_x = 2$ and thrice in y-direction i.e. $S_y = 3$

$$\therefore \quad S_1 = \begin{bmatrix} 2 & 0 & 0 \\ 0 & 3 & 0 \\ 0 & 0 & 1 \end{bmatrix}$$

Then reduction by 1/3 in x-direction.

$\therefore \quad S_x = 1/3$ and $S_y = 1$

$$\therefore \quad S_2 = \begin{bmatrix} 1/3 & 0 & 0 \\ 0 & 1 & 0 \\ 0 & 0 & 1 \end{bmatrix}$$

The resultant matrix will be,

$$R_S = S_1 \cdot S_2$$

$$= \begin{bmatrix} 2 & 0 & 0 \\ 0 & 3 & 0 \\ 0 & 0 & 1 \end{bmatrix} \begin{bmatrix} 1/3 & 0 & 0 \\ 0 & 1 & 0 \\ 0 & 0 & 1 \end{bmatrix}$$

$$R_S = \begin{bmatrix} 2/3 & 0 & 0 \\ 0 & 3 & 0 \\ 0 & 0 & 1 \end{bmatrix}$$

$$A' = A \cdot R_S$$

$$= [0\ 2\ 0] \begin{bmatrix} 2/3 & 0 & 0 \\ 0 & 3 & 0 \\ 0 & 0 & 1 \end{bmatrix}$$

$$= [0\ 6\ 1]$$

$$A' = (0, 0)$$

$$B' = B \cdot R_S$$

$$= [2\ 0\ 1] \begin{bmatrix} 2/3 & 0 & 0 \\ 0 & 3 & 0 \\ 0 & 0 & 1 \end{bmatrix}$$

$$= [4/3\ 0\ 1]$$

$$B' = (4/3, 0)$$

$$C' = C \cdot R_S$$

$$= [3\ 2\ 1] \begin{bmatrix} 2/3 & 0 & 0 \\ 0 & 3 & 0 \\ 0 & 0 & 1 \end{bmatrix}$$

$$= [2\ 6\ 1]$$

$$C' = (2, 6)$$

Thus, the co-ordinates of new triangle will be,

A' (0, 0), B' (4/3, 0), C' (2, 6).

Example 3.5:

A line (1, 1), (3, 4) is rotated 30° anticlockwise find out end points of the resultant line and transformation matrix.

Solution:

The end points of line are (1, 1) and (3, 4).

First translate the line to origin.

$$\therefore \quad t_x = -1,\ t_y = -1$$

The translation matrix will be,
$$T = \begin{bmatrix} 1 & 0 & 0 \\ 0 & 1 & 0 \\ -1 & -1 & 1 \end{bmatrix}$$

Now rotate the line in anticlockwise direction by 30°.
∴ Rotation matrix will be,
$$R = \begin{bmatrix} \cos\theta & \sin\theta & 0 \\ -\sin\theta & \cos\theta & 0 \\ 0 & 0 & 1 \end{bmatrix}$$

Put θ = 30°
cos 30° = 0.3
sin 30° = 0.5

∴
$$R = \begin{bmatrix} 0.3 & 0.5 & 0 \\ -0.5 & 0.3 & 0 \\ 0 & 0 & 1 \end{bmatrix}$$

Retranslate the line to original position.
∴ $t_x = 1, t_y = 1$

$$T^{-1} = \begin{bmatrix} 1 & 0 & 0 \\ 0 & 1 & 0 \\ 1 & 1 & 1 \end{bmatrix}$$

The resultant matrix will be,
$$R_S = [T][R][T^{-1}]$$
$$= \begin{bmatrix} 1 & 0 & 0 \\ 0 & 1 & 0 \\ -1 & -1 & 1 \end{bmatrix} \begin{bmatrix} 0.3 & 0.5 & 0 \\ -0.5 & 0.3 & 0 \\ 0 & 0 & 1 \end{bmatrix} \begin{bmatrix} 1 & 0 & 0 \\ 0 & 1 & 0 \\ 1 & 1 & 1 \end{bmatrix}$$
$$= \begin{bmatrix} 0.3 & 0.5 & 0 \\ -0.5 & 0.3 & 0 \\ 0.2 & -0.8 & 1 \end{bmatrix} \begin{bmatrix} 1 & 0 & 0 \\ 0 & 1 & 0 \\ 1 & 1 & 1 \end{bmatrix}$$
$$R_S = \begin{bmatrix} 0.3 & 0.5 & 0 \\ -0.5 & 0.3 & 0 \\ 1.2 & 0.2 & 1 \end{bmatrix}$$

Thus, the co-ordinates of resultant line will be,
$A' = A \cdot R_S$
$$= [1\ 1\ 1] \begin{bmatrix} 0.3 & 0.5 & 0 \\ -0.5 & 0.3 & 0 \\ 1.2 & 0.2 & 1 \end{bmatrix}$$
$= [1\ 1\ 1]$
$A' = (1, 1)$
$B' = B \cdot R_S$

COMPUTER GRAPHICS   GEOMETRIC TRANSFORMATION

$$= [3\ 4\ 1] \begin{bmatrix} 0.3 & 0.5 & 0 \\ -0.5 & 0.3 & 0 \\ 1.2 & 0.2 & 1 \end{bmatrix}$$

$$= [0.3\ 2.5\ 1]$$

B' = (0.3, 2.5)

Thus, the co-ordinates are (1, 1) and (0.3, 2.5).

Example 3.6:
Find the new co-ordinates of triangle A(0, 0), B(1, 1), C(5, 2) after it has been –
   (a) magnified to twice its size.
   (b) reduces to half of its size.

Solution:

   (a) To magnify the triangle to twice its size, scaling matrix will be needed. The scaling factor will be 2 i.e. $S_x = 2$, $S_y = 2$.

$$\therefore \quad S = \begin{bmatrix} 2 & 0 & 0 \\ 0 & 2 & 0 \\ 0 & 0 & 1 \end{bmatrix}$$

$$\therefore \quad A' = A[S]$$

$$= [0\ 0\ 1] \begin{bmatrix} 2 & 0 & 0 \\ 0 & 2 & 0 \\ 0 & 0 & 1 \end{bmatrix}$$

$$= [0\ 0\ 1]$$

$$\therefore \quad A' = (0, 0)$$

$$B' = B[S]$$

$$= [1\ 1\ 1] \begin{bmatrix} 2 & 0 & 0 \\ 0 & 2 & 0 \\ 0 & 0 & 1 \end{bmatrix}$$

$$= [2\ 2\ 1]$$

$$\therefore \quad B' = (2, 2)$$

$$C' = C[S]$$

$$= [5\ 2\ 1] \begin{bmatrix} 2 & 0 & 0 \\ 0 & 2 & 0 \\ 0 & 0 & 1 \end{bmatrix}$$

$$C' = [10, 4, 1]$$

Thus, the co-ordinates of new triangle will be,
   A' (0, 0), B' (2, 2), C' (10, 4)

   (b) To reduce the triangle by half its size, scaling factor will be,
   $S_x = 1/2$, $S_y = 1/2$.

$$\therefore \quad S = \begin{bmatrix} 1/2 & 0 & 0 \\ 0 & 1/2 & 0 \\ 0 & 0 & 1 \end{bmatrix}$$

$$A' = A[S]$$

$$= [0\ 0\ 1] \begin{bmatrix} 1/2 & 0 & 0 \\ 0 & 1/2 & 0 \\ 0 & 0 & 1 \end{bmatrix}$$

$$= [0\ 0\ 1]$$

$$\therefore \quad A' = (0, 0)$$

$$B' = B[S]$$

$$= [1\ 1\ 1] \begin{bmatrix} 1/2 & 0 & 0 \\ 0 & 1/2 & 0 \\ 0 & 0 & 1 \end{bmatrix}$$

$$= [1/2\ 1/2\ 1]$$

$$\therefore \quad B' = (1/2, 1/2)$$

$$C' = C[S]$$

$$= [5\ 2\ 1] \begin{bmatrix} 1/2 & 0 & 0 \\ 0 & 1/2 & 0 \\ 0 & 0 & 1 \end{bmatrix}$$

$$= [5/2\ 1\ 1]$$

$$\therefore \quad C' = (5/2, 1)$$

Thus, the co-ordinates of new triangle will be, A'(0, 0), B'(1/2, 1/2), C'(5/2, 1).

Example 3.7:

Magnify a triangle defined by vertices A(1, 1), B(2, 2), C(6, 3) to twice its size. Then rotate by 90° in clockwise direction keeping point C invariant. Give the co-ordinates of new triangle.

Solution:

To keep point C invariant first the triangle needs to be translated to origin with respect to point C. Thus, the translation factors will be, $t_x = -6$, $t_y = -3$.

$$\therefore \quad T = \begin{bmatrix} 1 & 0 & 0 \\ 0 & 1 & 0 \\ -6 & -3 & 1 \end{bmatrix}$$

Now to magnify the triangle by twice its size, the scaling matrix is needed. The scaling factors will be $S_x = S_y = 2$.

$$\therefore \quad S = \begin{bmatrix} 2 & 0 & 0 \\ 0 & 2 & 0 \\ 0 & 0 & 1 \end{bmatrix}$$

To rotate the triangle in a clockwise direction by angle of 90°, rotation matrix will be needed where θ = 90°.

(**Note:** If direction is not mentioned always consider clockwise direction)

$$\therefore R = \begin{bmatrix} \cos\theta & -\sin\theta & 0 \\ \sin\theta & \cos\theta & 0 \\ 0 & 0 & 1 \end{bmatrix}$$

$$\because \theta = 90°$$

$$\therefore R = \begin{bmatrix} \cos 90° & -\sin 90° & 0 \\ \sin 90° & \cos 90° & 0 \\ 0 & 0 & 1 \end{bmatrix}$$

$$R = \begin{bmatrix} 0 & -1 & 0 \\ 1 & 0 & 0 \\ 0 & 0 & 1 \end{bmatrix} \quad [\because \cos 90 = 0, \sin 90 = 1]$$

Then the triangle needs to be retranslated to its original point C. Thus, the translation factors will be $t_x = 6$, $t_y = 3$.

$$\therefore T = \begin{bmatrix} 1 & 0 & 0 \\ 0 & 1 & 0 \\ 6 & 3 & 1 \end{bmatrix}$$

Thus, the resultant transformation matrix will be,

$$R_S = [T][S][R][T]$$

$$R_S = \begin{bmatrix} 1 & 0 & 0 \\ 0 & 1 & 0 \\ -6 & -3 & 1 \end{bmatrix} \begin{bmatrix} 2 & 0 & 0 \\ 0 & 2 & 0 \\ 0 & 0 & 1 \end{bmatrix} \begin{bmatrix} 0 & -1 & 0 \\ 1 & 0 & 0 \\ 0 & 0 & 1 \end{bmatrix} \begin{bmatrix} 1 & 0 & 0 \\ 0 & 1 & 0 \\ 6 & 3 & 1 \end{bmatrix}$$

$$= \begin{bmatrix} 2 & 0 & 0 \\ 0 & 2 & 0 \\ -12 & -6 & 1 \end{bmatrix} \begin{bmatrix} 0 & -1 & 0 \\ 1 & 0 & 0 \\ 0 & 0 & 1 \end{bmatrix} \begin{bmatrix} 1 & 0 & 0 \\ 0 & 1 & 0 \\ 6 & 3 & 1 \end{bmatrix}$$

$$= \begin{bmatrix} 0 & -2 & 0 \\ 2 & 0 & 0 \\ -6 & 12 & 1 \end{bmatrix} \begin{bmatrix} 1 & 0 & 0 \\ 0 & 1 & 0 \\ 6 & 3 & 1 \end{bmatrix}$$

$$\therefore R_S = \begin{bmatrix} 0 & -2 & 0 \\ 2 & 0 & 0 \\ 0 & 15 & 1 \end{bmatrix}$$

For point A',

$$A' = A[R_S]$$

$$= [1 \; 1 \; 1] \begin{bmatrix} 0 & -2 & 0 \\ 2 & 0 & 0 \\ 0 & 15 & 1 \end{bmatrix}$$

$$= [2 \; 13 \; 1]$$

$$A' = [2, 13]$$

For point B', B' = B[R_S]

$$= [2\ 2\ 1] \begin{bmatrix} 0 & -2 & 0 \\ 2 & 0 & 0 \\ 0 & 15 & 1 \end{bmatrix}$$

$$= [4,\ 11,\ 1]$$

∴ B' = (4, 11)

Point C', C' = C[R_S]

$$= [6\ 3\ 1] \begin{bmatrix} 0 & -2 & 0 \\ 2 & 0 & 0 \\ 0 & 15 & 1 \end{bmatrix}$$

$$= [6\ 3\ 1]$$

∴ C' = (6, 3)

The co-ordinates of new triangle will be,

A'(2, 3), B'(4, 11), C'(6, 3)

Here the point C' remains invariant.

Example 3.8:

Write the general form of scaling with respect to fixed points (h, k).

Solution:

The scaling transformation not only alters the size of an object but also shifts it from original position. Thus, to scale an object keeping points (h, k) fixed first translate the object with respect to (h, k).

∴ $t_x = -h,\ t_y = -k$.

The translation matrix will be,

$$T = \begin{bmatrix} 1 & 0 & 0 \\ 0 & 1 & 0 \\ -h & -k & 1 \end{bmatrix}$$

Scaling matrix will be, $S = \begin{bmatrix} S_x & 0 & 0 \\ 0 & S_y & 0 \\ 0 & 0 & 1 \end{bmatrix}$

Now, to retranslate the object, put $t_x = h,\ t_y = k$.

∴ $$T = \begin{bmatrix} 1 & 0 & 0 \\ 0 & 1 & 0 \\ h & k & 1 \end{bmatrix}$$

The resultant transformation matrix will be,

$$R_S = [T]\ [S]\ [T]$$

COMPUTER GRAPHICS   GEOMETRIC TRANSFORMATION

$$= \begin{bmatrix} 1 & 0 & 0 \\ 0 & 1 & 0 \\ -h & -k & 1 \end{bmatrix} \begin{bmatrix} S_x & 0 & 0 \\ 0 & S_y & 0 \\ 0 & 0 & 1 \end{bmatrix} \begin{bmatrix} 1 & 0 & 0 \\ 0 & 1 & 0 \\ h & k & 1 \end{bmatrix}$$

$$= \begin{bmatrix} S_x & 0 & 0 \\ 0 & S_y & 0 \\ -h\,S_x & -k\,S_y & 1 \end{bmatrix} \begin{bmatrix} 1 & 0 & 0 \\ 0 & 1 & 0 \\ h & k & 1 \end{bmatrix} = \begin{bmatrix} S_x & 0 & 0 \\ 0 & S_y & 0 \\ -h\,S_x + h & -k\,S_y + k & 1 \end{bmatrix}$$

The new point co-ordinates will be,

$$[x'\ y'\ 1] = [x\ y\ 1] \begin{bmatrix} S_x & 0 & 0 \\ 0 & S_y & 0 \\ -h\,S_x + h & -k\,S_y + k & 1 \end{bmatrix}$$

$$= [x\,S_x - h\,S_x + h \quad y\,S_y - k\,S_y + k\ 1]$$

$$= [S_x\,(x - h) + h \quad S_y\,(y - k) + k\ 1]$$

$$= [(x - h)\,S_x + h \quad (y - k)\,S_y + k\ 1]$$

Example 3.9:
Consider the square P(0, 0), Q(0, 10), R(10, 10), S(10, 0). Rotate the square about fixed point R(10, 10) by an angle 45° (anticlockwise) followed by scaling of 2 units in x-direction and 2 units in y-direction.

Solution:
To keep the point R(10, 10) fixed, first the square is to be translated to origin with respect to point R.

∴ $t_x = -10$, $t_y = -10$

Thus, the translation matrix will be,

$$T = \begin{bmatrix} 1 & 0 & 0 \\ 0 & 1 & 0 \\ -10 & -10 & 1 \end{bmatrix}$$

To rotate the square in anticlockwise direction by angle 45°.
The rotation matrix will be,

Here,   θ = 45°

∴ $\cos 45 = \sin 45 = \dfrac{1}{\sqrt{2}}$

$$R = \begin{bmatrix} \cos 45° & \sin 45° & 0 \\ -\sin 45° & \cos 45° & 0 \\ 0 & 0 & 1 \end{bmatrix}$$

$$= \begin{bmatrix} \dfrac{1}{\sqrt{2}} & \dfrac{1}{\sqrt{2}} & 0 \\ \dfrac{-1}{\sqrt{2}} & \dfrac{1}{\sqrt{2}} & 0 \\ 0 & 0 & 1 \end{bmatrix}$$

After rotation, the square is again retranslated to point R.

$\therefore$ $t_x = 10$, $t_y = 10$

$$T^{-1} = \begin{bmatrix} 1 & 0 & 0 \\ 0 & 1 & 0 \\ 10 & 10 & 1 \end{bmatrix}$$

Now, to scale the square by 2 units in x direction and 2 units in y-direction, $S_x = 2$, $S_y = 2$. The scaling matrix will be,

$$S = \begin{bmatrix} 2 & 0 & 0 \\ 0 & 2 & 0 \\ 0 & 0 & 1 \end{bmatrix}$$

The resultant transformation matrix will be,

$$R_S = [T][R][T^{-1}][S]$$

$$= \begin{bmatrix} 1 & 0 & 0 \\ 0 & 1 & 0 \\ -10 & -10 & 1 \end{bmatrix} \begin{bmatrix} \frac{1}{\sqrt{2}} & \frac{1}{\sqrt{2}} & 0 \\ \frac{-1}{\sqrt{2}} & \frac{1}{\sqrt{2}} & 0 \\ 0 & 0 & 1 \end{bmatrix} \begin{bmatrix} 1 & 0 & 0 \\ 0 & 1 & 0 \\ 10 & 10 & 1 \end{bmatrix} \begin{bmatrix} 2 & 0 & 0 \\ 0 & 2 & 0 \\ 0 & 0 & 1 \end{bmatrix}$$

$$= \begin{bmatrix} \frac{1}{\sqrt{2}} & \frac{1}{\sqrt{2}} & 0 \\ \frac{-1}{\sqrt{2}} & \frac{1}{\sqrt{2}} & 0 \\ 0 & \frac{-20}{\sqrt{2}} & 1 \end{bmatrix} \begin{bmatrix} 1 & 0 & 0 \\ 0 & 1 & 0 \\ 10 & 10 & 1 \end{bmatrix} \begin{bmatrix} 2 & 0 & 0 \\ 0 & 2 & 0 \\ 0 & 0 & 1 \end{bmatrix}$$

$$= \begin{bmatrix} \frac{1}{\sqrt{2}} & \frac{1}{\sqrt{2}} & 0 \\ \frac{-1}{\sqrt{2}} & \frac{1}{\sqrt{2}} & 0 \\ 10 & -\frac{20}{\sqrt{2}} + 10 & 1 \end{bmatrix} \begin{bmatrix} 2 & 0 & 0 \\ 0 & 2 & 0 \\ 0 & 0 & 1 \end{bmatrix} = \begin{bmatrix} \sqrt{2} & \sqrt{2} & 0 \\ -\sqrt{2} & \sqrt{2} & 0 \\ 20 & -20\sqrt{2} + 20 & 1 \end{bmatrix}$$

For, $P' = P[R_S]$

$$= [0\ 0\ 1] \begin{bmatrix} \sqrt{2} & \sqrt{2} & 0 \\ -\sqrt{2} & \sqrt{2} & 0 \\ 20 & -20\sqrt{2} + 20 & 1 \end{bmatrix}$$

$$= [20\ \ -20\sqrt{2} + 20\ \ 1]$$

$$Q' = Q[R_S]$$
$$= [0\ 10\ 1] \begin{bmatrix} \sqrt{2} & \sqrt{2} & 0 \\ -\sqrt{2} & \sqrt{2} & 0 \\ 20 & -20\sqrt{2}+20 & 1 \end{bmatrix}$$

$$R' = R[R_S]$$
$$= [10\ 10\ 1] \begin{bmatrix} \sqrt{2} & \sqrt{2} & 0 \\ -\sqrt{2} & \sqrt{2} & 0 \\ 20 & -20\sqrt{2}+20 & 1 \end{bmatrix}$$
$$= [20\ 20\ 1]$$

$$S' = S[R_S]$$
$$= [10\ 0\ 1] \begin{bmatrix} \sqrt{2} & \sqrt{2} & 0 \\ -\sqrt{2} & \sqrt{2} & 0 \\ 20 & -20\sqrt{2}+20 & 1 \end{bmatrix}$$
$$= \begin{bmatrix} -10\sqrt{2}+20 & -10\sqrt{2}+20 & 1 \end{bmatrix}$$

∴ The co-ordinates of transformed square are:
P'(20, −20√2 + 20)
Q'(−10√2 + 20, −10√2 + 20)
R'(20, 20)
and S'(−10√2 + 20, −10√2 + 20).

Example 3.10:
Perform a 45° rotation of triangle A(0, 0), B(1, 1), C(5, 2)
   (i) about origin, (ii) about P(−1, −1)

Solution:
Assume clockwise direction −

(i) About origin: The rotation matrix for clockwise direction will be,
$$R = \begin{bmatrix} \cos\theta & -\sin\theta & 0 \\ \sin\theta & \cos\theta & 0 \\ 0 & 0 & 1 \end{bmatrix}$$

$\theta = 45°$

∴ $\cos\theta = \dfrac{1}{\sqrt{2}}$

$\sin\theta = \dfrac{1}{\sqrt{2}}$

∴ $R = \begin{bmatrix} \frac{1}{\sqrt{2}} & \frac{-1}{\sqrt{2}} & 0 \\ \frac{1}{\sqrt{2}} & \frac{1}{\sqrt{2}} & 0 \\ 0 & 0 & 1 \end{bmatrix}$

∴ A' = A[R]

$= \begin{bmatrix} 0 & 0 & 1 \end{bmatrix} \begin{bmatrix} \frac{1}{\sqrt{2}} & \frac{-1}{\sqrt{2}} & 0 \\ \frac{1}{\sqrt{2}} & \frac{1}{\sqrt{2}} & 0 \\ 0 & 0 & 1 \end{bmatrix}$

$= \begin{bmatrix} 0 & 0 & 1 \end{bmatrix}$

∴ A' = (0, 0)

B' = B[R]

$= \begin{bmatrix} 1 & 1 & 1 \end{bmatrix} \begin{bmatrix} \frac{1}{\sqrt{2}} & \frac{-1}{\sqrt{2}} & 0 \\ \frac{1}{\sqrt{2}} & \frac{1}{\sqrt{2}} & 0 \\ 0 & 0 & 1 \end{bmatrix}$

$= \begin{bmatrix} \sqrt{2} & 0 & 1 \end{bmatrix}$

∴ B' = ($\sqrt{2}$, 0)

C' = C[R]

$= \begin{bmatrix} 5 & 2 & 1 \end{bmatrix} \begin{bmatrix} \frac{1}{\sqrt{2}} & \frac{-1}{\sqrt{2}} & 0 \\ \frac{1}{\sqrt{2}} & \frac{1}{\sqrt{2}} & 0 \\ 0 & 0 & 1 \end{bmatrix}$

$= \begin{bmatrix} \frac{7}{\sqrt{2}} & \frac{-3}{\sqrt{2}} & 1 \end{bmatrix}$

∴ $C' = \left(\frac{7}{\sqrt{2}}, \frac{-3}{\sqrt{2}} \right)$

After rotation, the co-ordinates of triangle will be,

A'(0, 0), B'($\sqrt{2}$, 0), C' $\left(\frac{7}{\sqrt{2}}, \frac{-3}{\sqrt{2}} \right)$

(ii) About P(–1, –1): To rotate the triangle about point P first the triangle needs to be translate to origin with respect to point P.

∴ Translation matrix will be, $t_x = 1$, $t_y = 1$

$$T = \begin{bmatrix} 1 & 0 & 0 \\ 0 & 1 & 0 \\ 1 & 1 & 1 \end{bmatrix}$$

Now, to rotate the triangle by 45° in clockwise direction, rotation matrix will be,

$$R = \begin{bmatrix} \cos\theta & -\sin\theta & 0 \\ \sin\theta & \cos\theta & 0 \\ 0 & 0 & 1 \end{bmatrix}$$

$\theta = 45°$

$\cos\theta = \dfrac{1}{\sqrt{2}}$

$\sin\theta = \dfrac{1}{\sqrt{2}}$

∴ $$R = \begin{bmatrix} \dfrac{1}{\sqrt{2}} & \dfrac{-1}{\sqrt{2}} & 0 \\ \dfrac{1}{\sqrt{2}} & \dfrac{1}{\sqrt{2}} & 0 \\ 0 & 0 & 1 \end{bmatrix}$$

Now, again triangle needs to be retranslated to point P.

∴ $t_x = -1$, $t_y = -1$

$$T^{-1} = \begin{bmatrix} 1 & 0 & 0 \\ 0 & 1 & 0 \\ -1 & -1 & 1 \end{bmatrix}$$

The resultant transformation matrix will be,

$R_S = [T][R][T^{-1}]$

$$= \begin{bmatrix} 1 & 0 & 0 \\ 0 & 1 & 0 \\ 1 & 1 & 1 \end{bmatrix} \begin{bmatrix} \dfrac{1}{\sqrt{2}} & \dfrac{-1}{\sqrt{2}} & 0 \\ \dfrac{1}{\sqrt{2}} & \dfrac{1}{\sqrt{2}} & 0 \\ 0 & 0 & 1 \end{bmatrix} \begin{bmatrix} 1 & 0 & 0 \\ 0 & 1 & 0 \\ -1 & -1 & 1 \end{bmatrix}$$

$$= \begin{bmatrix} \dfrac{1}{\sqrt{2}} & \dfrac{-1}{\sqrt{2}} & 0 \\ \dfrac{1}{\sqrt{2}} & \dfrac{1}{\sqrt{2}} & 0 \\ \dfrac{2}{\sqrt{2}} & 0 & 1 \end{bmatrix} \begin{bmatrix} 1 & 0 & 0 \\ 0 & 1 & 0 \\ -1 & -1 & 1 \end{bmatrix}$$

$$R_S = \begin{bmatrix} \frac{1}{\sqrt{2}} & \frac{-1}{\sqrt{2}} & 0 \\ \frac{1}{\sqrt{2}} & \frac{1}{\sqrt{2}} & 0 \\ \sqrt{2}-1 & -1 & 1 \end{bmatrix}$$

$A' = A[R_S]$

$$= [0\ 0\ 1] \begin{bmatrix} \frac{1}{\sqrt{2}} & \frac{-1}{\sqrt{2}} & 0 \\ \frac{1}{\sqrt{2}} & \frac{1}{\sqrt{2}} & 0 \\ \sqrt{2}-1 & -1 & 1 \end{bmatrix}$$

$= [\sqrt{2}-1\ \ -1\ \ 1]$

∴ $A' = (\sqrt{2}-1\ \ -1)$

$B' = B[R_S]$

$$= [1\ 1\ 1] \begin{bmatrix} \frac{1}{\sqrt{2}} & \frac{-1}{\sqrt{2}} & 0 \\ \frac{1}{\sqrt{2}} & \frac{1}{\sqrt{2}} & 0 \\ \sqrt{2}-1 & -1 & 1 \end{bmatrix}$$

$= (2\sqrt{2}-1,\ -1)$

∴ $B' = (2\sqrt{2}-1,\ -1)$

$C' = C[R_S]$

$$= [5\ 2\ 1] \begin{bmatrix} \frac{1}{\sqrt{2}} & \frac{-1}{\sqrt{2}} & 0 \\ \frac{1}{\sqrt{2}} & \frac{1}{\sqrt{2}} & 0 \\ \sqrt{2}-1 & -1 & 1 \end{bmatrix}$$

$= \left(\frac{9}{\sqrt{2}} - 1,\ -\frac{3}{\sqrt{2}} - 1\ \ 1 \right)$

∴ $C' = \left[\frac{9}{\sqrt{2}} - 1\ \ -\frac{3}{\sqrt{2}}\ \ -1 \right]$

∴ After rotation the co-ordinates of new triangle will be,

$A' = (\sqrt{2}-1, -1)$ $B' = (2\sqrt{2}-1, -1)$ and

$C' = \left(\frac{9}{\sqrt{2}} - 1,\ \frac{-3}{\sqrt{2}} - 1 \right)$

Example 3.11:

Consider the square A(1, 0), B(0, 0), C(0, 1) D(1, 1). Rotate the square ABCD by 45° anticlockwise about point A(1, 0).

Solution:

To rotate the square about fixed point A, first the square is translated to origin with respect to A(1, 0). Thus $t_x = -1$, $t_y = 0$.

The translation matrix will be,

$$T = \begin{bmatrix} 1 & 0 & 0 \\ 0 & 1 & 0 \\ -1 & 0 & 1 \end{bmatrix}$$

Now, to rotate the square in anticlockwise direction by $\theta = 45°$. The rotation matrix will be,

$$R = \begin{bmatrix} \cos 45° & \sin 45° & 0 \\ -\sin 45° & \cos 45° & 0 \\ 0 & 0 & 1 \end{bmatrix}$$

∴ $\cos 45° = \dfrac{1}{\sqrt{2}}$

$\sin 45° = \dfrac{1}{\sqrt{2}}$

$$R = \begin{bmatrix} \dfrac{1}{\sqrt{2}} & \dfrac{1}{\sqrt{2}} & 0 \\ \dfrac{-1}{\sqrt{2}} & \dfrac{1}{\sqrt{2}} & 0 \\ 0 & 0 & 1 \end{bmatrix}$$

The square is then retranslated to point A'.

∴ $t_x = 1$, $t_y = 0$

∴ $$T^{-1} = \begin{bmatrix} 1 & 0 & 0 \\ 0 & 1 & 0 \\ 1 & 0 & 1 \end{bmatrix}$$

The resultant transformation matrix will be,

$$R_S = [T]\,[R]\,[T^{-1}]$$

$$= \begin{bmatrix} 1 & 0 & 0 \\ 0 & 1 & 0 \\ -1 & 0 & 1 \end{bmatrix} \begin{bmatrix} \dfrac{1}{\sqrt{2}} & \dfrac{1}{\sqrt{2}} & 0 \\ \dfrac{-1}{\sqrt{2}} & \dfrac{1}{\sqrt{2}} & 0 \\ 0 & 0 & 1 \end{bmatrix} \begin{bmatrix} 1 & 0 & 0 \\ 0 & 0 & 1 \\ 1 & 0 & 1 \end{bmatrix}$$

$$= \begin{bmatrix} \frac{1}{\sqrt{2}} & \frac{1}{\sqrt{2}} & 0 \\ \frac{-1}{\sqrt{2}} & \frac{1}{\sqrt{2}} & 0 \\ \frac{-1}{\sqrt{2}} & \frac{-1}{\sqrt{2}} & 1 \end{bmatrix} \begin{bmatrix} 1 & 0 & 0 \\ 0 & 1 & 0 \\ 1 & 0 & 1 \end{bmatrix}$$

$$R_S = \begin{bmatrix} \frac{1}{\sqrt{2}} & \frac{1}{\sqrt{2}} & 0 \\ \frac{-1}{\sqrt{2}} & \frac{1}{\sqrt{2}} & 0 \\ \frac{-1}{\sqrt{2}}+1 & \frac{-1}{\sqrt{2}} & 1 \end{bmatrix}$$

Now, $A' = A[R_S]$

$$= \begin{bmatrix} 1 & 0 & 1 \end{bmatrix} \begin{bmatrix} \frac{1}{\sqrt{2}} & \frac{1}{\sqrt{2}} & 0 \\ \frac{-1}{\sqrt{2}} & \frac{1}{\sqrt{2}} & 0 \\ \frac{-1}{\sqrt{2}}+1 & \frac{-1}{\sqrt{2}} & 1 \end{bmatrix}$$

$$= \begin{bmatrix} 1 & 0 & 1 \end{bmatrix}$$

$B' = B[R_S]$

$$= \begin{bmatrix} 0 & 0 & 1 \end{bmatrix} \begin{bmatrix} \frac{1}{\sqrt{2}} & \frac{1}{\sqrt{2}} & 0 \\ \frac{-1}{\sqrt{2}} & \frac{1}{\sqrt{2}} & 0 \\ \frac{-1}{\sqrt{2}}+1 & \frac{-1}{\sqrt{2}} & 1 \end{bmatrix}$$

$$= \begin{bmatrix} \frac{-1}{\sqrt{2}}+1 & \frac{-1}{\sqrt{2}} & 1 \end{bmatrix}$$

$C' = C[R_S]$

$$= \begin{bmatrix} 0 & 1 & 1 \end{bmatrix} \begin{bmatrix} \frac{1}{\sqrt{2}} & \frac{1}{\sqrt{2}} & 0 \\ \frac{-1}{\sqrt{2}} & \frac{1}{\sqrt{2}} & 0 \\ \frac{-1}{\sqrt{2}}+1 & \frac{-1}{\sqrt{2}} & 1 \end{bmatrix}$$

$$= \begin{bmatrix} 1-\sqrt{2} & 0 & 1 \end{bmatrix}$$

$$D' = D[R_S]$$

$$= \begin{bmatrix} 1 & 1 & 1 \end{bmatrix} \begin{bmatrix} \frac{1}{\sqrt{2}} & \frac{1}{\sqrt{2}} & 0 \\ \frac{-1}{\sqrt{2}} & \frac{1}{\sqrt{2}} & 0 \\ \frac{-1}{\sqrt{2}} + 1 & \frac{-1}{\sqrt{2}} & 1 \end{bmatrix}$$

$$= \begin{bmatrix} 1 - \frac{1}{\sqrt{2}} & \frac{1}{\sqrt{2}} & 1 \end{bmatrix}$$

Hence, the co-ordinates of rotated square will be,

$$A' = (1, 0) \quad B' = \left(-\frac{1}{\sqrt{2}} + 1, \frac{-1}{\sqrt{2}}\right), \quad C' = (1 - \sqrt{2}, 0) \text{ and } D' = \left(1 - \frac{1}{\sqrt{2}}, \frac{1}{\sqrt{2}}\right).$$

Example 3.12:

Prove that two scaling transformation commute, i.e. $S_1 S_2 = S_2 \cdot S_1$.

Solution:

The scaling transformation is given by,

$$S_1 = \begin{bmatrix} S_{x_1} & 0 & 0 \\ 0 & S_{y_1} & 0 \\ 0 & 0 & 1 \end{bmatrix}$$

$$S_2 = \begin{bmatrix} S_{x_2} & 0 & 0 \\ 0 & S_{y_2} & 0 \\ 0 & 0 & 1 \end{bmatrix}$$

$$\therefore \quad S_1 \cdot S_2 = \begin{bmatrix} S_{x_1} & 0 & 0 \\ 0 & S_{y_1} & 0 \\ 0 & 0 & 1 \end{bmatrix} \begin{bmatrix} S_{x_2} & 0 & 0 \\ 0 & S_{y_2} & 0 \\ 0 & 0 & 1 \end{bmatrix}$$

$$= \begin{bmatrix} S_{x_1} S_{x_2} & 0 & 0 \\ 0 & S_{y_1} S_{y_2} & 0 \\ 0 & 0 & 1 \end{bmatrix} \text{ and,}$$

$$S_2 \cdot S_1 = \begin{bmatrix} S_{x_2} & 0 & 0 \\ 0 & S_{y_2} & 0 \\ 0 & 0 & 1 \end{bmatrix} \begin{bmatrix} S_{x_1} & 0 & 0 \\ 0 & S_{y_1} & 0 \\ 0 & 0 & 1 \end{bmatrix}$$

$$= \begin{bmatrix} S_{x_2} S_{x_1} & 0 & 0 \\ 0 & S_{y_2} S_{y_1} & 0 \\ 0 & 0 & 1 \end{bmatrix}$$

Since multiplication is commutative

$$S_{x_1} S_{x_2} = S_{x_2} S_{x_1}$$

and

$$S_{y_1} \cdot S_{y_2} = S_{y_1} S_{y_2}$$

∴ $\boxed{S_1 S_2 = S_2 \cdot S_1}$ (Hence Proved)

Example 3.13:

Show that scaling and rotation do not commute in general. What is the condition under which the scaling transformation is commutative to rotation.

Solution:

The scaling matrix is,

$$S = \begin{bmatrix} S_x & 0 & 0 \\ 0 & S_y & 0 \\ 0 & 0 & 1 \end{bmatrix}$$

The rotation matrix is,

$$R = \begin{bmatrix} \cos\theta & \sin\theta & 0 \\ -\sin\theta & \cos\theta & 0 \\ 0 & 0 & 1 \end{bmatrix}$$

(i) S.R.:

$$= \begin{bmatrix} S_x & 0 & 0 \\ 0 & S_y & 0 \\ 0 & 0 & 1 \end{bmatrix} \begin{bmatrix} \cos\theta & \sin\theta & 0 \\ -\sin\theta & \cos\theta & 0 \\ 0 & 0 & 1 \end{bmatrix}$$

$$= \begin{bmatrix} S_x \cos\theta & S_x \sin\theta & 0 \\ -S_y \sin\theta & S_y \cos\theta & 0 \\ 0 & 0 & 1 \end{bmatrix} \quad \ldots (i)$$

(ii) R.S.:

$$= \begin{bmatrix} \cos\theta & \sin\theta & 0 \\ -\sin\theta & \cos\theta & 0 \\ 0 & 0 & 1 \end{bmatrix} \begin{bmatrix} S_x & 0 & 0 \\ 0 & S_y & 0 \\ 0 & 0 & 1 \end{bmatrix}$$

$$= \begin{bmatrix} S_x \cos\theta & S_y \sin\theta & 0 \\ -S_x \sin\theta & S_y \cos\theta & 0 \\ 0 & 0 & 1 \end{bmatrix} \quad \ldots (ii)$$

From (i) and (ii)

∴ SR ≠ RS

When $S_x = S_y$ then only scaling transformation is commutative to rotation transformation.

Example 3.14:

Prove that two rotations about origin are commutative i.e. $R_1 R_2 = R_2 R_1$.

Solution:

$$R_1 = \begin{bmatrix} \cos\theta_1 & \sin\theta_1 & 0 \\ -\sin\theta_1 & \cos\theta_1 & 0 \\ 0 & 0 & 1 \end{bmatrix}$$

$$R_2 = \begin{bmatrix} \cos\theta_2 & \sin\theta_2 & 0 \\ -\sin\theta_2 & \cos\theta_2 & 0 \\ 0 & 0 & 1 \end{bmatrix}$$

$$R_1 \cdot R_2 = \begin{bmatrix} \cos\theta_1 & \sin\theta_1 & 0 \\ -\sin\theta_1 & \cos\theta_1 & 0 \\ 0 & 0 & 1 \end{bmatrix} \begin{bmatrix} \cos\theta_2 & \sin\theta_2 & 0 \\ -\sin\theta_2 & \cos\theta_2 & 0 \\ 0 & 0 & 1 \end{bmatrix}$$

$$= \begin{bmatrix} \cos\theta_1\cos\theta_2 - \sin\theta_1\sin\theta_2 & \cos\theta_1\sin\theta_2 + \sin\theta_1\cos\theta_2 & 0 \\ -\sin\theta_1\cos\theta_2 - \cos\theta_1\sin\theta_2 & -\sin\theta_1\sin\theta_2 + \cos\theta_1\cos\theta_2 & 0 \\ 0 & 0 & 1 \end{bmatrix} \quad \ldots (i)$$

$$R_2 \cdot R_1 = \begin{bmatrix} \cos\theta_2 & \sin\theta_2 & 0 \\ -\sin\theta_2 & \cos\theta_2 & 0 \\ 0 & 0 & 1 \end{bmatrix} \begin{bmatrix} \cos\theta_1 & \sin\theta_1 & 0 \\ -\sin\theta_1 & \cos\theta_1 & 0 \\ 0 & 0 & 1 \end{bmatrix}$$

$$= \begin{bmatrix} \cos\theta_2\cos\theta_1 - \sin\theta_2\sin\theta_1 & \cos\theta_2\sin\theta_1 + \sin\theta_2\cos\theta_1 & 0 \\ -\sin\theta_2\cos\theta_1 - \sin\theta_1\cos\theta_2 & -\sin\theta_1\sin\theta_2 + \cos\theta_1\cos\theta_2 & 0 \\ 0 & 0 & 1 \end{bmatrix} \quad \ldots (ii)$$

Applying (i) and (ii) to point (x' y').

$$[x' \; y' \; 1] = [x \quad y \quad 1] \begin{bmatrix} \cos\theta_1\cos\theta_2 - \sin\theta_1\sin\theta_2 & \cos\theta_1\sin\theta_2 + \sin\theta_1\cos\theta_2 & 0 \\ -\sin\theta_1\cos\theta_2 - \cos\theta_1\sin\theta_2 & -\sin\theta_1\sin\theta_2 + \cos\theta_1\cos\theta_2 & 0 \\ 0 & 0 & 1 \end{bmatrix}$$

$$= \begin{bmatrix} x\cos\theta_1\cos\theta_2 - y\sin\theta_2\cos\theta_1 & x\cos\theta_2\sin\theta_1 - y\sin\theta_1\sin\theta_2 & 1 \\ -x\sin\theta_1\sin\theta_2 - y\cos\theta_2\sin\theta_1 & +x\sin\theta_2\cos\theta_1 + y\cos\theta_1\cos\theta_2 & \end{bmatrix}$$

$$= [x\cos(\theta_1+\theta_2) - y\sin(\theta_1+\theta_2) \quad x\sin(\theta_1+\theta_2) + y\cos(\theta_1+\theta_2) \quad 1] \quad \ldots (a)$$

$$[x' \; y' \; 1] = [x \quad y \quad 1] \begin{bmatrix} \cos\theta_2\cos\theta_1 - \sin\theta_2\sin\theta_1 & \cos\theta_2\sin\theta_1 + \sin\theta_2\cos\theta_1 & 0 \\ -\sin\theta_2\cos\theta_1 - \sin\theta_1\cos\theta_2 & -\sin\theta_1\sin\theta_2 + \cos\theta_1\cos\theta_2 & 0 \\ 0 & 0 & 1 \end{bmatrix}$$

$$= \begin{bmatrix} x\cos\theta_1\cos\theta_2 - x\sin\theta_2\sin\theta_1 & x\cos\theta_2\sin\theta_1 + x\sin\theta_2\cos\theta_1 & 1 \\ -y\sin\theta_2\cos\theta_1 - y\sin\theta_1\cos\theta_2 & -y\sin\theta_1\sin\theta_2 + y\cos\theta_1\cos\theta_2 & \end{bmatrix}$$

$$= [x\cos(\theta_1+\theta_2) - y\sin(\theta_1+\theta_2) \quad x\sin(\theta_1+\theta_2) + y\cos(\theta_1+\theta_2) \quad 1] \quad \ldots (b)$$

From (a) and (b),

$$\boxed{R_1 \cdot R_2 = R_2 \cdot R_1} \quad \text{(Hence Proved)}$$

3.4 REFLECTION

This type of transformation generates the mirror image of an object. To carry out the reflection it is necessary to define the axis of reflection.

(i) Reflection about x-axis: Consider point P(x, y)

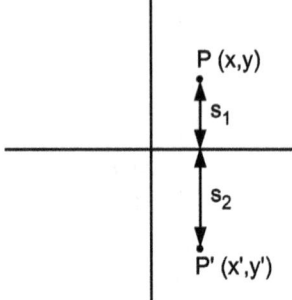

Fig. 3.5

Here P' is the mirror image of P.

$\therefore \quad S_1 = S_2$
$$x' = x$$
$$y' = -y$$

In matrix representation,

$$[x'\ y'\ 1] = [x\ y\ 1] \begin{bmatrix} 1 & 0 & 0 \\ 0 & -1 & 0 \\ 0 & 0 & 1 \end{bmatrix}$$

(ii) Reflection about y-axis: Consider point P(x, y)

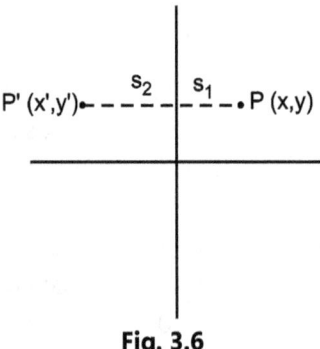

Fig. 3.6

Here P' is the mirror image of P.

$\therefore \quad S_1 = S_2$
$$x' = -x$$
$$y' = y$$

$$[x'\ y'\ 1] = [x\ y\ 1] \begin{bmatrix} -1 & 0 & 0 \\ 0 & 1 & 0 \\ 0 & 0 & 1 \end{bmatrix}$$

Similarly, the transformation matrix for y = x axis will be,

$$[x'\ y'\ 1] = [x\ y\ 1] \begin{bmatrix} 0 & 1 & 0 \\ 1 & 0 & 0 \\ 0 & 0 & 1 \end{bmatrix}$$

and for y = –x axis the transformation matrix will be,

$$[x'\ y'\ 1] = [x\ y\ 1] \begin{bmatrix} 0 & -1 & 0 \\ -1 & 0 & 0 \\ 0 & 0 & 1 \end{bmatrix}$$

3.4.1 Reflection about Arbitrary Axis

If the reflection is to be made about an axis which is not the standard one such as x, y, y = x, y = –x, then this must be first coincide with one of the standard axis and then the reflection is performed. The steps are as follows:

Step – I : **Translation:** First translate the line to the origin.
Step – II : **Rotation:** If needed then rotate it to coincide it with one of the standard axis.
Step – III : **Reflection:** Take reflection.
Step – IV : **Rerotation:** If the line is rotated in Step – II then rerotation is performed in reverse direction.
Step – V : **Retranslation:** Retranslate the line back to its original position.

3.5 COMPOSITE TRANSFORMATION OR CONCATENATION

Combination of fundamental matrices to produce the desired general result is called as composite transformation or concatenation. The basic purpose of concatenation is to efficiently apply single composed or concatenated transformation to a point and to apply a series of transformation one after another which is applied by multiplying transformation matrices. If m_1 and m_2 indicates a fundamental transformation matrices then concatenation is $m_1 \cdot m_2$ where '·' specifies operation of matrix multiplication.

The properties of composite transformation are:

A matrix multiplication and hence concatenation are not commutative. However for concatenation to be commutative following cases must hold good.

(a) If m_1 and m_2 represents rotation, then $m_1 \cdot m_2 = m_2 \cdot m_1$.
(b) If m_1 and m_2 represents translation then $m_1 \cdot m_2 = m_2 \cdot m_1$.
(c) If m_1 and m_2 represents scaling then $m_1 \cdot m_2 = m_2 \cdot m_1$.
(d) If m_1 is scaling and m_2 is rotation then $m_1 \cdot m_2 = m_2 \cdot m_1$ provided $S_x = S_y$ i.e. uniform scaling.

Example 3.15:

Reflect a figure defined by the vertices A(−1, 0), B(0, −2), C(1, 0), D(0, 2) about the following axis:
  (a) x = 2
  (b) y = 2
  (c) y = x + 2.

Solution:

(a) **x = 2:** First translate the line to origin.

∴ $t_x = -2, t_y = 0$

The translation matrix will be,

$$T = \begin{bmatrix} 1 & 0 & 0 \\ 0 & 1 & 0 \\ -2 & 0 & 1 \end{bmatrix}$$

Since, x = 2, the line is parallel to y-axis. After translation line comes in y-axis. Thus, reflection matrix about y-axis is,

$$R_e = \begin{bmatrix} -1 & 0 & 0 \\ 0 & 1 & 0 \\ 0 & 0 & 1 \end{bmatrix}$$

Again retranslate the axis to original position $t_x = 2, t_y = 0$,

∴ $$T^{-1} = \begin{bmatrix} 1 & 0 & 0 \\ 0 & 1 & 0 \\ 2 & 0 & 1 \end{bmatrix}$$

∴ The resultant transformation matrix will be,

$$R_S = [T][R_e][T^{-1}]$$

$$= \begin{bmatrix} 1 & 0 & 0 \\ 0 & 1 & 0 \\ -2 & 0 & 1 \end{bmatrix} \begin{bmatrix} -1 & 0 & 0 \\ 0 & 1 & 0 \\ 0 & 0 & 1 \end{bmatrix} \begin{bmatrix} 1 & 0 & 0 \\ 0 & 1 & 0 \\ 2 & 0 & 1 \end{bmatrix}$$

$$= \begin{bmatrix} -1 & 0 & 0 \\ 0 & 1 & 0 \\ 2 & 0 & 1 \end{bmatrix} \begin{bmatrix} 1 & 0 & 0 \\ 0 & 1 & 0 \\ 2 & 0 & 1 \end{bmatrix}$$

$$R_S = \begin{bmatrix} -1 & 0 & 0 \\ 0 & 1 & 0 \\ 4 & 0 & 1 \end{bmatrix}$$

For, A' = A[R_S]

$$= [-1 \ 0 \ 1] \begin{bmatrix} -1 & 0 & 0 \\ 0 & 1 & 0 \\ 4 & 0 & 1 \end{bmatrix}$$

A' = [5 0 1]

$$\therefore \quad A' = (5, 0)$$
$$B' = B[R_S]$$
$$= [0\ -2\ 1] \begin{bmatrix} -1 & 0 & 0 \\ 0 & 1 & 0 \\ 4 & 0 & 1 \end{bmatrix}$$
$$= [4\ -2\ 1]$$
$$\therefore \quad B' = (4, -2)$$
$$C' = C[R_S]$$
$$= [1\ 0\ 1] \begin{bmatrix} -1 & 0 & 0 \\ 0 & 1 & 0 \\ 4 & 0 & 1 \end{bmatrix}$$
$$= [3\ 0\ 1]$$
$$\therefore \quad C' = (3, 0)$$
$$D' = D[R_S]$$
$$= [0\ 2\ 1] \begin{bmatrix} -1 & 0 & 0 \\ 0 & 1 & 0 \\ 4 & 0 & 1 \end{bmatrix}$$
$$= [4\ 2\ 1]$$
$$\therefore \quad D' = (4, 2)$$

The co-ordinates of reflected figure are A'(5, 0), B'(4, −2), C'(3, 0) and D'(4, 2).

(b) y = 2:

First translate the line to origin.

$\therefore \quad t_x = 0,\ t_y = -2.$

The translation matrix will be,

$$T = \begin{bmatrix} 1 & 0 & 0 \\ 0 & 1 & 0 \\ 0 & -2 & 1 \end{bmatrix}$$

Since y = 2, the line is parallel to x-axis. After translation it comes in x-axis. Thus, the reflection matrix for x-axis will be,

$$R_e = \begin{bmatrix} 1 & 0 & 0 \\ 0 & -1 & 0 \\ 0 & 0 & 1 \end{bmatrix}$$

Now, retranslate the axis to original position, $t_x = 0,\ t_y = 2$.

$$\therefore \quad T^{-1} = \begin{bmatrix} 1 & 0 & 0 \\ 0 & 1 & 0 \\ 0 & 2 & 1 \end{bmatrix}$$

The resultant transformation matrix will be,

$$R_S = [T]\ [R_e]\ [T^{-1}]$$

$$= \begin{bmatrix} 1 & 0 & 0 \\ 0 & 1 & 0 \\ 0 & -2 & 1 \end{bmatrix} \begin{bmatrix} 1 & 0 & 0 \\ 0 & -1 & 0 \\ 0 & 0 & 1 \end{bmatrix} \begin{bmatrix} 1 & 0 & 0 \\ 0 & 1 & 0 \\ 0 & 2 & 1 \end{bmatrix}$$

$$= \begin{bmatrix} 1 & 0 & 0 \\ 0 & -1 & 0 \\ 0 & 2 & 1 \end{bmatrix} \begin{bmatrix} 1 & 0 & 0 \\ 0 & 1 & 0 \\ 0 & 2 & 1 \end{bmatrix}$$

∴ $R_S = \begin{bmatrix} 1 & 0 & 0 \\ 0 & -1 & 0 \\ 0 & 4 & 1 \end{bmatrix}$

For, A' $= A[R_S]$

$$= [-1 \ 0 \ 1] \begin{bmatrix} 1 & 0 & 0 \\ 0 & -1 & 0 \\ 0 & 4 & 1 \end{bmatrix}$$

$= [-1 \ 4 \ 1]$

∴ A' = (−1, 4)

B' = B[R_S]

$$= [0 \ -2 \ 1] \begin{bmatrix} 1 & 0 & 0 \\ 0 & -1 & 0 \\ 0 & 4 & 1 \end{bmatrix}$$

$= [0 \ 6 \ 1]$

∴ B' = (0, 6)

C' = C[R_S]

$$= [1 \ 0 \ 1] \begin{bmatrix} 1 & 0 & 0 \\ 0 & -1 & 0 \\ 0 & 4 & 1 \end{bmatrix}$$

$= [1 \ 4 \ 1]$

∴ C' = (1, 4)

D' = D[R_S]

$$= [0 \ 2 \ 1] \begin{bmatrix} 1 & 0 & 0 \\ 0 & -1 & 0 \\ 0 & 4 & 1 \end{bmatrix}$$

$= [0 \ 2 \ 1]$

∴ D' = (0, 2)

∴ The co-ordinates of reflected figure are A'(−1, 4), B'(0, 6), C'(4, 1), D'(0, 2).

(c) y = x + 2:

The end points of line are,

$y = x + 2$

Put $\quad x = 0, y = 2$

Put $\quad y = 0, x = -2$

Thus, the end points are (0, 2) and (−2, 0).

First translate the axis with respect to point (0, 2).

∴ $t_x = 0, t_y = -2$.

The translation matrix will be,

$$T = \begin{bmatrix} 1 & 0 & 0 \\ 0 & 1 & 0 \\ 0 & -2 & 1 \end{bmatrix}$$

After translation axis gets coincide with y = x-axis. Thus, reflection matrix about y = x-axis is,

$$R_e = \begin{bmatrix} 0 & 1 & 0 \\ 1 & 0 & 0 \\ 0 & 0 & 1 \end{bmatrix}$$

Retranslate the axis to original position with respect to (0, 2)

$t_x = 0, t_y = 2$

∴ $$T^{-1} = \begin{bmatrix} 1 & 0 & 0 \\ 0 & 1 & 0 \\ 0 & 2 & 1 \end{bmatrix}$$

The resultant transformation matrix will be,

$$R_S = [T][R_e][T^{-1}]$$

$$= \begin{bmatrix} 1 & 0 & 0 \\ 0 & 1 & 0 \\ 0 & -2 & 1 \end{bmatrix} \begin{bmatrix} 0 & 1 & 0 \\ 1 & 0 & 0 \\ 0 & 0 & 1 \end{bmatrix} \begin{bmatrix} 1 & 0 & 0 \\ 0 & 1 & 0 \\ 0 & 2 & 1 \end{bmatrix}$$

$$= \begin{bmatrix} 0 & 1 & 0 \\ 1 & 0 & 0 \\ -2 & 0 & 1 \end{bmatrix} \begin{bmatrix} 1 & 0 & 0 \\ 0 & 1 & 0 \\ 0 & 2 & 1 \end{bmatrix}$$

∴ $$R_S = \begin{bmatrix} 0 & 1 & 0 \\ 1 & 0 & 0 \\ -2 & 2 & 1 \end{bmatrix}$$

For, $\quad A' = A[R_S]$

$$= [-1\ 0\ 1] \begin{bmatrix} 0 & 1 & 0 \\ 1 & 0 & 0 \\ -2 & 2 & 1 \end{bmatrix}$$

∴ $\quad A' = [-2\ 1\ 1]$

$B' = B[R_S]$

$$= [0\ -2\ 1] \begin{bmatrix} 0 & 1 & 0 \\ 1 & 0 & 0 \\ -2 & 2 & 1 \end{bmatrix}$$

$\therefore \quad B' = [-4\ 2\ 1]$

$C' = C[R_S]$

$$= [1\ 0\ 1] \begin{bmatrix} 0 & 1 & 0 \\ 1 & 0 & 0 \\ -2 & 2 & 1 \end{bmatrix}$$

$\therefore \quad C' = [-2\ 3\ 1]$

$D' = D[R_S]$

$$= [0\ 2\ 1] \begin{bmatrix} 1 & 0 & 0 \\ 0 & 1 & 0 \\ -2 & 2 & 1 \end{bmatrix}$$

$D' = [0\ 2\ 1]$

The co-ordinates of reflected figure are A'(–2, 1), B'(–4, 2), C'(–2, 3) and D'(0, 2).

Example 3.16:
Show that rotation about origin by 270° is equivalent to reflection about two axes.

Solution:
Consider rotation in a counter clockwise direction. The rotation matrix will be,

$$R = \begin{bmatrix} \cos\theta & \sin\theta & 0 \\ -\sin\theta & \cos\theta & 0 \\ 0 & 0 & 1 \end{bmatrix}$$

Put $\theta = 270°$

$\cos 270° = 0$

$\sin 270° = -1$

$$\therefore \quad R = \begin{bmatrix} 0 & -1 & 0 \\ 1 & 0 & 0 \\ 0 & 0 & 1 \end{bmatrix}$$

Let us take an arbitrary point P(x, y). After rotation by 270° in counter clockwise direction, the resultant co-ordinates will be,

$$[x'\ y'\ 1] = [x\ y\ 1] \begin{bmatrix} 0 & -1 & 0 \\ 1 & 0 & 0 \\ 0 & 0 & 1 \end{bmatrix}$$

$$= [y\ -x\ 1] \qquad \ldots (i)$$

Now take the reflection at P(x, y) about y-axis.
The reflection matrix for y-axis is

$$R_{e_1} = \begin{bmatrix} -1 & 0 & 0 \\ 0 & 1 & 0 \\ 0 & 0 & 1 \end{bmatrix}$$

Then take the reflection about y = x-axis.

The reflection matrix is,

$$R_{e_2} = \begin{bmatrix} 0 & 1 & 0 \\ 1 & 0 & 0 \\ 0 & 0 & 1 \end{bmatrix}$$

The resultant matrix is, $R_S = [R_{e_1}][R_{e_2}]$

$$= \begin{bmatrix} -1 & 0 & 0 \\ 0 & 1 & 0 \\ 0 & 0 & 1 \end{bmatrix} \begin{bmatrix} 0 & 1 & 0 \\ 1 & 0 & 0 \\ 0 & 0 & 1 \end{bmatrix}$$

The co-ordinates of reflected point P' will be,

$$[x' \; y' \; 1] = [x \; y \; 1] \begin{bmatrix} 0 & -1 & 0 \\ 1 & 0 & 0 \\ 0 & 0 & 1 \end{bmatrix}$$

$$= [y \; -x \; 1] \qquad \qquad \ldots \text{(ii)}$$

From equations (i) and (ii) it is clear that a point rotated about 270° is equivalent to reflection about two axes.

Example 3.17:
Show how reflection in the line y = x and y = –x can be performed by scaling operation followed by rotation.

Solution:
The matrix for reflection about y = x will be,

$$R_{e_1} = \begin{bmatrix} 0 & 1 & 0 \\ 1 & 0 & 0 \\ 0 & 0 & 1 \end{bmatrix}$$

The matrix for reflection about y = –x,

$$R_{e_2} = \begin{bmatrix} 0 & -1 & 0 \\ -1 & 0 & 0 \\ 0 & 0 & 1 \end{bmatrix}$$

The resultant matrix will be,

$$R_S = [R_{e_1}] \cdot [R_{e_2}]$$

$$= \begin{bmatrix} 0 & 1 & 0 \\ 1 & 0 & 0 \\ 0 & 0 & 1 \end{bmatrix} \begin{bmatrix} 0 & -1 & 0 \\ -1 & 0 & 0 \\ 0 & 0 & 1 \end{bmatrix}$$

$$R_S = \begin{bmatrix} -1 & 0 & 0 \\ 0 & -1 & 0 \\ 0 & 0 & 1 \end{bmatrix} \qquad \qquad \ldots \text{(i)}$$

COMPUTER GRAPHICS — GEOMETRIC TRANSFORMATION

The scaling matrix is,
$$S = \begin{bmatrix} S_x & 0 & 0 \\ 0 & S_y & 0 \\ 0 & 0 & 1 \end{bmatrix}$$

Put $S_x = S_y = 1$,

$$\therefore \quad S = \begin{bmatrix} 1 & 0 & 0 \\ 0 & 1 & 0 \\ 0 & 0 & 1 \end{bmatrix}$$

Now rotation matrix in clockwise direction is,
$$R = \begin{bmatrix} \cos\theta & -\sin\theta & 0 \\ \sin\theta & \cos\theta & 0 \\ 0 & 0 & 1 \end{bmatrix}$$

Put, $\theta = 180°$

$\cos 180° = -1$
$\sin 180° = 0$

$$\therefore \quad R = \begin{bmatrix} -1 & 0 & 0 \\ 0 & -1 & 0 \\ 0 & 0 & 1 \end{bmatrix}$$

The resultant matrix is, $R_S = [S][R]$

$$= \begin{bmatrix} 1 & 0 & 0 \\ 0 & 1 & 0 \\ 0 & 0 & 1 \end{bmatrix} \begin{bmatrix} -1 & 0 & 0 \\ 0 & -1 & 0 \\ 0 & 0 & 1 \end{bmatrix}$$

$$R_S = \begin{bmatrix} -1 & 0 & 0 \\ 0 & -1 & 0 \\ 0 & 0 & 1 \end{bmatrix} \quad \ldots (i)$$

From equation (i) and (ii). It is clear that the reflection about line $y = x$ and $y = -x$ can be performed by scaling followed by rotation.

Example 3.18:

A triangle with vertices (2, 2), (4, 2) and (3, 5) is reflected about the line $x + y = -2$. Find out the final position of triangle.

Solution:

The triangle in matrix notation will be,
$$\begin{bmatrix} 2 & 2 & 1 \\ 4 & 2 & 1 \\ 3 & 5 & 1 \end{bmatrix}$$

Line is given by equation $x + y = -2$. To find the end points of a line,
Put $x = 0$, $y = -2$
Put $y = 0$, $x = -2$

Thus, the end points are (0, –2) and (–2, 0).
First translate the line, so that it will pass through origin.
$t_x = 2, t_y = 0$

$$\therefore \quad T = \begin{bmatrix} 1 & 0 & 0 \\ 0 & 1 & 0 \\ 2 & 0 & 1 \end{bmatrix}$$

Now after translation the line coincides with y = –x a-axis.
The reflection matrix for y = –x axis is,

$$R_e = \begin{bmatrix} 0 & -1 & 0 \\ -1 & 0 & 0 \\ 0 & 0 & 1 \end{bmatrix}$$

Retranslate the line to original position.
$\therefore \quad t_x = -2, t_y = 0.$
The translation matrix is,

$$T^{-1} = \begin{bmatrix} 1 & 0 & 0 \\ 0 & 1 & 0 \\ -2 & 0 & 1 \end{bmatrix}$$

The resultant matrix is, $R_S = [T][R_e][T^{-1}]$

$$= \begin{bmatrix} 1 & 0 & 0 \\ 0 & 1 & 0 \\ 2 & 0 & 1 \end{bmatrix} \begin{bmatrix} 0 & -1 & 0 \\ -1 & 0 & 0 \\ 0 & 0 & 1 \end{bmatrix} \begin{bmatrix} 1 & 0 & 0 \\ 0 & 1 & 0 \\ -2 & 0 & 1 \end{bmatrix}$$

$$= \begin{bmatrix} 0 & -1 & 0 \\ -1 & 0 & 0 \\ 0 & -2 & 1 \end{bmatrix} \begin{bmatrix} 1 & 0 & 0 \\ 0 & 1 & 0 \\ -2 & 0 & 1 \end{bmatrix}$$

$$\therefore \quad R_S = \begin{bmatrix} 0 & -1 & 0 \\ -1 & 0 & 0 \\ -2 & -2 & 1 \end{bmatrix}$$

The position of resultant vertices will be,

$$\begin{bmatrix} 2 & 2 & 1 \\ 4 & 2 & 1 \\ 3 & 5 & 1 \end{bmatrix} \begin{bmatrix} 0 & -1 & 0 \\ -1 & 0 & 0 \\ -2 & -2 & 1 \end{bmatrix} = \begin{bmatrix} -4 & -4 & 1 \\ -4 & -6 & 1 \\ -7 & -5 & 1 \end{bmatrix}$$

Thus, the co-ordinates of reflected triangle are (–4, –4) (–4, –6) and (–7, –5).

Example 3.19:

Find reflection of a triangle whose vertices are A(1, 1) B(5, 1) C(1, 5) about line y = 2x + 10.

Solution:

The line is defined by equation y = 2x + 10.

To determine the end points of line,
  Put x = 0, y = 10
  Put y = 0, x = −5
Thus, end points are (−5, 0) and (0, 10).
First translate the line to origin.
∴ $t_x = 0, t_y = -10$

$$T = \begin{bmatrix} 1 & 0 & 0 \\ 0 & 1 & 0 \\ 0 & -10 & 1 \end{bmatrix}$$

[**Note:** In above case point (0, 10) is considered. If x-intercept has been taken then the translation matrix will be,

$$T = \begin{bmatrix} 1 & 0 & 0 \\ 0 & 1 & 0 \\ 5 & 0 & 1 \end{bmatrix} \qquad (\because \text{ X-intercept is } -5)$$

Rotate the line in clockwise direction to coincide it with x-axis.
The rotation matrix for clockwise direction is,

$$R = \begin{bmatrix} \cos\theta & -\sin\theta & 0 \\ \sin\theta & \cos\theta & 0 \\ 0 & 0 & 1 \end{bmatrix}$$

To find θ: Where m → slope.
We have, $\theta = \tan^{-1} m$
The equation of line is,   y = mx + c
               y = 2x + 10
∴   m = 2
               $\theta = \tan^{-1}(2)$
∴   θ = 63.43
       cos (63.43) = 0.4472
∴   sin (63.43) = 0.8944

$$R = \begin{bmatrix} 0.4472 & -0.8944 & 0 \\ 0.8944 & 0.4472 & 0 \\ 0 & 0 & 1 \end{bmatrix}$$

Now, take reflection of given triangle about x-axis. The reflection matrix is,

$$R_e = \begin{bmatrix} 1 & 0 & 0 \\ 0 & -1 & 0 \\ 0 & 0 & 1 \end{bmatrix}$$

Rerotate the line in anticlockwise direction by same angle i.e. θ = 63.43,

∴ $$R^{-1} = \begin{bmatrix} \cos\theta & \sin\theta & 0 \\ -\sin\theta & \cos\theta & 0 \\ 0 & 0 & 1 \end{bmatrix}$$

Put $\theta = 63.43$

$$\therefore \quad R^{-1} = \begin{bmatrix} 0.4472 & 0.8944 & 0 \\ -0.8944 & 0.4472 & 0 \\ 0 & 0 & 1 \end{bmatrix}$$

Retranslate the line to original position

$\therefore \quad t_x = 0, t_y = 10$

The translation matrix will be,

$$T^{-1} = \begin{bmatrix} 1 & 0 & 0 \\ 0 & 1 & 0 \\ 0 & 10 & 1 \end{bmatrix}$$

The resultant transformation matrix is,

$R_S = [T][R][R_e][R^{-1}][T^{-1}]$

$$= \begin{bmatrix} 1 & 0 & 0 \\ 0 & 1 & 0 \\ 0 & -10 & 1 \end{bmatrix} \begin{bmatrix} 0.4472 & -0.8944 & 0 \\ 0.8944 & 0.4472 & 0 \\ 0 & 0 & 1 \end{bmatrix} \begin{bmatrix} 1 & 0 & 0 \\ 0 & -1 & 0 \\ 0 & 0 & 1 \end{bmatrix}$$

$$\begin{bmatrix} 0.4472 & 0.8944 & 0 \\ -0.8944 & 0.4472 & 0 \\ 0 & 0 & 1 \end{bmatrix}$$

$$\begin{bmatrix} 1 & 0 & 0 \\ 0 & 1 & 0 \\ 0 & 10 & 1 \end{bmatrix}$$

$$= \begin{bmatrix} 0.4472 & -0.8944 & 0 \\ 0.8944 & 0.4472 & 0 \\ -8.944 & -4.472 & 1 \end{bmatrix} \begin{bmatrix} 1 & 0 & 0 \\ 0 & -1 & 0 \\ 0 & 0 & 1 \end{bmatrix} \begin{bmatrix} 0.4472 & 0.8944 & 0 \\ -0.8944 & 0.4472 & 0 \\ 0 & 0 & 1 \end{bmatrix} \begin{bmatrix} 1 & 0 & 0 \\ 0 & 1 & 0 \\ 0 & 10 & 1 \end{bmatrix}$$

$$= \begin{bmatrix} 0.4472 & 0.8944 & 0 \\ 0.8944 & -0.4472 & 0 \\ -8.944 & -4.472 & 1 \end{bmatrix} \begin{bmatrix} 0.4472 & 0.8944 & 0 \\ -0.8944 & 0.4472 & 0 \\ 0 & 0 & 1 \end{bmatrix} \begin{bmatrix} 1 & 0 & 0 \\ 0 & 1 & 0 \\ 0 & 10 & 1 \end{bmatrix}$$

$$= \begin{bmatrix} -0.6 & 0.8 & 0 \\ 0.8 & 0.6 & 0 \\ -8 & -6 & 1 \end{bmatrix} \begin{bmatrix} 1 & 0 & 0 \\ 0 & 1 & 0 \\ 0 & 10 & 1 \end{bmatrix}$$

$$RS = \begin{bmatrix} -0.6 & 0.8 & 0 \\ 0.8 & 0.6 & 0 \\ -8 & 4 & 1 \end{bmatrix}$$

For, $A' = A[R_S]$

$$= \begin{bmatrix} 1 & 1 & 1 \end{bmatrix} \begin{bmatrix} -0.6 & 0.8 & 0 \\ 0.8 & 0.6 & 0 \\ -8 & 4 & 1 \end{bmatrix}$$

$= [-7.8 \quad 5.4 \quad 1]$

$$B' = B[R_S]$$
$$= [5\ 1\ 1]\begin{bmatrix} -0.6 & 0.8 & 0 \\ 0.8 & 0.6 & 0 \\ -8 & 4 & 1 \end{bmatrix}$$
$$= [-10.2\ 8.6\ 1]$$
$$C' = C[R_S]$$
$$= [1\ 5\ 1]\begin{bmatrix} -0.6 & 0.8 & 0 \\ 0.8 & 0.6 & 0 \\ -8 & 4 & 1 \end{bmatrix}$$
$$= [-4.6\ 7.8\ 1]$$

The co-ordinates of resultant figure will be,
A'(–7.8, 5.4), B'(–10.2, 8.6) and C'(–4.6, 7.8).

Example 3.20:
Find the general form of matrix for reflection about line L with slope m and y intercept (0, b).
Solution:
Reflection is to be taken about the line y = mx + b.

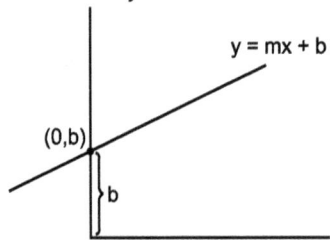

Fig. 3.7

Firstly translate the line y = mx + b to shift it from point (0, b) to origin.
The translation matrix will be,
$$T = \begin{bmatrix} 1 & 0 & 0 \\ 0 & 1 & 0 \\ 0 & -b & 1 \end{bmatrix}$$

Then rotate the line in clockwise direction by an angle θ about origin to make it align with x-axis.
$$y = mx + b$$
$$\theta = \tan^{-1} m$$

The rotation matrix will be,
$$R = \begin{bmatrix} \cos\theta & -\sin\theta & 0 \\ \sin\theta & \cos\theta & 0 \\ 0 & 0 & 1 \end{bmatrix}$$

Take reflection about x-axis.
$$\therefore \quad R_e = \begin{bmatrix} 1 & 0 & 0 \\ 0 & -1 & 0 \\ 0 & 0 & 1 \end{bmatrix}$$

Then rerotate the line in counterclockwise direction by angle θ.

$$\therefore \quad R^{-1} = \begin{bmatrix} \cos\theta & \sin\theta & 0 \\ -\sin\theta & \cos\theta & 0 \\ 0 & 0 & 1 \end{bmatrix}$$

Retranslate the line to original position. Therefore, $t_x = 0$, $t_y = b$.

$$\therefore \quad T^{-1} = \begin{bmatrix} 1 & 0 & 0 \\ 0 & 1 & 0 \\ 0 & b & 1 \end{bmatrix}$$

The resultant transformation matrix will be,

$$R_S = [T][R][R_e][R^{-1}][T^{-1}]$$

$$= \begin{bmatrix} 1 & 0 & 0 \\ 0 & 1 & 0 \\ 0 & -b & 1 \end{bmatrix} \begin{bmatrix} \cos\theta & -\sin\theta & 0 \\ \sin\theta & \cos\theta & 0 \\ 0 & 0 & 1 \end{bmatrix} \begin{bmatrix} 1 & 0 & 0 \\ 0 & -1 & 0 \\ 0 & 0 & 1 \end{bmatrix} \begin{bmatrix} \cos\theta & \sin\theta & 0 \\ -\sin\theta & \cos\theta & 0 \\ 0 & 0 & 1 \end{bmatrix} \begin{bmatrix} 1 & 0 & 0 \\ 0 & 1 & 0 \\ 0 & b & 1 \end{bmatrix}$$

$$= \begin{bmatrix} \cos^2\theta - \sin^2\theta & \sin 2\theta & 0 \\ \sin 2\theta & \sin^2\theta - \cos^2\theta & 0 \\ -b \sin 2\theta & -b(\sin 2\theta + \cos 2\theta) + b & 1 \end{bmatrix}$$

Example 3.21:
Derive a transformation matrix to reflect an object about a line L having y intercept (0, –b) and angle of inclination θ° with respect to axis.
Solution:
Similar as Example 3.20.

Example 3.22:
Find the reflection of an arbitrary point about the line x = m, where m is constant.
Solution:

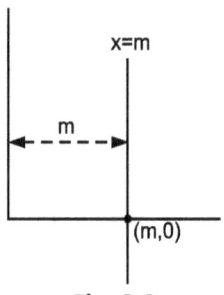

Fig. 3.8

The line x = m is parallel to y-axis at a distance of m from origin. Let the arbitrary point be (x, y).

First perform translation so that the line will merge with y-axis.

$\therefore \quad t_x = -m$, $t_y = 0$

The translation matrix will be,

$$T = \begin{bmatrix} 1 & 0 & 0 \\ 0 & 1 & 0 \\ -m & 0 & 1 \end{bmatrix}$$

Now, reflect the line about y-axis.

$$\therefore \quad R_e = \begin{bmatrix} -1 & 0 & 0 \\ 0 & 1 & 0 \\ 0 & 0 & 1 \end{bmatrix}$$

Retranslate the line to original position.

$\therefore \quad t_x = m_1,\ t_y = 0$

$$T^{-1} = \begin{bmatrix} 1 & 0 & 0 \\ 0 & 1 & 0 \\ m & 0 & 1 \end{bmatrix}$$

The resultant transformation matrix will be,

$$R_S = [T][R_e][T^{-1}]$$

$$= \begin{bmatrix} 1 & 0 & 0 \\ 0 & 1 & 0 \\ -m & 0 & 1 \end{bmatrix} \begin{bmatrix} -1 & 0 & 0 \\ 0 & 1 & 0 \\ 0 & 0 & 1 \end{bmatrix} \begin{bmatrix} 1 & 0 & 0 \\ 0 & 1 & 0 \\ m & 0 & 1 \end{bmatrix}$$

$$= \begin{bmatrix} -1 & 0 & 0 \\ 0 & 1 & 0 \\ m & 0 & 1 \end{bmatrix} \begin{bmatrix} 1 & 0 & 0 \\ 0 & 1 & 0 \\ m & 0 & 1 \end{bmatrix}$$

$$R_S = \begin{bmatrix} -1 & 0 & 0 \\ 0 & 1 & 0 \\ 2m & 0 & 1 \end{bmatrix}$$

The co-ordinates of reflected point will be,

$$[x'\ y'\ 1] = [x\ y\ 1] \begin{bmatrix} -1 & 0 & 0 \\ 0 & 1 & 0 \\ 2m & 0 & 1 \end{bmatrix}$$

$$= [-x + 2m\ y\ 1]$$

$\therefore$ The co-ordinates are $(-x + 2m,\ y)$

Example 3.23:

Consider the square A(1, 0), B(0, 0), C(0, 1), D(1, 1). Rotate the square by 45° in anticlockwise direction followed by reflection about x-axis.

Solution:

The rotation matrix for anticlockwise direction is,

$$R = \begin{bmatrix} \cos\theta & \sin\theta & 0 \\ -\sin\theta & \cos\theta & 0 \\ 0 & 0 & 1 \end{bmatrix}$$

Put, $\theta = 45°$

$\therefore \quad \cos\theta = \cos 45° = \dfrac{1}{\sqrt{2}}$

and, $$\sin 45° = \frac{1}{\sqrt{2}}$$

$$\therefore \quad R = \begin{bmatrix} \frac{1}{\sqrt{2}} & \frac{1}{\sqrt{2}} & 0 \\ \frac{-1}{\sqrt{2}} & \frac{1}{\sqrt{2}} & 0 \\ 0 & 0 & 1 \end{bmatrix}$$

Reflection matrix about x-axis is

$$R_e = \begin{bmatrix} 1 & 0 & 0 \\ 0 & -1 & 0 \\ 0 & 0 & 1 \end{bmatrix}$$

The resultant matrix will be,

$$R_S = [R][R_e]$$

$$= \begin{bmatrix} \frac{1}{\sqrt{2}} & \frac{1}{\sqrt{2}} & 0 \\ \frac{-1}{\sqrt{2}} & \frac{1}{\sqrt{2}} & 0 \\ 0 & 0 & 1 \end{bmatrix} \begin{bmatrix} 1 & 0 & 0 \\ 0 & -1 & 0 \\ 0 & 0 & 1 \end{bmatrix}$$

$$R_S = \begin{bmatrix} \frac{1}{\sqrt{2}} & \frac{-1}{\sqrt{2}} & 0 \\ \frac{-1}{\sqrt{2}} & \frac{-1}{\sqrt{2}} & 0 \\ 0 & 0 & 1 \end{bmatrix}$$

For, $$A' = A[R_S]$$

$$= [1\ 0\ 1] \begin{bmatrix} \frac{1}{\sqrt{2}} & \frac{-1}{\sqrt{2}} & 0 \\ \frac{-1}{\sqrt{2}} & \frac{-1}{\sqrt{2}} & 0 \\ 0 & 0 & 1 \end{bmatrix}$$

$$\therefore \quad A' = \begin{bmatrix} \frac{1}{\sqrt{2}} & \frac{-1}{\sqrt{2}} & 1 \end{bmatrix}$$

$$B' = B[R_S]$$

$$= [0\ 0\ 1] \begin{bmatrix} \frac{1}{\sqrt{2}} & \frac{-1}{\sqrt{2}} & 0 \\ \frac{-1}{\sqrt{2}} & \frac{-1}{\sqrt{2}} & 0 \\ 0 & 0 & 1 \end{bmatrix}$$

$$\therefore \quad B' = [0\ 0\ 1]$$

$$C' = C[R_S]$$

$$= \begin{bmatrix} 0 & 1 & 1 \end{bmatrix} \begin{bmatrix} \frac{1}{\sqrt{2}} & \frac{-1}{\sqrt{2}} & 0 \\ \frac{-1}{\sqrt{2}} & \frac{-1}{\sqrt{2}} & 0 \\ 0 & 0 & 1 \end{bmatrix}$$

$$= \begin{bmatrix} \frac{-1}{\sqrt{2}} & \frac{-1}{\sqrt{2}} & 1 \end{bmatrix}$$

$$D' = D[R_S]$$

$$= \begin{bmatrix} 1 & 1 & 1 \end{bmatrix} \begin{bmatrix} \frac{1}{\sqrt{2}} & \frac{-1}{\sqrt{2}} & 0 \\ \frac{-1}{\sqrt{2}} & \frac{-1}{\sqrt{2}} & 0 \\ 0 & 0 & 1 \end{bmatrix}$$

$$= \begin{bmatrix} 0 & -\sqrt{2} & 1 \end{bmatrix}$$

The co-ordinates are $A'\left(\frac{1}{\sqrt{2}}, \frac{-1}{\sqrt{2}}\right)$, $B'(0, 0)$, $C'\left(\frac{-1}{\sqrt{2}}, \frac{-1}{\sqrt{2}}\right)$ and $D'(0, -\sqrt{2})$.

Example 3.24:
Show that the transformation matrix for reflection about line y = x is equivalent to reflection relative to x-axis followed by anticlockwise rotation of 90°.

Solution:
Transformation matrix for reflection about y = x is,

$$R_e = \begin{bmatrix} 0 & 1 & 0 \\ 1 & 0 & 0 \\ 0 & 0 & 1 \end{bmatrix} \quad \ldots \text{(i)}$$

Transformation matrix for reflection about x-axis is,

$$R_e = \begin{bmatrix} 1 & 0 & 0 \\ 0 & -1 & 0 \\ 0 & 0 & 1 \end{bmatrix}$$

Rotation matrix for anticlockwise direction is

$$R = \begin{bmatrix} \cos\theta & \sin\theta & 0 \\ -\sin\theta & \cos\theta & 0 \\ 0 & 0 & 1 \end{bmatrix}$$

Put, $\theta = 90°$

$$R = \begin{bmatrix} 0 & 1 & 0 \\ -1 & 0 & 0 \\ 0 & 0 & 1 \end{bmatrix}$$

$$= [R_e][R]$$

$$= \begin{bmatrix} 1 & 0 & 0 \\ 0 & -1 & 0 \\ 0 & 0 & 1 \end{bmatrix} \begin{bmatrix} 0 & 1 & 0 \\ -1 & 0 & 0 \\ 0 & 0 & 1 \end{bmatrix}$$

$$\therefore \quad R = \begin{bmatrix} 0 & 1 & 0 \\ 1 & 0 & 0 \\ 0 & 0 & 1 \end{bmatrix} \quad \text{... (ii)}$$

From equations (i) and (ii), it is clear that transformation matrix of reflection about y = x is equivalent to reflection about x-axis followed by anticlockwise rotation of 90°.

3.6 CO-ORDINATE TRANSFORMATION

The co-ordinate system can be changed by using transformations.

Transformations are of many types each of them is having a specific use.

Translation is a transformation which is used when the origins are not aligned.

Rotations can also be used, generally for angles $\pi/2$.

When the orientation of y-axis is along the long edge and x-axis along short edge then it is a referred as a **portrait mode**.

When the orientation of y-axis is along the short edge and x-axis along the long edge then it is referred as **landscape mode**.

The transformation from normalized co-ordinates to actual device co-ordinates is given by example.

The arithmetic use for the conversion.

$$X_1 \leftarrow X_x \text{ width} + \text{width} - \text{start}$$

$$Y_1 \leftarrow Y_x \text{ height} + \text{height} - \text{start}$$

The above equation represents a scale by width for x and for y which is followed by a translation by width-start and height-start.

The transformation matrix for the above change will be,

$$\Delta = \begin{vmatrix} \text{Width} & 0 & 0 \\ 0 & \text{Height} & 0 \\ \text{Width-start} & \text{Height-start} & 1 \end{vmatrix}$$

3.7 INVERSE TRANSFORMATION

This type of transformation is used to undo the effect of any transformation. For undoing the effect of some transformation, the transformation must be carried out in reverse direction. Carrying out transformation is nothing but a transformation itself, which is called as inverse transformation.

For instance, rotating an object by angle θ in counterclockwise direction using transformation matrix is given by,

$$R = \begin{bmatrix} \cos\theta & \sin\theta & 0 \\ -\sin\theta & \cos\theta & 0 \\ 0 & 0 & 1 \end{bmatrix}$$

$$R^{-1} = \begin{bmatrix} \cos\theta & -\sin\theta & 0 \\ \sin\theta & \cos\theta & 0 \\ 0 & 0 & 1 \end{bmatrix}$$

To undo the effect of above transformation rotation by an angle of θ in opposite direction is required i.e. in clockwise direction which is again a transformation and is referred as inverse rotation.

$$R \cdot R^{-1} = \begin{bmatrix} \cos\theta & \sin\theta & 0 \\ -\sin\theta & \cos\theta & 0 \\ 0 & 0 & 1 \end{bmatrix} \begin{bmatrix} \cos\theta & -\sin\theta & 0 \\ \sin\theta & \cos\theta & 0 \\ 0 & 0 & 1 \end{bmatrix}$$

$$= \begin{bmatrix} \cos^2\theta + \sin^2\theta & -\cos\theta\sin\theta + \sin\theta\cos\theta & 0 \\ -\sin\theta\cos\theta + \cos\theta\sin\theta & \sin^2\theta + \cos^2\theta & 0 \\ 0 & 0 & 1 \end{bmatrix}$$

∵ $\cos^2\theta + \sin^2\theta = 1$
$\sin\theta\cos\theta - \cos\theta\sin\theta = 0$

∴ $$R \cdot R^{-1} = \begin{bmatrix} 1 & 0 & 0 \\ 0 & 1 & 0 \\ 0 & 0 & 1 \end{bmatrix}$$

Thus, $R \cdot R^{-1}$ will give a unity matrix which nullify the effect.

Similarly, for undoing the transformation application of inverse transformation is required if 'S' is a scaling.

$$S = \begin{bmatrix} S_x & 0 & 0 \\ 0 & S_y & 0 \\ 0 & 0 & 1 \end{bmatrix}$$

Then inverse transformation will be

$$S^{-1} = \begin{bmatrix} 1/S_x & 0 & 0 \\ 0 & 1/S_y & 0 \\ 0 & 0 & 1 \end{bmatrix}$$

COMPUTER GRAPHICS   GEOMETRIC TRANSFORMATION

If T is a translation matrix,

$$T = \begin{bmatrix} 1 & 0 & 0 \\ 0 & 1 & 0 \\ T_x & T_y & 1 \end{bmatrix}$$

Then the inverse transformation will be,

$$T^{-1} = \begin{bmatrix} 1 & 0 & 0 \\ 0 & 1 & 0 \\ -T_x & -T_y & 1 \end{bmatrix}$$

The inverse of a matrix in terms of determinants can be expressed as –

Inverse of a matrix:
$$T = \begin{bmatrix} a & d & 0 \\ b & e & 0 \\ c & f & 1 \end{bmatrix}$$

$$t_{ij} = \frac{(-1)^{i+j} \det. m_{ji}}{\Delta T}$$

$$T^{-1} = \begin{bmatrix} e & -d & 0 \\ -b & a & 0 \\ (bf - ce) & -(af - cd) & (ae - bd) \end{bmatrix}$$

$$= \frac{1}{ae - bd}$$

Example 3.25:

Find the inverse transformation which converts the figure defined by vertices (3, 2), (2, 1) and (4, 1) into another figure which is defined by vertices (−3, −1), (−4, −2) and (−2, −2).

Solution: Consider original Fig. as A and resulting Fig. as B.

$$A \rightarrow B$$

$$A \cdot T \rightarrow B$$
$$T \rightarrow BA^{-1}$$

$$A = \begin{bmatrix} 3 & 2 & 1 \\ 2 & 1 & 1 \\ 4 & 1 & 1 \end{bmatrix} \quad B = \begin{bmatrix} -3 & -1 & 1 \\ -4 & -2 & 1 \\ -2 & -2 & 1 \end{bmatrix}$$

$$\Delta A = 3(0) - 2(-2) + 1(-2)$$
$$\Delta A = 2$$

To find A^{-1}:

$$\begin{bmatrix} (1 \times 1 - 1 \times 1) & (2 \times 1 - 4 \times 1) & (2 \times 1 - 4 \times 1) \\ (2 \times 1 - 1 \times 1) & (3 \times 1 - 4 \times 1) & (3 \times 1 - 4 \times 2) \\ (2 \times 1 - 1 \times 1) & (3 \times 1 - 2 \times 1) & (3 \times 1 - 2 \times 2) \end{bmatrix}$$

$$= \begin{bmatrix} 0 & -2 & -2 \\ 1 & -1 & -5 \\ 1 & 1 & -1 \end{bmatrix}$$

Chp 3 | 3.45

The transpose of above matrix can be obtained by changing rows into columns and vice versa.

$$\begin{bmatrix} 0 & \underline{1} & 1 \\ \underline{-2} & -1 & \underline{1} \\ -2 & \underline{-5} & -1 \end{bmatrix}$$

Then change the sign of marked position. The resultant matrix will be,

$$R = \begin{bmatrix} 0 & -1 & 1 \\ 2 & -1 & -1 \\ -2 & 5 & -1 \end{bmatrix}$$

$$A^{-1} = \frac{1}{\Delta R} \cdot R$$

$$= \frac{1}{2} \begin{bmatrix} 0 & -1 & 1 \\ 2 & -1 & -1 \\ -2 & 5 & -1 \end{bmatrix}$$

$$T = A^{-1} \cdot B$$

$$= \frac{1}{2} \begin{bmatrix} 0 & -1 & 1 \\ 2 & -1 & -1 \\ -2 & 5 & -1 \end{bmatrix} \begin{bmatrix} -3 & -1 & 1 \\ -4 & -2 & 1 \\ -2 & -2 & 1 \end{bmatrix}$$

$$= \frac{1}{2} \begin{bmatrix} 2 & 0 & 0 \\ 0 & 2 & 0 \\ -12 & -6 & 2 \end{bmatrix}$$

$$T = \begin{bmatrix} 1 & 0 & 0 \\ 0 & 1 & 0 \\ -6 & 3 & 1 \end{bmatrix}$$

To verify the result $A \cdot T = B$

$$A \cdot T = \begin{bmatrix} 3 & 2 & 1 \\ 2 & 1 & 1 \\ 4 & 1 & 1 \end{bmatrix} \begin{bmatrix} 1 & 0 & 0 \\ 0 & 1 & 0 \\ -6 & 3 & 1 \end{bmatrix}$$

$$= \begin{bmatrix} -3 & -1 & 1 \\ -4 & -2 & 1 \\ -2 & -2 & 1 \end{bmatrix}$$

$$= B \quad \text{(Hence Proved)}.$$

Example 3.26: Find the inverse transformation for converting a figure defined by the vertices A(1, 1), B(3, 1), C(3, 3) into another Fig. defined by vertices A'(−3, −2), B'(−2, −2), and C'(−2, 1).

Solution:
$$P \rightarrow Q$$
$$P \cdot T \rightarrow Q$$
$$T \rightarrow P^{-1} Q$$

$$P = \begin{bmatrix} 1 & 1 & 1 \\ 3 & 1 & 1 \\ 3 & 3 & 1 \end{bmatrix} \quad Q = \begin{bmatrix} -3 & -2 & 1 \\ -2 & -2 & 1 \\ -2 & 1 & 1 \end{bmatrix}$$

$$\Delta P = 1(1-3) - 1(3-3) + 1(9-3)$$
$$= 4$$

$$P^{-1} = \frac{1}{4} \begin{bmatrix} -2 & 2 & 0 \\ 0 & -2 & 2 \\ 6 & 0 & -2 \end{bmatrix}$$

$$= \frac{1}{2} \begin{bmatrix} -1 & 1 & 0 \\ 0 & -1 & 1 \\ 3 & 0 & -1 \end{bmatrix}$$

$$T = P^{-1} Q$$

$$= \frac{1}{2} \begin{bmatrix} -1 & 1 & 0 \\ 0 & -1 & 1 \\ 3 & 0 & -1 \end{bmatrix} \begin{bmatrix} -3 & -2 & 1 \\ -2 & -2 & 1 \\ -2 & 1 & 1 \end{bmatrix}$$

$$T = \frac{1}{2} \begin{bmatrix} 1 & 0 & 0 \\ 0 & 3 & 0 \\ -7 & -7 & 2 \end{bmatrix}$$

3.8 SHEAR TRANSFORMATION

This type of transformation produces shape distortions that represents a twisting of shearing effect. There are two types of shearing transformations. x-shear and y-shear.

(i) x-shear: The x-shear preserves the y co-ordinates, but changes the x values which causes vertical lines to tilt right or left as shown in Fig. 3.9.

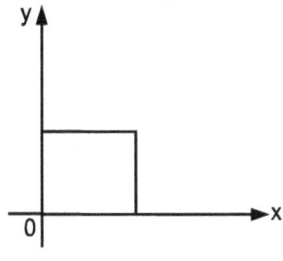
(a) Original Object

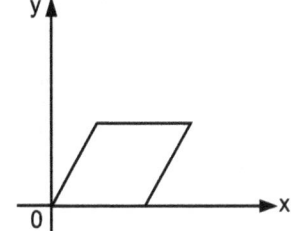
(B) Object after x-shear

Fig. 3.9

$$X_{sh} = \begin{bmatrix} 1 & 0 & 0 \\ Sh_x & 1 & 0 \\ 0 & 0 & 1 \end{bmatrix}$$

$$x' = x + y \cdot sh_x$$

and $\quad y' = y$

(ii) y-shear: The y-shear preserves the x co-ordinates but changes the y values which causes horizontal lines to transform into lines which slope up or down, as shown in Fig. 3.10.

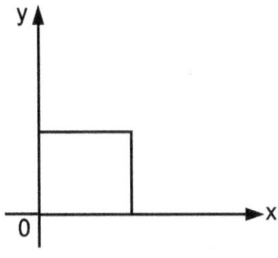

(a) Original Object   (B) Object after y-shear

Fig. 3.10

$$Y_{sh} = \begin{bmatrix} 1 & S_{hy} & 0 \\ 0 & 1 & 0 \\ 0 & 0 & 1 \end{bmatrix}$$

$$x' = x$$

and

$$y' = y + x \cdot Sh_y$$

Example 3.27:
Find the co-ordinates of figure bounded by (0, 0) (1, 5) (6, 3) (−3, −4) column reflected along line whose equation is y = 2x + 4 and sheared by 2 units in x and 2 units in y-direction.

Solution:
To find the end points of line,

$$y = 2x + 4$$

Put $\quad x = 0, \; y = 4$

Put $\quad y = 0, \; x = -2$

Thus, the end points or (0, 4) and (−2, 0).

Translate the line to origin with respect (0, 4), $t_x = 0$, $t_y = -4$

Translation matrix will be,

$$T = \begin{bmatrix} 1 & 0 & 0 \\ 0 & 1 & 0 \\ 0 & -4 & 1 \end{bmatrix}$$

Rotate the line in clockwise direction,

Rotation matrix will be, $\quad R = \begin{bmatrix} \cos\theta & -\sin\theta & 0 \\ \sin\theta & \cos\theta & 0 \\ 0 & 0 & 1 \end{bmatrix}$

To find θ:

$$\theta = \tan^{-1} m$$
$$\theta = \tan^{-1} 2$$
$$\theta = 63.43$$

$$\cos(63.43°) = 0.4472$$
$$\sin(63.43°) = 0.8944$$

$$\therefore R = \begin{bmatrix} 0.4472 & -0.8944 & 0 \\ 0.8944 & 0.4472 & 0 \\ 0 & 0 & 1 \end{bmatrix}$$

Reflection about x-axis.

The matrix will be,

$$R_e = \begin{bmatrix} 1 & 0 & 0 \\ 0 & -1 & 1 \\ 0 & 0 & 1 \end{bmatrix}$$

Rerotate the line in anticlockwise direction by angle θ,

$$\therefore R^{-1} = \begin{bmatrix} \cos\theta & \sin\theta & 0 \\ -\sin\theta & \cos\theta & 0 \\ 0 & 0 & 1 \end{bmatrix}$$

Put $\theta = 63.43$

$$R^{-1} = \begin{bmatrix} 0.4472 & 0.8944 & 0 \\ -0.8944 & 0.4472 & 0 \\ 0 & 0 & 1 \end{bmatrix}$$

Retranslate the line to original position,

$$T^{-1} = \begin{bmatrix} 1 & 0 & 0 \\ 0 & 1 & 0 \\ 0 & 4 & 1 \end{bmatrix}$$

For shearing along x-axis,

$$T_{Sh_x} = \begin{bmatrix} 1 & 0 & 0 \\ Sh_x & 1 & 0 \\ 0 & 0 & 1 \end{bmatrix}$$

Put $Sh_x = 2$

$$\therefore T_{Sh_x} = \begin{bmatrix} 1 & 0 & 0 \\ 2 & 1 & 0 \\ 0 & 0 & 1 \end{bmatrix}$$

For shearing along y-axis,

$$T_{Sh_y} = \begin{bmatrix} 1 & Sh_y & 0 \\ 0 & 1 & 0 \\ 0 & 0 & 1 \end{bmatrix}$$

Put $Sh_y = 2$

$$T_{Sh_y} = \begin{bmatrix} 1 & 2 & 0 \\ 0 & 1 & 0 \\ 0 & 0 & 1 \end{bmatrix}$$

The resultant transformation matrix will be,
$$R_S = [T][R][R_e][R^{-1}][T^{-1}][T_{Shx}][T_{Shy}]$$
$$R_S = \begin{bmatrix} -0.6 & 0.8 & 0 \\ 0.8 & 0.6 & 0 \\ -3.2 & 1.6 & 1 \end{bmatrix}$$

Example 3.28:

Perform x-shear and y-shear on a triangle having A(2, 1), B(4, 3), C(2, 3). Consider the constant value a = b = 2.

Solution:

Triangle ABC in matrix form is,
$$A = \begin{bmatrix} 2 & 1 & 1 \\ 4 & 3 & 1 \\ 2 & 3 & 1 \end{bmatrix}$$

For shearing along x-axis,
$$T_{Shx} = \begin{bmatrix} 1 & 0 & 0 \\ Sh_x & 1 & 0 \\ 0 & 0 & 1 \end{bmatrix}$$

Put $Sh_x = 2$

$$= \begin{bmatrix} 1 & 0 & 0 \\ 2 & 1 & 0 \\ 0 & 0 & 1 \end{bmatrix}$$

For shearing along y-axis,
$$T_{Shy} = \begin{bmatrix} 1 & Sh_y & 0 \\ 0 & 1 & 0 \\ 0 & 0 & 1 \end{bmatrix}$$

Put $Sh_y = 2$

$$T_{Shy} = \begin{bmatrix} 1 & 2 & 0 \\ 0 & 1 & 0 \\ 0 & 0 & 1 \end{bmatrix}$$

The resultant matrix will be,
$$R_S = T_{shx} \cdot T_{shy}$$
$$= \begin{bmatrix} 1 & 0 & 0 \\ 2 & 1 & 0 \\ 0 & 0 & 1 \end{bmatrix} \begin{bmatrix} 1 & 2 & 0 \\ 0 & 1 & 0 \\ 0 & 0 & 1 \end{bmatrix} = \begin{bmatrix} 1 & 2 & 0 \\ 2 & 5 & 0 \\ 0 & 0 & 1 \end{bmatrix}$$

The co-ordinates of resultant figure will be,
$$= \begin{bmatrix} 2 & 1 & 1 \\ 4 & 3 & 1 \\ 2 & 3 & 1 \end{bmatrix} \begin{bmatrix} 1 & 2 & 0 \\ 2 & 5 & 0 \\ 0 & 0 & 1 \end{bmatrix} = \begin{bmatrix} 4 & 9 & 1 \\ 10 & 23 & 1 \\ 8 & 19 & 1 \end{bmatrix}$$

Thus, coordinates are (4, 9), B'(10, 23) and C'(8, 19).

Example 3.29:

Show how shear transformation can be expressed in terms of rotation and scaling. Show how rotations can be expressed in terms of shear and scales. What scaling operations can be expressed as shear?

Solution:

The shear transformation matrix for x, and y are combinely given as,

$$T_{Sh_x} \cdot T_{Sh_y} = \begin{bmatrix} 1 & Sh_y & 0 \\ Sh_x & 1 & 0 \\ 0 & 0 & 1 \end{bmatrix} \quad \ldots (i)$$

The scaling matrix is, $\quad S = \begin{bmatrix} S_x & 0 & 0 \\ 0 & S_y & 0 \\ 0 & 0 & 1 \end{bmatrix}$

The rotation matrix is, $\quad R = \begin{bmatrix} \cos\theta & \sin\theta & 0 \\ -\sin\theta & \cos\theta & 0 \\ 0 & 0 & 1 \end{bmatrix}$

$$S \cdot R = \begin{bmatrix} S_x & 0 & 0 \\ 0 & S_y & 0 \\ 0 & 0 & 1 \end{bmatrix} \begin{bmatrix} \cos\theta & \sin\theta & 0 \\ -\sin\theta & \cos\theta & 0 \\ 0 & 0 & 1 \end{bmatrix}$$

$$= \begin{bmatrix} S_x \cos\theta & S_x \sin\theta & 0 \\ -S_y \sin\theta & S_y \cos\theta & 0 \\ 0 & 0 & 1 \end{bmatrix} \quad \ldots (ii)$$

Comparing (i) and (ii), $\quad Sh_x = -S_y \sin\theta$

$$Sh_y = S_x \sin\theta$$

$$S_x \cos\theta = 1$$

$$S_y \cos\theta = 1$$

$$S_x = \frac{1}{\cos\theta}$$

and $\quad S_y = \dfrac{1}{\cos\theta}$

Substituting values of S_x and S_y,

$$Sh_x = -S_y \sin\theta$$

$$= \frac{-1}{\cos\theta} \cdot \sin\theta$$

$$= -\tan\theta$$

$$Sh_y = S_x \sin\theta$$

$$= \frac{1}{\cos\theta} \cdot \sin\theta$$

$$= \tan\theta$$

Therefore, the shear transformation matrix expressed in terms of rotation and scales is,

$$\begin{bmatrix} 1 & \tan\theta & 0 \\ -\tan\theta & 1 & 0 \\ 0 & 0 & 1 \end{bmatrix} \quad \because S_x \cos\theta = S_y \cos\theta = 1$$

$\theta \rightarrow$ Angle of rotation
$S_x \rightarrow$ x scale
$S_y \rightarrow$ y scale

The transformation matrix for scaling and rotation are –

$$S = \begin{bmatrix} S_x & 0 & 0 \\ 0 & S_y & 0 \\ 0 & 0 & 1 \end{bmatrix}$$

$$R = \begin{bmatrix} S_x \cos\theta & S_x \sin\theta & 0 \\ -S_y \sin\theta & S_y \cos\theta & 0 \\ 0 & 0 & 1 \end{bmatrix}$$

$$S \cdot R = \begin{bmatrix} S_x \cos\theta & S_x \sin\theta & 0 \\ -S_y \sin\theta & S_y \cos\theta & 0 \\ 0 & 0 & 1 \end{bmatrix}$$

The reflection matrix for y = x is,

$$R_e = \begin{bmatrix} 0 & 1 & 0 \\ 1 & 0 & 0 \\ 0 & 0 & 1 \end{bmatrix}$$

Equating the reflection matrix for y = x and $S \cdot R$,

$$\begin{bmatrix} 0 & 1 & 0 \\ 1 & 0 & 0 \\ 0 & 0 & 1 \end{bmatrix} \begin{bmatrix} S_x \cos\theta & S_x \sin\theta & 0 \\ -S_y \sin\theta & S_y \cos\theta & 0 \\ 0 & 0 & 1 \end{bmatrix}$$

$S_x \cos\theta = S_y \cos\theta = 0 \qquad \therefore \theta = 90°$

$S_x \sin 90 = 1 \qquad\qquad \therefore S_x = 1$ and

$-S_y \cdot \sin 90° = 1 \qquad\qquad S_y = -1$

Therefore, with $S_x = 1$, $S_y = -1$ and $\theta = 90°$ the reflection about the line y = x can be expressed by scaling operation followed by rotation.

(ii) The reflection matrix for y = –x is,

$$R_e = \begin{bmatrix} 0 & -1 & 0 \\ -1 & 0 & 0 \\ 0 & 0 & 1 \end{bmatrix}$$

Equating the reflection matrix for y = –x with $S \cdot R$,

$$\begin{bmatrix} 0 & -1 & 0 \\ -1 & 0 & 0 \\ 0 & 0 & 1 \end{bmatrix} = \begin{bmatrix} S_x \cos\theta & S_x \sin\theta & 0 \\ -S_y \sin\theta & S_y \cos\theta & 0 \\ 0 & 0 & 1 \end{bmatrix}$$

$S_x \cos\theta = S_y \cos\theta = 0$ ∴ $\theta = 90°$
$S_x \sin\theta = -1$ ∴ $S_x = -1$
$-S_y \cdot \sin\theta = -1$ $S_y = 1$

Thus, with $S_x = -1$ and $S_y = 1$ and $\theta = 90°$ the reflection about the line $y = -x$ can be expressed in terms of scaling followed by rotation.

Example 3.30:
Convert the square defined by vertices A(0, 0), B(1, 0), C(1, 1), D(0, 1) into a parallelogram by applying appropriate transformation.

Solution:
The square can be converted into parallelogram by applying shearing transformation.

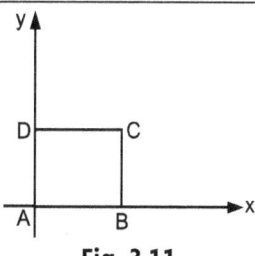

Fig. 3.11

First apply y-shear, $T_{Shy} = \begin{bmatrix} 1 & Sh_y & 0 \\ 0 & 1 & 0 \\ 0 & 0 & 1 \end{bmatrix}$

Put $Sh_y = 1$

$T_{Shy} = \begin{bmatrix} 1 & 1 & 0 \\ 0 & 1 & 0 \\ 0 & 0 & 1 \end{bmatrix}$

Then apply x-shear, $T_{Shx} = \begin{bmatrix} 1 & 0 & 0 \\ Sh_x & 1 & 0 \\ 0 & 0 & 1 \end{bmatrix}$

Put $Sh_x = 1$

$T_{Shx} = \begin{bmatrix} 1 & 0 & 0 \\ 1 & 1 & 0 \\ 0 & 0 & 1 \end{bmatrix}$

The resultant transformation matrix will be,

$R_S = T_{Shy} \cdot T_{Shx}$

$= \begin{bmatrix} 1 & 1 & 0 \\ 0 & 1 & 0 \\ 0 & 0 & 1 \end{bmatrix} \begin{bmatrix} 1 & 0 & 0 \\ 1 & 1 & 0 \\ 0 & 0 & 1 \end{bmatrix}$

$R_S = \begin{bmatrix} 2 & 1 & 0 \\ 1 & 1 & 0 \\ 0 & 0 & 1 \end{bmatrix}$

The new co-ordinates are:

$\begin{bmatrix} 0 & 0 & 1 \\ 1 & 0 & 1 \\ 1 & 1 & 1 \\ 0 & 1 & 1 \end{bmatrix} \begin{bmatrix} 2 & 1 & 0 \\ 1 & 1 & 0 \\ 0 & 0 & 1 \end{bmatrix} \begin{bmatrix} 0 & 0 & 1 \\ 2 & 1 & 1 \\ 3 & 2 & 1 \\ 1 & 1 & 1 \end{bmatrix}$

Thus, A' = (0, 0), B' = (2, 1), C' = (3, 2) and D' = (1, 1)

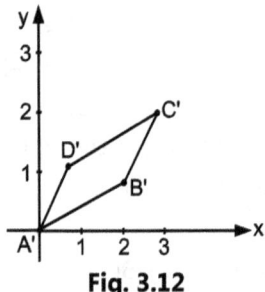

Fig. 3.12

Example 3.31:
What transformation are required to convert a Fig. defined as A(0, 0) B(1, 0) C(1, 1) D(0, 1) into figure defined as A'(0, 0), B'(2, 1), C'(3, 3), D'(1, 2).

Solution:
Shearing transformation. Applying y-shear and then x-shear will convert the original Fig. into the resultant figure.

Example 3.32:
Prove that parallel lines remain parallel after applying transformation on them.

Solution:
Consider square having co-ordinates A(0, 0), B(2, 0), C(2, 2) and D(0, 2).

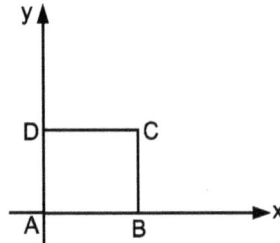

Fig. 3.13

Here opposite sides of a square are parallel. Now applying shear transformation to above square.

Apply y-shear, $T_{Shy} = \begin{bmatrix} 1 & Sh_y & 0 \\ 0 & 1 & 0 \\ 0 & 0 & 1 \end{bmatrix}$

Put $Sh_y = 1$

$T_{Shy} = \begin{bmatrix} 1 & 1 & 0 \\ 0 & 1 & 0 \\ 0 & 0 & 1 \end{bmatrix}$

Then apply x-shear, $T_{Shx} = \begin{bmatrix} 1 & 0 & 0 \\ Sh_x & 1 & 0 \\ 0 & 0 & 1 \end{bmatrix}$

Put $Sh_x = 1$

$$T_{Shx} = \begin{bmatrix} 1 & 0 & 0 \\ 1 & 1 & 0 \\ 0 & 0 & 1 \end{bmatrix}$$

The resultant transformation matrix will be,

$$R_S = T_{Shy} \cdot T_{Shx} = \begin{bmatrix} 1 & 1 & 0 \\ 0 & 1 & 0 \\ 0 & 0 & 1 \end{bmatrix} \begin{bmatrix} 1 & 0 & 0 \\ 1 & 1 & 0 \\ 0 & 0 & 1 \end{bmatrix}$$

$$R_S = \begin{bmatrix} 2 & 1 & 0 \\ 1 & 1 & 0 \\ 0 & 0 & 1 \end{bmatrix}$$

For,
$$A' = A[R_S] = [0\ 0\ 1] \begin{bmatrix} 2 & 1 & 0 \\ 1 & 1 & 0 \\ 0 & 0 & 1 \end{bmatrix}$$

$$= [0\ 0\ 1]$$

$$B' = B[R_S]$$

$$= [2\ 0\ 1] \begin{bmatrix} 2 & 1 & 0 \\ 1 & 1 & 0 \\ 0 & 0 & 1 \end{bmatrix} = [4\ 2\ 1]$$

$$C' = C[R_S] = [2\ 2\ 1] \begin{bmatrix} 2 & 1 & 0 \\ 1 & 1 & 0 \\ 0 & 0 & 1 \end{bmatrix}$$

$$= [6\ 4\ 1]$$

$$D' = D[R_S] = [0\ 2\ 1] \begin{bmatrix} 2 & 1 & 0 \\ 1 & 1 & 0 \\ 0 & 0 & 1 \end{bmatrix}$$

$$= [2\ 2\ 1]$$

A' = (0, 0), B' = (4, 2), C' = (6, 4), D' = (2, 2)
The resultant figure will be,

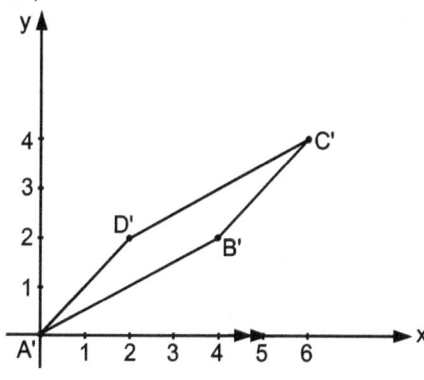

Fig. 3.14

The opposite sides are parallel in the resultant figure. Hence proved.

3.9 THREE DIMENSIONAL TRANSFORMATIONS (3-D TRANSFORMATION)

3.9.1 Introduction

Some graphics applications are two-dimensional such as graphs, charts, certain maps etc. But we live in three-dimensional world and deal with many design applications which describe three-dimensional objects. For example, if the architect wants to see how the structure will actually look, then a three-dimensional model can allow him to view the structure from different viewpoints. Some simulation applications, such as docking a spaceship or landing an airplane, also needs a three-dimensional view of the world.

In three-dimensional space we shall extend the transformations to allow translation and rotation, but the viewing surface is only two-dimensional, we must consider ways of projecting the object onto this flat surface to form the image.

The 3D co-ordinate system is divided into two types:
  (a) Right-handed system.
  (b) Left-handed system.

If the thumb of the right hand points in the positive z direction as one curls the fingers of the right hand from x into y, then the coordinates are called a right-handed system. If the thumb points in the negative z direction then it is left handed-system.

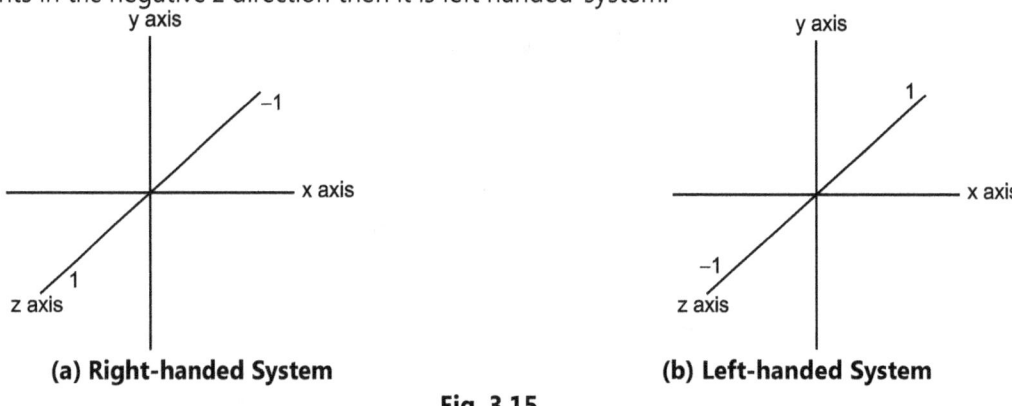

(a) Right-handed System   (b) Left-handed System

Fig. 3.15

3.9.2 Translation

Consider point p with the coordinates (x, y, z). To shift this point to new position p'(x', y', z').

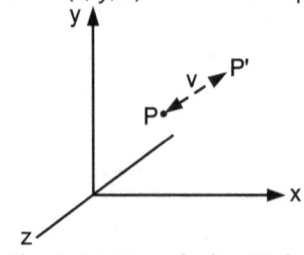

Fig. 3.16: Translating Point

As shown in previous figure the shifting and direction of the translation is now defined by vector $v = a_i + b_j + c_k$. Thus,

$$x' = x + a$$
$$y' = y + b$$
$$z' = z + c$$

where, a, b, c are the translation factors in x, y and z directions respectively.

The matrix representation will be,

$$T = \begin{bmatrix} 1 & 0 & 0 & 0 \\ 0 & 1 & 0 & 0 \\ 0 & 0 & 1 & 0 \\ a & b & c & 1 \end{bmatrix}$$

or

$$T = \begin{bmatrix} 1 & 0 & 0 & 0 \\ 0 & 1 & 0 & 0 \\ 0 & 0 & 1 & 0 \\ t_x & t_y & t_z & 1 \end{bmatrix}$$

$$P' = P \cdot T$$

$$[x' \ y' \ z' \ 1] = [x \ y \ z \ 1] \begin{bmatrix} 1 & 0 & 0 & 0 \\ 0 & 1 & 0 & 0 \\ 0 & 0 & 1 & 0 \\ t_x & t_y & t_z & 1 \end{bmatrix}$$

$$= [x + t_x \ \ y + t_y \ \ z + t_z \ \ 1]$$

Like two dimensional transformation an object is translated in three-dimensions by transforming each vertex of the object.

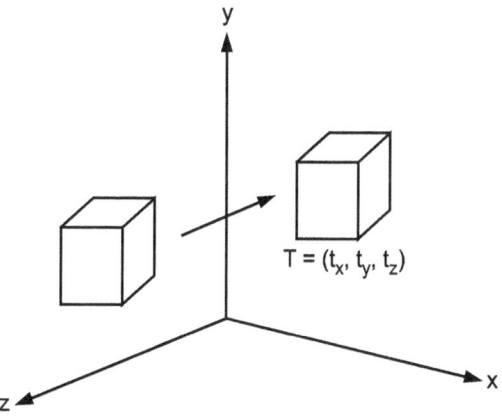

Fig. 3.17: Translating Object

3.9.3 Scaling

Scaling transformation alters the size of the object. This transformation either magnifies or reduces the size depending on the value of the scaling factor. If the scaling factor is less than 1, it reduces and if it is greater than 1 it magnifies.

Consider point P(x, y, z) which is to be scaled by S_x, S_y, S_z. Then the new coordinates will be,

$$x' = x \cdot S_x$$
$$y' = y \cdot S_y$$
$$z' = z \cdot S_z$$

The scaling matrix will be,

$$S = \begin{bmatrix} S_x & 0 & 0 & 0 \\ 0 & S_y & 0 & 0 \\ 0 & 0 & S_z & 0 \\ 0 & 0 & 0 & 1 \end{bmatrix}$$

$$[x'\ y'\ z'\ 1] = [x\ y\ z\ 1] \begin{bmatrix} S_x & 0 & 0 & 0 \\ 0 & S_y & 0 & 0 \\ 0 & 0 & S_z & 0 \\ 0 & 0 & 0 & 1 \end{bmatrix}$$

The scaling transformation is done with respect to origin i.e. the origin is kept fixed.

3.9.4 Rotation

In 2D transformation the rotation was prescribed by the angle of rotation and the point of rotation. But in case of 3D rotation, the angle of rotation as well as the axis of rotation need to be mentioned. There are three axis, so the rotation can take place about any of these axis, i.e. about x-axis, y-axis and z-axis respectively.

Three-dimensional transformation matrix for each coordinate axes rotations with homogeneous coordinates are –

Rotation About z-axis: Let P be the point object in xy plane P(x, y, 0). Rotate it by an angle θ° in counterclockwise direction. The resultant point will be P'(x', y', 0).

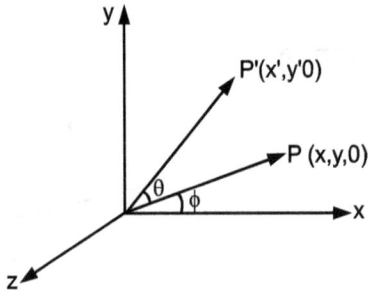

Fig. 3.18

As shown in figure,

$$x = r \cos \phi \quad \ldots (i)$$
$$y = r \sin \phi \quad \ldots (ii)$$
$$x' = r \cos (\theta + \phi)$$
$$y' = r \sin (\theta + \phi)$$
$$x' = r \cos \theta \cos \phi - r \sin \theta \sin \phi$$
$$y' = r \sin \theta \cos \phi + r \cos \theta \sin \phi$$

Put the values of $r \cos \phi$ and $r \sin \phi$ from equations (i) and (ii).

$$x' = x \cos \theta - y \sin \theta$$
$$y' = x \sin \theta + y \cos \theta$$

The resulting transformation will be,

$$R_z \Rightarrow x' = x \cos \theta - y \sin \theta$$
$$y' = x \sin \theta + y \cos \theta$$
$$z' = 0$$

$$[x'\ y'\ z'\ 1] = [x\ y\ z\ 1] \begin{bmatrix} \cos \theta & \sin \theta & 0 & 0 \\ -\sin \theta & \cos \theta & 0 & 0 \\ 0 & 0 & 1 & 0 \\ 0 & 0 & 0 & 1 \end{bmatrix}$$

Rotation about x-axis: This can be obtained similarly by circularly reshuffling y and z.

$$\therefore \quad R_x \Rightarrow x' = x$$
$$y' = y \cos \theta - z \sin \theta$$
$$z = y \sin \theta + z \cos \theta$$

$$[x'\ y'\ z'\ 1] = [x\ y\ z\ 1] \begin{bmatrix} 1 & 0 & 0 & 0 \\ 0 & \cos \theta & \sin \theta & 0 \\ 0 & -\sin \theta & \cos \theta & 0 \\ 0 & 0 & 0 & 1 \end{bmatrix}$$

Rotation About y-axis:

$$R_y \Rightarrow x' = x \cos \theta + z \sin \theta$$
$$y' = y$$
$$z = -x \sin \theta + z \cos \theta$$

$$[x'\ y'\ z'\ 1] = [x\ y\ z\ 1] \begin{bmatrix} \cos \theta & 0 & -\sin \theta & 0 \\ 0 & 1 & 0 & 0 \\ +\sin \theta & 0 & \cos \theta & 0 \\ 0 & 0 & 0 & 1 \end{bmatrix}$$

All the above rotation matrix are for rotation in counterclockwise direction. To obtain the rotation matrix in clockwise direction, change the sign of 't sin θ'.

$$\therefore R_z = \begin{bmatrix} \cos\theta & -\sin\theta & 0 & 0 \\ \sin\theta & \cos\theta & 0 & 0 \\ 0 & 0 & 1 & 0 \\ 0 & 0 & 0 & 1 \end{bmatrix}$$

$$R_y = \begin{bmatrix} \cos\theta & 0 & +\sin\theta & 0 \\ 0 & 1 & 0 & 0 \\ -\sin\theta & 0 & \cos\theta & 0 \\ 0 & 0 & 0 & 1 \end{bmatrix}$$

$$R_x = \begin{bmatrix} 1 & 0 & 0 & 0 \\ 0 & \cos\theta & -\sin\theta & 0 \\ 0 & \sin\theta & \cos\theta & 0 \\ 0 & 0 & 0 & 1 \end{bmatrix}$$

3.10 ROTATION ABOUT AN ARBITRARY AXIS

Any line in a space can be used as axis of rotation. For deriving the transformation matrix for rotation by an angle θ° about any arbitrary line in a space, the following transformation must be carried out in a sequence.

   (i) **Translation:** Perform translation, so that the line will coincide with origin.

   (ii) **Rotation:** Perform rotation to align with one of the co-ordinate axis for example, if the line is to be aligned with z-axis then first rotate it about x-axis to bring it in x-z plane and then rotate it about y-axis to align it with z-axis. Then perform rotation about z-axis.

   (iii) **Retranslation:** Then apply inverse translation to bring the line and coordinates to their original orientation.

Consider point P(x, y, z) which is to be rotated about arbitrary line. The parametric equation for the line are –

$$x = x_1 + A_t$$
$$y = y_1 + B_t$$
$$z = z_1 + C_t$$

where,
$$A = (x_2 - x_1)$$
$$B = (y_2 - y_1)$$
$$C = (z_2 - z_1)$$

$x_1, y_1, z_1 \rightarrow$ Points on the line

$A, B, C \rightarrow$ Direction vectors

The first step is to translate the line to bring it in the origin. The translation matrix will be,

$$T = \begin{bmatrix} 1 & 0 & 0 & 0 \\ 0 & 1 & 0 & 0 \\ 0 & 0 & 1 & 0 \\ -x_1 & -y_1 & -z_1 & 1 \end{bmatrix}$$

The inverse transformation will be,

$$T^{-1} = \begin{bmatrix} 1 & 0 & 0 & 0 \\ 0 & 1 & 0 & 0 \\ 0 & 0 & 1 & 0 \\ x_1 & y_1 & z_1 & 1 \end{bmatrix}$$

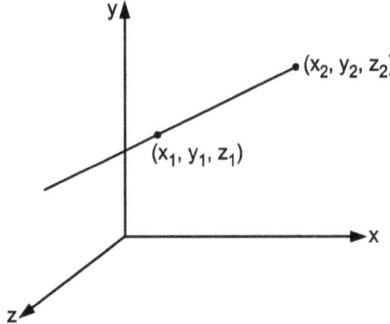

Fig. 3.19: Before Translation the Position of Line

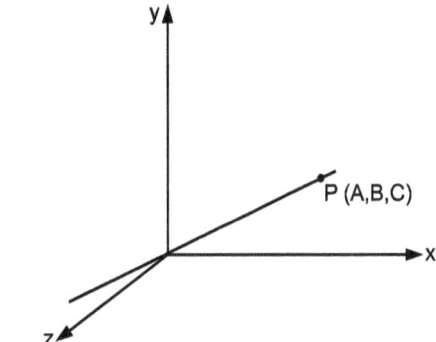

Fig. 3.20: After Translation the Position of Line

The second step is the rotation of line about x-axis to bring the line in x-z plane, for this the angle of rotation by which the line is to be rotated must be computed. For this, project a point P(A, B, C) in y-z plane.

Let P' be the point p in y-z plane.

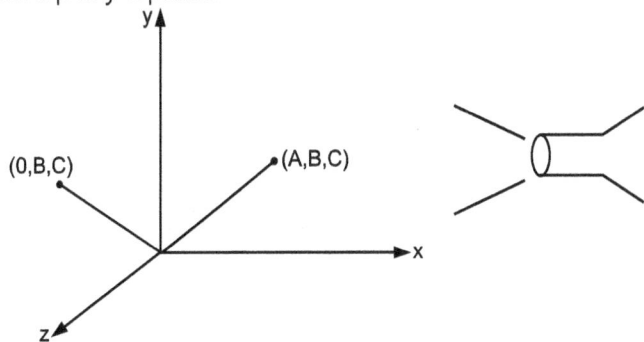

Fig. 3.21: Projection of a Line Segment on yz Plane

The coordinates of P' are (0, B, C). The length of segment OP' = $\sqrt{B^2 + C^2}$. The angle of rotation about x-axis is,

$$\cos I = \frac{C}{\sqrt{B^2 + C^2}} \qquad \sin I = \frac{B}{\sqrt{B^2 + C^2}}$$

Put, $\sqrt{B^2 + C^2} = V$

∴ $\cos I = C/V \qquad \sin I = B/V$

Now rotation matrix about x-axis, so that arbitrary axis will be in xz plane, the line segment's shadow will lie in z-axis.

$$R_x = \begin{bmatrix} 1 & 0 & 0 & 0 \\ 0 & C/V & B/V & 0 \\ 0 & -B/V & C/V & 0 \\ 0 & 0 & 0 & 1 \end{bmatrix}$$

The inverse rotation will be,

$$R_x^{-1} = \begin{bmatrix} 1 & 0 & 0 & 0 \\ 0 & C/V & -B/V & 0 \\ 0 & B/V & C/V & 0 \\ 0 & 0 & 0 & 1 \end{bmatrix}$$

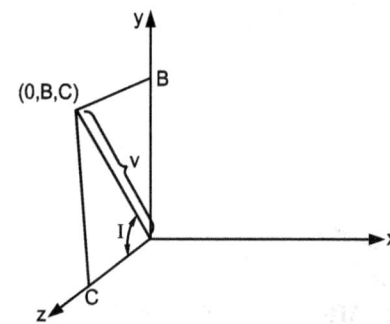

Fig. 3.22: Parameters of line segment projection

The rotation axis lying with x-z plane is shown in Fig. 3.23.

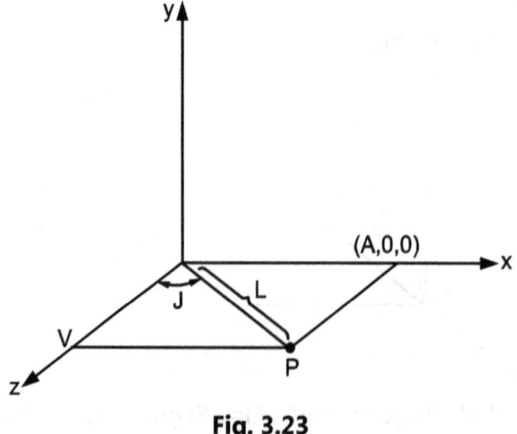

Fig. 3.23

The parameters will remain unchanged and equal to A as it is the rotation about x-axis. The y co-ordinate becomes zero and z co-ordinate will be,
$$z = \sqrt{R^2 + C^2} = V$$
The co-ordinates of point P are P(A, 0, 0), the length OP will be $\sqrt{A^2 + B^2 + C^2}$.
Put, $\sqrt{A^2 + B^2 + C^2} = L$
∴ (OP) = L

Now perform the rotation of line about y-axis by an angle J to make it align with z-axis. As shown in above figure 3.23 is an angle between segment OP and z-axis.
$$\cos J = V/L \quad \sin J = A/L$$
The rotation matrix about y-axis will be,
$$R_y = \begin{bmatrix} V/L & 0 & A/L & 0 \\ 0 & 1 & 0 & 0 \\ -A/L & 0 & V/L & 0 \\ 0 & 0 & 0 & 1 \end{bmatrix}$$

The inverse transformation will be,
$$R_y^{-1} = \begin{bmatrix} V/L & 0 & A/L & 0 \\ 0 & 1 & 0 & 0 \\ -A/L & 0 & V/L & 0 \\ 0 & 0 & 0 & 1 \end{bmatrix}$$

Now after performing rotation about y-axis the line will get aligned with z-axis. Then perform the rotation about z-axis by an angle θ. The matrix will be,
$$R_z = \begin{bmatrix} \cos\theta & \sin\theta & 0 & 0 \\ -\sin\theta & \cos\theta & 0 & 0 \\ 0 & 0 & 1 & 0 \\ 0 & 0 & 0 & 1 \end{bmatrix}$$

Then apply inverse transformation in sequence R_y^{-1}, R_x^{-1}, T^{-1} to rotate the axis to their original position. The resultant transformation matrix will be,
$$R_S = [T][R_x][R_y][R_z][R_y]^{-1}[R_x]^{-1}[T^{-1}]$$

3.11 REFLECTION

The reflection in 3D transformation is similar to the concept of 2D transformation. In this case the reference plane i.e. plane about which the reflection is to be taken must be known. Thus, there are three standard reflections about xy plane, xz plane and yz plane. Each plane reference implies that those co-ordinates will remain same which are constituting that plane.

3.11.1 Reflection with Respect to any Plane

It is necessary to reflect an object through a plane other than x = 0 (yz-plane), y = 0 (xz-plane) or z = 0 (xy-plane). Procedure to achieve such a reflection i.e. reflection about any plane can be given as follows.

(i) Translate a known point P_0, that lies in the reflection plane to the origin of the co-ordinate system.

(ii) Rotate the normal vector to the reflection plane at the origin until it is coincident with the z axis, this makes the reflection plane z = 0 coordinate plane i.e. xy-plane.

(iii) Reflect the object through z = 0 (xy-plane) co-ordinate plane.

(iv) Perform the inverse transformation to those given above to achieve the result.

Let $P_0(x_0, y_0, z_0)$ be the given known point. Translate this point to the origin by using corresponding translation matrix.

$$T = \begin{bmatrix} 1 & 0 & 0 & 0 \\ 0 & 1 & 0 & 0 \\ 0 & 0 & 1 & 0 \\ -x_0 & -y_0 & -z_0 & 1 \end{bmatrix}$$

The normal vector will be,

$$N = h_1 I + h_2 J + h_3 K$$
$$|N| = \sqrt{n_1^2 + n_2^2 + n_3^2}$$
$$\lambda = \sqrt{n_2^2 + n_3^2}$$

To match this vector with z-axis, so that the plane of reflection will be parallel to xy plane, the same procedure will be used as used in rotation.

$$R_{xy} = \begin{bmatrix} \frac{\lambda}{|N|} & 0 & \frac{n_1}{|N|} & 0 \\ \frac{-n_1 n_2}{\lambda |N|} & \frac{n_3}{\lambda} & \frac{n_2}{|N|} & 0 \\ \frac{-n_1 n_3}{\lambda |N|} & \frac{-n_2}{\lambda} & \frac{n_3}{|N|} & 0 \\ 0 & 0 & 0 & 1 \end{bmatrix}$$

For reflection about xy plane,

$$R_e = \begin{bmatrix} 1 & 0 & 0 & 0 \\ 0 & 1 & 0 & 0 \\ 0 & 0 & -1 & 0 \\ 0 & 0 & 0 & 1 \end{bmatrix}$$

The inverse translation will be,

$$T^{-1} = \begin{bmatrix} 1 & 0 & 0 & 0 \\ 0 & 1 & 0 & 0 \\ 0 & 0 & 1 & 0 \\ x_0 & y_0 & z_0 & 1 \end{bmatrix}$$

The inverse rotation will be,

$$R_{xy}^{-1} = \begin{bmatrix} \frac{\lambda}{|N|} & \frac{-n_2 n_2}{\lambda |N|} & \frac{-n_1 n_3}{\lambda |N|} & 0 \\ 0 & \frac{n_3}{\lambda} & \frac{-n_3}{\lambda} & 0 \\ \frac{n_1}{|N|} & \frac{n_2}{|N|} & \frac{n_3}{|N|} & 0 \\ 0 & 0 & 0 & 1 \end{bmatrix}$$

∴ Resultant transformation matrix will be,

$$R_S = [T][R_{xy}][R_e][R_{xy}]^{-1}[T]^{-1}$$

3.12 3-DIMENSIONAL VIEWING TRANSFORMATION

In two-dimensional viewing there are 2D window and 2D viewport and the objects in the world co-ordinates are clipped against the window and are then transformed into the viewport for display. The three dimensional viewing transformation is more complex than the 2D viewing transformation. The complexity added because of the added dimension and the fact that even though objects are three-dimensional the display devices are only 2D.

The mismatch between 3D objects and 2D displays is compensated by introducing projections. The projections transforms 3D objects into a 2D projection plane. Fig. 3.24 shows the conceptual model of the 3D transformation process.

In 3D viewing, a view plane is specified in the world coordinates using modeling transformation. The world co-ordinate positions of the objects are then converted into viewing co-ordinates by viewing transformation. The projection transformation is then used to convert 3D descriptions of objects in viewing co-ordinates to the 2D projection co-ordinates.

For example, to write a flight simulator program. The first thing to be done is to construct a model of the world over which the pilot is to fly. Buildings, fields, runways, lakes and other scenes maybe constructed using 3D line and polygon primitives. Windowing and modeling allows to use real world dimensions. Therefore, model of the world is represented using the world co-ordinates. Then object description is converted from world co-ordinates to viewing co-ordinates. This produces the view which the pilot can see from his airplane.

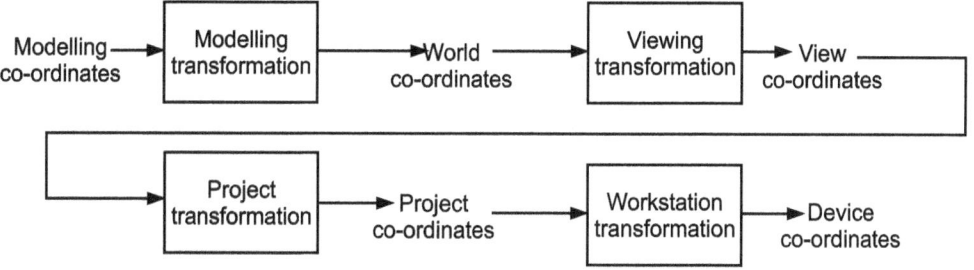

Fig. 3.24: Conceptual Model of 3D Transformation

The projection transformation is then used to convert 3D description of the object in viewing co-ordinates to the 2D co-ordinates are converted into device co-ordinates which are used to display the picture on the view display.

3.12.1 Viewing Parameters

To view the object from the side, top or even from the behind it is needed to apply some rotation transformation before projection. There are two ways:
    (i) Keeping the view plane as fixed and the object as rotated.
    (ii) Keeping the object as fixed and the view plane as repositioned.

Consider the second way then if the view plane were the film in a camera, every display file segment represents a photograph taken by this camera. By moving a camera anywhere, the object can be viewed from any angle. The user is given routines by which he may change a number of viewing parameters. By setting the parameters, he can position the synthetic camera.

The viewing parameters are:
    (a) View reference point (XR, YR, ZR).
    (b) View plane normal vector (DXN, DYN, DZN).
    (c) VIEW-DISTANCE parameter.
    (d) View-up direction (XUP, YUP, ZUP).

(a) View Reference Point (XR, YR, ZR): The view reference point is the center of attention. All other viewing parameters are expressed relative to this point. If the view is rotated, it will be at about the view reference point and not about the origin. View reference point can be considered as an anchor to which a string is tied. The synthetic camera is attached to the other end of the string. By changing other viewing parameter the camera can swing through an arc or change the length of the string. One end of the string is always attached to the view reference point as shown Fig. 3.25.

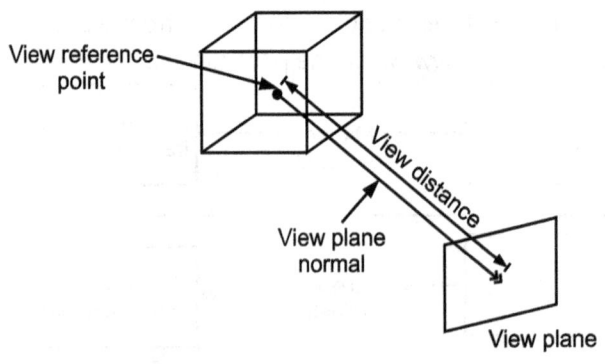

Fig. 3.25

(b) View Plane Normal Vector (DXN, DYN, DZN): The direction of the imaginary string is given by this viewing parameter. This normal is the direction perpendicular to the view plane i.e. the film in the camera. Thus, the camera always looks along the string towards the view reference point. The camera is pointed in the direction of the view plane normal.

(c) VIEW-DISTANCE Parameter: The length of the string is given by this parameter. This tells how the camera is positioned from the view reference point. The view plane is positioned **VIEW-DISTANCE** away from the view reference point in the direction of the view plane normal.

(d) View-up Direction (XUP, YUP, ZUP): This parameter fixes the camera angle. Imagine an arrow extending from the view reference point in the view-up direction. Looking through the camera's view finder and spinning camera until the arrow appears to be in the camera's "up" direction. Changing the view reference point will change the part of the object that is shown at the origin.

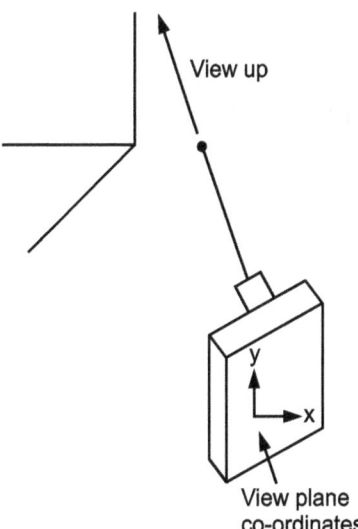

Fig. 3.26

There are two co-ordinate systems. The object co-ordinates which is used to model the object and the view plane co-ordinates, which are attached to the view plane. These parameters allow the user to select how to view the object. The system must provide the user with a means of setting the parameters to the values which he desires. The values are saved as global variables.

3.13 3D PRIMITIVES

Like 2D primitives, there are 3D primitives to draw points, lines and planes in three dimensions. Here instead of two, the three coordinates need to be specified.

(1) 3D Absolute Move:

MOVE_ABS_3 (X, Y, Z): This is 3D absolute move command, where X, Y, Z are co-ordinates of new position.

Global DF_PEN_X, DF_PEN_Y, DF_PEN_Z are current pen positions.
BEGIN
    DF_PEN_X ← X ;
    DF_PEN_Y ← Y ;
    DF_PEN_Z ← Z ;
    DF_ENTER (1) ;
    RETURN;
END;

(2) 3D Relative Move:

MOVE_REL_3 (DX, DY, DZ):

Arguments DX, DY, DZ – Changes done in the current pen position.
Global   DF_PEN_X, DF_PEN_Y, DF_PEN_Z – current pen position.
BEGIN
    DF_PEN_X ← DF_PEN_X + DX;
    DF_PEN_Y ← DF_PEN_Y + DY;
    DF_PEN_Z ← DF_PEN_Z + DZ;
    DF_ENTER (1);
    RETURN;
END;

(3) Absolute Line Drawing Routine:

LINE_ABS_3 (X, Y, Z):

Arguments X, Y, Z are coordinates of point to draw the line.
Global   DF_PEN_X, DF_PEN_Y, DF_PEN_Z – current pen position.
BEGIN
    DF_PEN_X ← X;
    DF_PEN_Y ← Y;
    DF_PEN_Z ← Z;
    DF_ENTER (2);
END;

(4) 3-D Relative Line Drawing Routine:

LINE_REL_3 (DX, DY, DZ):

Arguments D_X, D_Y, D_Z are displacement over which a line is to be drawn.
Global   DF_PEN_X, DF_PEN_Y, DF_PEN_Z – the current pen postion.
BEGIN
    DF_PEN_X ← DF_PEN_X + DX;
    DF_PEN_Y ← DF_PEN_Y + DY;
    DF_PEN_Z ← DF_PEN_Z + DZ;
    DF_ENTER (2);
    RETURN;
END;

(5) Absolute Polygon Drawing Routine:

POLYGON_ABS_3 (AX, AY, AZ, N):

Arguments N – number of polygon sides AX, AY, AZ – array of the co-ordinates of vertices.

Global   DF_PEN_X, DF_PEN_Y, DF_PEN_Z – the current pen position.
BEGIN
    If N < 3 then RETURN ERROR 'SIZE ERROR' ;
    DF_PEN_X ← AX[N] ;
    DF_PEN_Y ← AY[N] ;
    DF_PEN_Z ← AZ[N] ;
    DF_ENTER (N) ;
    FOR I = I to N
    LINE_ABS_3 (AX[I], AY[I], AZ[I])
    RETURN;
END;

(6) 3-D Relative Polygon Drawing Algorithm:

POLYGON_REL_3 (AX, AY, AZ, N):

Arguments N – number of polygon sides AX, AY, AZ – array of displacement for the polygon sides.

Global   DF_PEN_X, DF_PEN_Y, DF_PEN_Z – the current pen postion.
BEGIN
    If N < 3 then RETURN ERROR 'SIZE ERROR' ;
    DF_PEN_X ← DF_PEN_X + AX[I];
    DF_PEN_Y ← DF_PEN_Y + AY[I];
    DF_PEN_Z ← DF_PEN_Z + AZ[I];
    Save vertex for closing polygon
    TEMP X ← DF_PEN_X;
    TEMP Y ← DF_PEN_Y;
    TEMP Z ← DF_PEN_Z;
    DF_ENTER (N);
    Enter polygon sides,
    FOR I = 2 to N DO;
    LINE_REL_3 (AX[I], AY[I], AZ[I]);
    Close the polygon
    LINE_ABS_3 (TEMPX, TEMPY, TEMPZ);
    RETURN;
END;

3.14 PROJECTION

The process of representing a three dimensional object or scene into two dimensional medium is referred as projection.

Hierarchy of projection is –

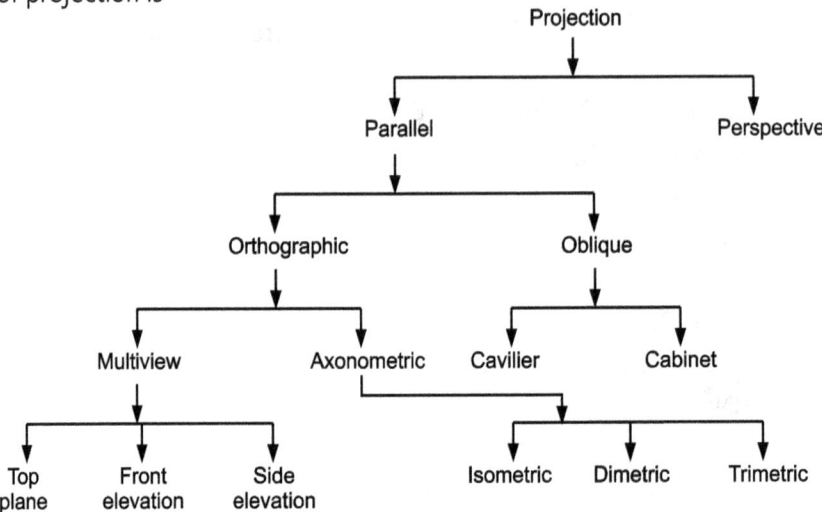

The plane geometric projections of objects are formed by the intersection of lines referred as projectors with a plane called the projection plane. Projectors are nothing but lines form an arbitrary point called as center of projection. In three dimensional space, if the center of projection is located at a finite point, then the result is a perspective projection. If the projectors are parallel and the center of projection is located at infinity then the result is a parallel projection.

3.14.1 Parallel Projection

This technique is used in drawing or drafting for producing scale drawings of three dimensional objects. This method is very useful for obtaining the accurate views of the various sides of an object. It also preserves the relative dimensions of objects. But the drawback of parallel projection is that, it does not give a realistic representation of the appearance of three dimensional object. In parallel projection, z coordinate is discarded and parallel lines from each vertex on the object are extended until they intersect the view plane.

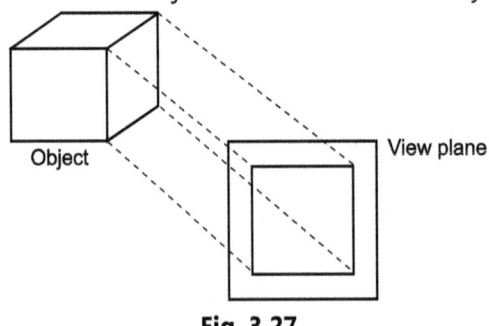

Fig. 3.27

Parallel projection is further classified into two types:
(i) Orthographic projection.
(ii) Oblique projection.

(i) Orthographic Projection: In orthographic projection, the direction of projection is perpendicular to the projection plane. It is used in the projection of front, side and top views of the object. The orthographic top views are referred as "**planes**" and orthographic front, side and rear views are referred as "**elevations**". These projections always show the correct or true size and shape of a single face or plane of an object. Engineering drawings employ these projections because the angles and lengths are accurately depicted.

The orthographic projection is divided into following types:
(1) Multiview,
(2) Axonometric.

In multiview projection, the projection plane is parallel to the principal plane. It is categorized into three types viz. Three views, Auxiliary views and Sectional views.

In Axonometric projection, the projection plane is not parallel to the principle plane. This projection can display more than one face of an object.

The axonometric projection is further classified as –

Isometric, Diametric and Trimetric projection.

The most commonly used axonometric orthographic projection is the isometric projection. It can be generated by aligning the view plane so that it intersects each coordinate axis in which the object is defined at the same distance from the origin.

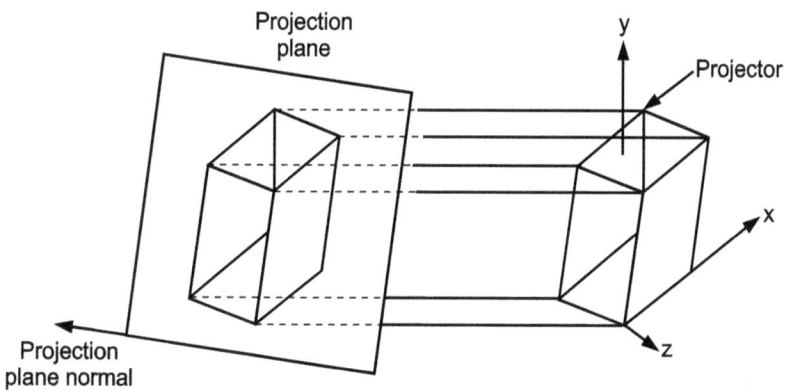

Fig. 3.28

As shown in Fig. 3.28 the isometric projection is obtained by aligning the projection vector with the cube diagonal. It uses an useful property that all the principle axes are equally foreshortened, allowing measurements along the axes to be made to the same scale hence the name iso for equal, metric for measure.

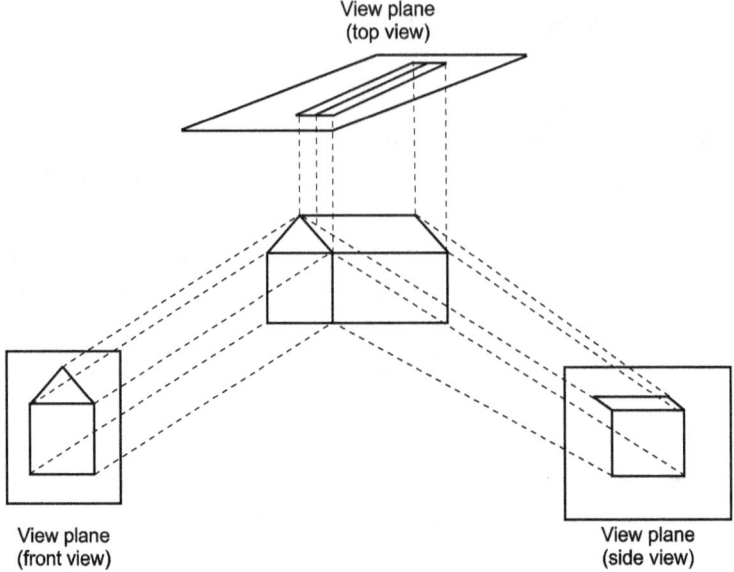

Fig. 3.29

Oblique Projection: An oblique projection is obtained by projecting points along parallel lines that are not perpendicular to the projection plane.

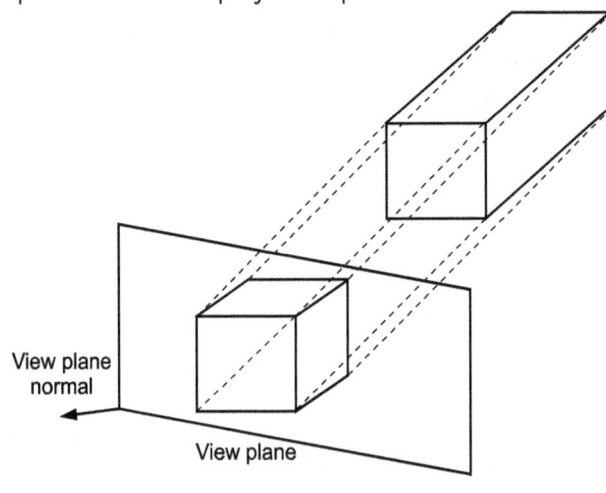

Fig. 3.30

As shown in Fig. 3.30, the view plane normal and direction of projection are not the same.
The oblique projection is further classified into:
(a) Cavalier projection,
(b) Cabinet projection.

For the cavalier projection the direction of projection makes a 45° angle with the view plane. As a result, the projection of a line perpendicular to the view plane has the same length as the line itself i.e. there is no foreshortening. Fig. 3.31 shows cavalier projection of a unit cube with α = 45° and α = 30°.

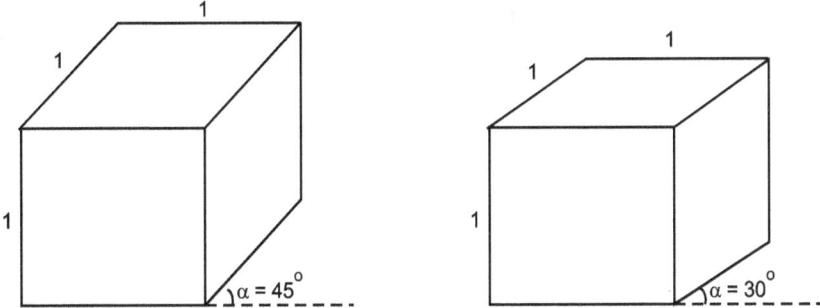

Fig. 3.31: Cavalier projections of a unit cube

In the cabinet projection, the direction of projection makes an angle of arc tan (2) = 63.4 with the view plane. For this angle, lines perpendicular to the viewing surface are projected at one half their actual length. Cabinet projections appear more realistic than cavalier because of the reduction in the length of perpendiculars. Fig. below shows the examples of cabinet projections for a unit cube.

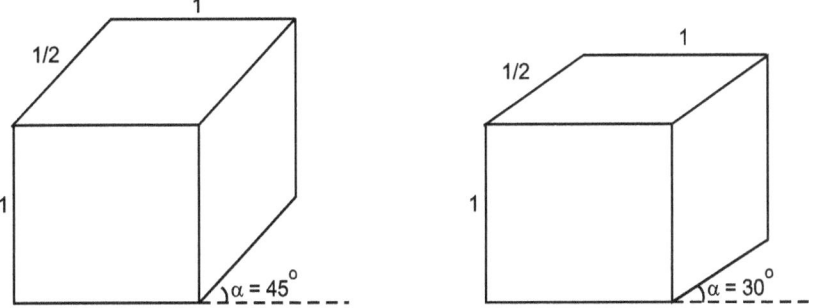

Fig. 3.32: Cabinet projections of a unit cube

3.14.2 General Equation of Parallel Projection

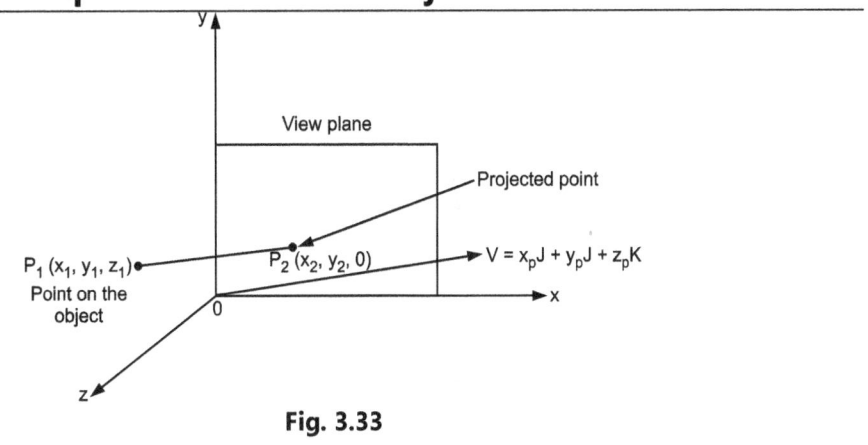

Fig. 3.33

COMPUTER GRAPHICS — GEOMETRIC TRANSFORMATION

In a general parallel projection, any direction may be selected for the lines of projection. Suppose that the direction of projection is given by the vector $[x_p, y_p, z_p]$ and that the object is to be projected onto the xy plane. If the point on the object is given as (x_1, y_1, z_1) then the projected point (x_2, y_2) can be determined as given below:

The equations in the parametric form for a line passing through the projected point (x_2, y_2, z_2) and in the direction of projection are given as –

$$x_2 = x_1 + x_p u$$
$$y_2 = y_1 + y_p u$$
$$z_2 = z_1 + z_p u$$

For projected point z_2 is 0, therefore the third equation can be written as,

$$0 = z_1 + z_p u$$

$$u = \frac{-z_1}{z_p}$$

Substituting the value of u in first two equations,

$$x_2 = x_1 + x_p \left(\frac{-z_1}{z_p}\right)$$

$$y_2 = y_1 + y_p \left(\frac{-z_1}{z_p}\right)$$

The above equation can be represented in matrix form as given below:

$$[x_2, y_2] = [x_1\ y_1\ z_1] \begin{bmatrix} 1 & 0 \\ 0 & 1 \\ \frac{-x_p}{z_p} & \frac{-y_p}{z_p} \end{bmatrix}$$

or in homogeneous co-ordinates.

$$[x_2, y_2, z_2\ 1] = [x_1\ y_1\ z_1\ 1] \begin{bmatrix} 1 & 0 & 0 & 0 \\ 0 & 1 & 0 & 0 \\ \frac{-x_p}{z_p} & \frac{-y_p}{z_p} & 0 & 0 \\ 0 & 0 & 0 & 1 \end{bmatrix}$$

i.e. $\qquad P_2 = P_1 \cdot Par_v$

This is the general equation of parallel projection on xy plane in matrix form.

3.15 PERSPECTIVE PROJECTION

In perspective projection, if the object is far away from the viewer then it appears smaller and it appears larger if the object is nearer to the viewer. This helps the viewer in determining depth cue. The depth cue is an indication of which portion of the image correspond to part of the object which are close or far away. In this projection the lines of projection converge at a single point which is referred as center of projection. The intersection of lines of projection with the plane of screen determines the projected image, as shown in Fig. 3.31.

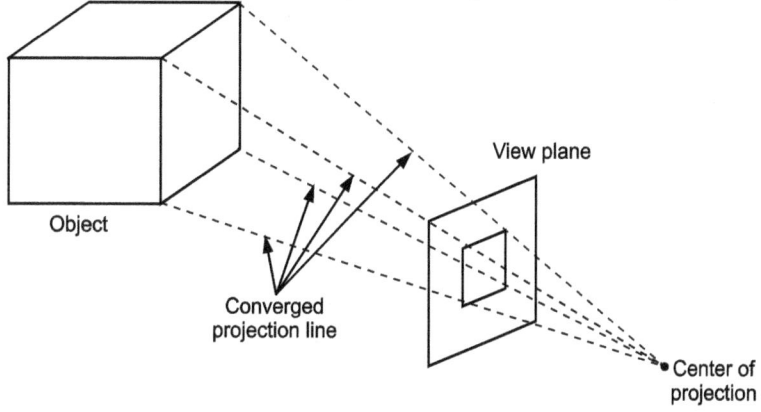

Fig. 3.34

To generate perspective projection of a three dimensional object, first of all project points along projection lines that will meet at the center of projection is selected. The center of projection is on the negative z-axis at a distance behind the projection plane.
However any position can be selected for the center of projection but for simplification of calculation it is better to choose a position along z-axis.
The transformation equation for a perspective projection can be obtained from the parametric equations which describes the projection line from point P to the center of projection.
If the center of projection is at (x_c, y_c, z_c) and point on the object is (x_1, y_1, z_1) then the projection ray will be,

$$x_1 = x_c + (x_1 - x_c) u$$
$$y = y_c + (y_1 - y_c) u$$
$$z = z_c + (z_1 - z_c) u$$

The projected point (x_2, y_2) will be the point where this line intersects the xy plane. For this intersection point $z = 0$,

$$z = z_c + (z_1 - z_c) u$$
$$0 = z_c + (z_1 - z_c) u$$

$$\therefore \quad u = \frac{-z_c}{z_1 - z_c}$$

$$\therefore \quad x_2 = x_c + (x_1 - x_c) \left(\frac{-z_c}{z_1 - z_c}\right)$$

$$x_2 = x_c - z_c \frac{x_1 - x_c}{z_1 - z_c}$$

$$y_2 = y_c - z_c \frac{y_1 - y_c}{z_1 - z_c}$$

$$x_2 = \frac{x_c z_1 - x_1 z_c}{z_1 - z_c}$$

$$y_2 = \frac{y_c z_1 - y_1 z_c}{z_1 - z_c}$$

In the matrix form –

$$P = \begin{bmatrix} -z_c & 0 & 0 & 0 \\ 0 & -z_c & 0 & 0 \\ x_c & y_c & 0 & 1 \\ 0 & 0 & 0 & -z_c \end{bmatrix}$$

Consider point (x_1, y_1, z_1), in homogeneous coordinates it is $[x_1\omega_1 \ y_1\omega_1 \ z_1\omega_1 \ \omega_1]$

$$[x_2\omega_2 \ y_2\omega_2 \ z_2\omega_2 \ \omega_2] = [x_1\omega_1 \ y_1\omega_1 \ z_1\omega_1 \ \omega_1] \begin{bmatrix} -z_c & 0 & 0 & 0 \\ 0 & -z_c & 0 & 0 \\ x_c & y_c & 0 & 1 \\ 0 & 0 & 0 & -z_c \end{bmatrix}$$

$$= [-x_1\omega_1 z_c + z_1\omega_1 x_c \ \ -y_1\omega_1 z_c + z_1\omega_1 y_c \ \ 0 \ \ z_1\omega_1 - z_c\omega_1]$$

∴ $\omega_2 = z_1\omega_1 - z_c\omega_1$

and $z_2\omega_2 = 0$

∴ $z_2 = 0$

$x_2\omega_2 = -x_1\omega_1 z_c + z_1\omega_1 x_c$

⇒ $x_2 = \dfrac{x_c z_1 - x_1 z_c}{z_1 - z_c}$

And $y_2\omega_2 = -y_1\omega_1 z_c + z_1\omega_1 y_c$

⇒ $y_2 = \dfrac{y_c z_1 - y_1 z_c}{z_1 - z_c}$

The resulting point (x_2, y_2) is then the correctly projected point.

∴ The projection transformation is,

$$P_1 = \begin{bmatrix} 1 & 0 & 0 & 0 \\ 0 & 1 & 0 & 0 \\ \frac{-x_c}{z_c} & \frac{-y_p}{z_c} & 0 & \frac{-1}{z_c} \\ 0 & 0 & 0 & 1 \end{bmatrix}$$

The change is the factor of $-\dfrac{1}{z_c}$. Because the first three coordinates $(x\omega, y\omega, z\omega)$ is divided by ω to obtain the actual position, changing all four co-ordinates by some common factor has no effect. The perspective projection is defined as that the center of projection is located at the origin and the view plane is positioned at z = d. Thus, the transformation matrix is given by,

$$P_2 = \begin{bmatrix} 1 & 0 & 0 & 0 \\ 0 & 1 & 0 & 0 \\ 0 & 0 & 0 & 1/d \\ 0 & 0 & 0 & 1 \end{bmatrix}$$

3.15.1 Types of Perspective Projection

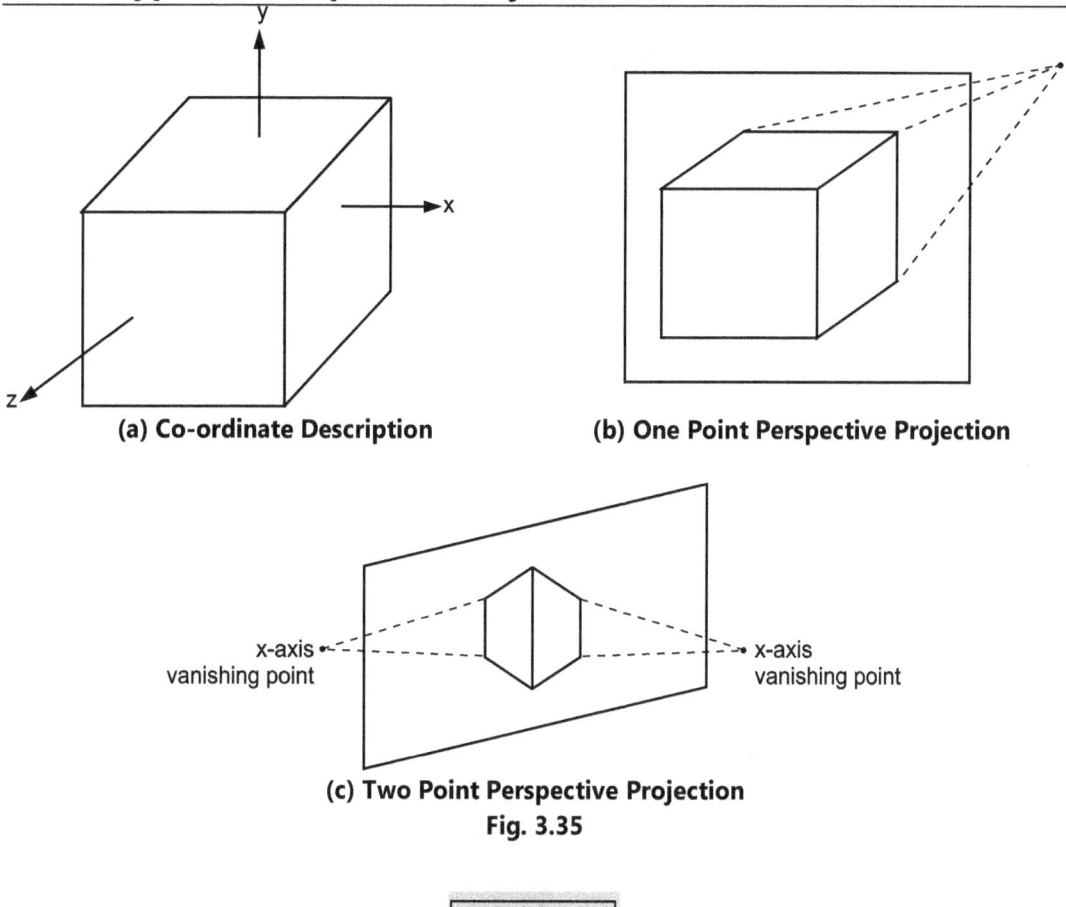

(a) Co-ordinate Description (b) One Point Perspective Projection

(c) Two Point Perspective Projection

Fig. 3.35

EXERCISE

1. Obtain the 3-D transformation matrices for:
   (i) Translation, (ii) Scaling, (iii) Rotation about an arbitrary axis.
2. Give the classification of perspective parallel projection.
3. Explain parallel projection in detail with transformation matrix.
4. Derive the 3D primitive transformation for the following rotation:
   Rotate object about z-axis such that x-axis passes through a point $P(x_p, y_p, 0)$ in x-y plane.

5. Consider the square A(1, 0), B(0, 0), (0, 1), D(1, 1). Rotate the square ABCD by 45° anticlockwise about point A(1, 0).
6. Perform a 45° rotation of triangle A(0, 0), B(1, 1), C(5, 2).
   (i) About the origin, (ii) About P(−1, −1).
7. What is homogeneous co-ordinate system? Explain the need of homogeneous co-ordinates.
8. Explain with example, 3-D viewing transformation.
9. What is the concept of vanishing point in perspective projection.
10. Explain classification of parallel projection in detail. Discuss applications of parallel projections.
11. Consider the square A(2, 0), B(0, 0), C(0, 1), D(1, 1). Rotate the square anticlockwise direction followed by reflection about x-axis.
12. Explain the following 3-D transformation:
    (i) Rotation about all co-ordinate axis
    (ii) Rotation about any arbitrary axis.
13. Derive the general equation of parallel projection onto a given view plane in the direction of given projector.
14. Consider the square P(0, 0), Q(0, 10), R(10,10), S(10, 0). Rotate the square about fixed point. R(10, 10) by an angle 45° (anticlockwise) followed by scaling by 2 units in X direction and 2 units in Y direction.
15. What are parallel and perspective projections? Give classification of both.
16. Explain inverse transformation. Derive the matrix for inverse transformation and what is the concept of homogeneous co-ordinates.
17. Prove that two scaling transformation. Commute i.e.
    $S_1S_2 = S_2S_1$
18. Explain the term shearing and reflection.
19. Explain various steps to perform rotation about x-axis, y-axis and z-axis in 3D.
20. Describe w.r.t. 2-D transformation:
    (i) Scaling, (ii) Rotation, (iii) Translation.
21. Show that the two dimensional scaling and rotation do not commute in general.
22. Explain: (i) 3-D co-ordinate system, (ii) 3-D primitives.
23. Explain the 3-D viewing process with various 3-D viewing parameters.
24. Perform x-shear and y-shear on a triangle having A(2, 1), B(4, 3), C(2, 3). Consider the constant value a = b = 2.
25. Show that the transformation matrix of reflection about a line y = x is equivalent to reflection relative to x-axis followed by anticlockwise rotation of 90°.
26. Drive transformation matrix for perspective projection.
27. Magnify the triangle with vertices A(0, 0), B(1, 1), C(5, 2) to twice its size as well as rotate it by 45°. Derive the translation matrices.

UNIT IV

WINDOWING AND CLIPPING

4.1 WINDOWING AND CLIPPING

- The process of selecting and viewing the picture with different views is called '**windowing**' and a process which divides each element of the picture into its visible and invisible portions, allowing the invisible portion to be discarded is called '**clipping**'.
- To extract a portion of interest the first thing to be done is to define a window enclosing a portion of interest called as clipping window.
- After that use a suitable algorithm to determine the points, lines or portion of lines which lie within the clipping window.
- Such algorithm is referred as clipping algorithm.
- After determining the lines or portion of lines, which lies within the clipping window they are retained for display discarding others.

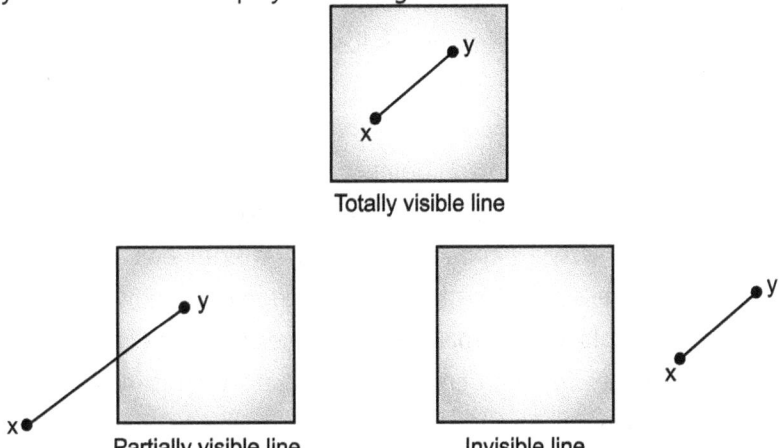

Fig. 4.1

- Since for a typical scene or picture, large number of lines is needed to be clipped, the amount of work done by clipping algorithm is substantial.
- Thus, it is desirable that the clipping algorithm must use simple visibility test to quickly discard and the totally invisible lines and equally accept the totally visible lines.

- Thus, only potential partially visible lines will be considered for performing expensive computation of point of intersection of a picture to be clipped in 2-dimension then the clipping window will be plane or polygon.
- One such algorithm to test the visibility of line is **sutherland cohen outcode algorithm**.

4.1.1 Sutherland Cohen Outcode Algorithm

- The Sutherland Cohen Technique is used to perform a visibility test. This technique makes the use of a four-bit code to indicate the regions that contains the end point of a line.
- If the end point lies to the left of the window then the first bit is set, if the end point lies to the right of the window then the second bit is set. If it lies below bottom of the window third bit is set while if it uses above top of window then the forth bit is set.

1001	1000	1010
0001	0000	0010
0101	0100	0110

The nine regions along with their four bit codes are shown above.
- Depending upon the region in which it lies, every end point has four bits associated with it.
- The end point codes can be used to detect the visibility of lines by performing logical AND operation of two end points codes of a given line.
- If the bit wise ANDing and the end point bit codes is non-zero then the line is totally invisible. This will happen if and only if both end points lie outside the windows and on the same side of a particular edge of window.
- The line may be totally or partially visible if the result of AND operation is zero. If the end point codes for both end points are zero then it indicates that the line is totally visible otherwise it is partially visible.

(a) Sutherland Cohen Algorithm for Clipping Line:
The Sutherland-Cohen algorithm is as follows:
For each widow edge do
{
    For each line segment P_1P_2 do
    {
        If P_1P_2 is totally invisible or partially visible then ignore and goto next line segment

```
        If P₁ is not outside the window then swap (P₁, P₂)
        Compute the point of intersection with window edge
        Replace P₁ with point of intersection
    }
}
```

To compute the point of intersection following formulae are used:
Consider $P_1(x_1, y_1)$ and $P_2(x_2, y_2)$ be the left edge of window.
Thus, point slope form is,

$$y - y_1 = \left(\frac{y_2 - y_1}{x_2 - x_1}\right)(x - x_1)$$

For right edge
$$\text{Put } x = x_R$$
Thus, the points will be
$$(x_R, y = y_1 + m(x_R - x_1))\ m \neq 0$$

For left edge
$$\text{Put } x = x_L$$
Thus, the points will be,
$$(x_L, y = y_1 + m(x_L - x_1))\ m \neq \infty$$

For top edge
$$\text{Put } y = y_T$$
Thus, the points will be,
$$\left(x = x_1 + \frac{1}{m}(y_T - y_1),\ y_T\right)\ m \neq 0$$

For bottom edge,
$$\text{Put } y = y_B$$
Thus, the points will be,
$$\left(x = x_1 + \frac{1}{m}(y_B - y_1),\ y_B\right)\ m \neq \infty$$

Note: If the point of intersection lies outside the window then it is rejected otherwise it is stressed to draw a line segment between those intersection which uses inside the window.

(b) Numericals:

Example 4.1:

Use the Cohen-Sutherland outcode algorithm to clip two lines.
$P_1(40, 15)$, $P_2(75, 45)$ and $P_3(70, 20)$, $P_4(100, 10)$ against a window A (50, 10), B (80, 10), C (80, 40), D (50, 40).

Solution:
$$P_1(40, 15)$$
$$P_2(75, 45)$$
$$wx_1 = 50 \quad wy_1 = 40$$
$$wx_2 = 80 \quad wy_2 = 10$$

Point	Encode	ANDing
P_1	0001	0000
P_2	0000	

∵ The bitwise ANDing is zero.

∴ Line is partially visible.

To determine the point of intersection:

$$y_1 = m(x_L - x) + y \qquad \left[m = \frac{45-15}{75-40} = \frac{6}{7}\right]$$

$$= \frac{6}{7}(50 - 40) + 15$$

$$y_1 = 23.57$$

$$x_1 = \frac{1}{m}(y_T - y) + x$$

$$= \frac{7}{6}(40 - 15) + 40$$

$$= 69.16$$

$$y_2 = m(x_R - x) + y$$

$$= \frac{6}{7}(80 - 40) + 15$$

$$= 49.28$$

$$x_2 = \frac{1}{m}(y_B - y) + x$$

$$= \frac{7}{6}(10 - 15) + 40$$

$$= 34.16$$

∴ Point of intersection are

(69.16, 23.57) and (34.16, 49.28)

Example 4.2:

P_3 (70, 20), P_4 (100, 10). Determine point of intersection.

Point	Encode	ANDing
P_3	0000	0000
P_4	0010	

∵ Bitwise ANDing is zero.

∴ Line is partially visible.

To determine the point of intersection:

$$m = \frac{10 - 20}{100 - 70} = -\frac{1}{3}$$

COMPUTER GRAPHICS — WINDOWING AND CLIPPING

$$y_1 = m(x_L - x) + y = -\frac{1}{3}(50 - 70) + 20$$
$$= 26.66$$

$$x_1 = \frac{1}{m}(y_T - y) + x = -3(40 - 20) + 70$$
$$= 10$$

$$y_2 = m(x_R - x) + y = -\frac{1}{3}(80 - 70) + 20$$
$$= 16.66$$

$$x_2 = \frac{1}{m}(y_B - y) + x = -3(10 - 20) + 70$$
$$= 100$$

Thus, the point of intersection are (10, 26.66) and (100, 16.66)

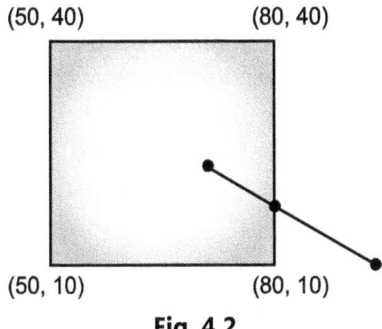

Fig. 4.2

4.1.2 2D Midpoint Subdivision Algorithm OR Sutherland Cohen Mid-point Subdivisional Algorithm

To avoid the computation of intersection of lines with window edge the mid-point subdivision algorithm has been developed. In this algorithm, the line which cannot be identified whether it is visible or not are subdivided into two equal parts. Then, the two segments are tested for visibility. If both of them can not be rejected then continue with each half until the intersection with the window edge is found or the length of divided segments becomes as small as it can be treated as a point. Then the visibility of the point is then checked to determine whether it is inside or outside the window.

(a) Algorithm:
Step I: Given line segment P_1P_2. Test is for totally visible or not.
Step II: If not then divide P_1P_2 at its mid-point P_m.
Step III: Then apply visibility test for segments P_1P_m and P_mP_2.
Step IV: If P_mP_2 is invisible then it can be discarded and continue visibility test with P_mP_2 and vice-versa.

Step V: If neither P_1P_m or P_mP_2 rejected then save one of the segment for later consideration and continue with P_1P_m until intersection with the window edge is obtained or the divided segment becomes so short that it can be treated as a point.

Step VI: Then evaluate visibility of point.

Example:
Consider a window having co-ordinates (−1, −1) to (1, 1).
Clip a line from P_1 (−3/2, 1/6) and P_2 (1/2, 3/2).
To solve the above problem according to mid-point subdivision algorithm first calculate the end point codes of a given line P_1P_2.
The end point codes are 0001 and 1000 respectively. Thus, the line is partially visible even it is outside the window. The intersection of line P_1P_2 with respect to left edge is (−1, 1/2). So replace P_1 with this point of intersection to yield a new line segment P_1 (−1, 1/2) and P_2 (1/2, 3/2) as shown in Fig. 4.3 (b).
Now the end point codes for new segment will be 0000 and 1000. This indicates that the line is partially visible. Since P_1 is inside the window hence swapping is needed. After swapping P_1 and P_2 new line segment will be P_1 (1/25, 3/2) and P_2 (−1, 1/2) as shown in Fig. 4.3 (c).
The end point codes for new line segment are both 0000. Thus, the line is completely visible, as shown in Fig. 4.3 (d).

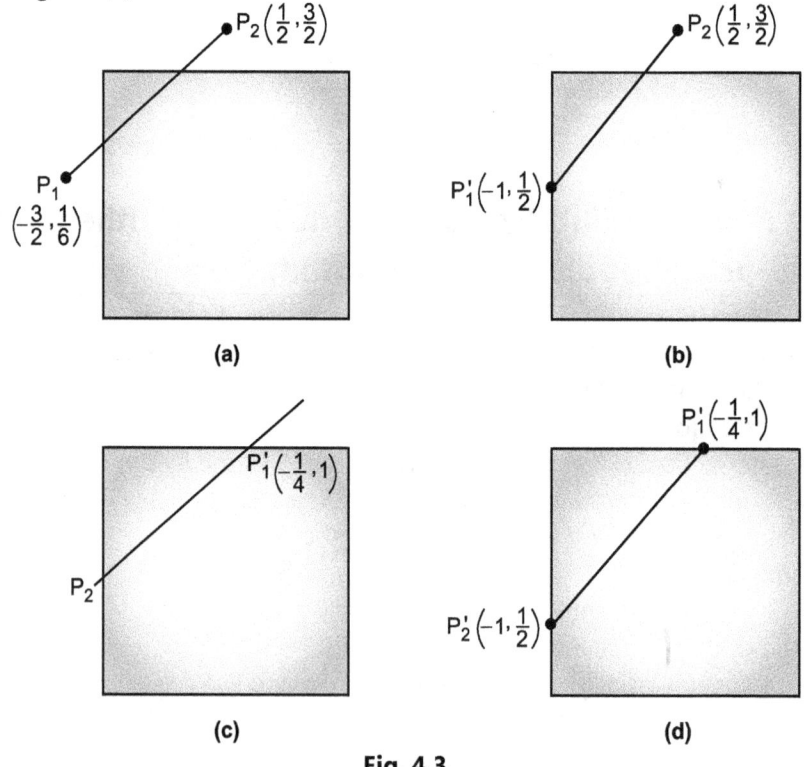

Fig. 4.3

4.2 LINE CLIPPING

(i) The lines are said to be interior to the clipping window and hence visible if both end points of a line are interior to the window e.g. line P_1P_2 in figure below.

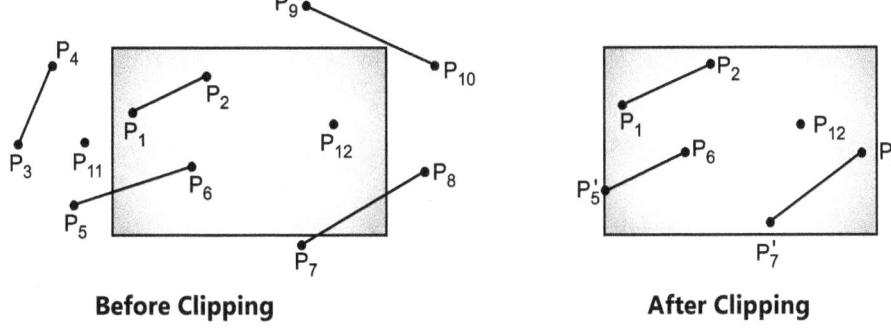

Before Clipping   **After Clipping**

Fig. 4.4

(ii) However, if both end points of a line are exterior to the window, the line is not necessarily completely exterior to the window, e.g. line P_7P_8 in above figure.

(iii) If both end points of a line are completely to the right of completely to the left of, completely above, or completely below the window, then the line is completely exterior to the window and hence invisible. For e.g. line P_3P_4 in above figure.

(iv) The lines which crosses one or more clipping boundaries require calculation of multiple intersection points.

4.3 3D CLIPPING AND WINDOWING

Clipping procedure identifies those portion of a picture that are either inside or outside of a specified region of space and windowing process select and view the picture with different views.

For 3D graphics the creation of realistic picture is an important task such as in simulation design. To create realistic view, the scene or process must be processed through viewing co-ordinate transformation and projection routines that transform three dimensional viewing co-ordinates into 2-dimensions.

Windowing and clipping allows to use real world co-ordinates. The actual objects are 3-dimensional but display devices are 2-dimensional.

In 3D clipping different views of an object can be focused using clipping volume or view volume. The commonly used volumes are rectangular parallolepiped and truncated pyramidal volume. These give clipped object with six sided rectangular portion for flight simulator program. The first thing to be done is to construct a model of world over which the pilot is to fly. So for viewing exact positions of object from airplane, pilot has to view the projections and highlight on specified region but airplane display is with 2D, so all projections are needed to view objects from plane.

4.3.1 Cohen-Suthreland End-Point Code

In three dimensional clipping the shape of clipping volume plays an important role. The clipping volume can be either a box or frustrum of vision. The box is normally used for parallel projections and the frustrum of vision is used for perspective projections.

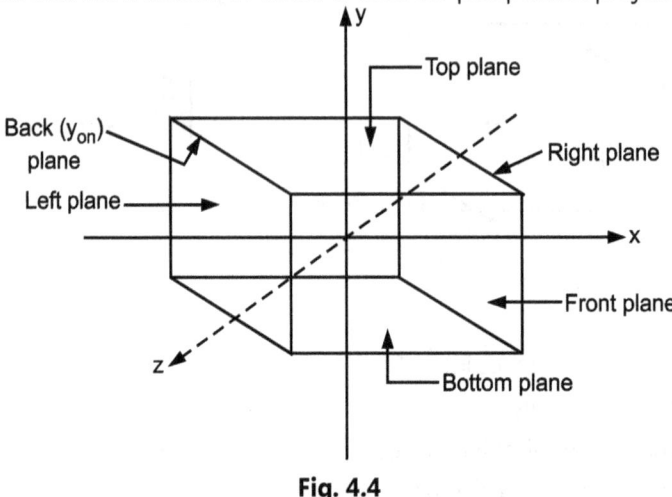

Fig. 4.4

Cohen suthreland end-point code can be used for identifying totally visible or partially visible lines. Here 6-bit end point code is used. Starting from left to right (1st bit is leftmost bit), the bit setting is as indicated below –

Bit 1 is set if the point is behind the volume.
Bit 2 is set if the point is in front the volume.
Bit 3 is set if the point is above the volume.
Bit 4 is set if the point is below the volume.
Bit 5 is set if the point is the right of the volume.
Bit 6 is set if the point is to left of the volume.

Bit	1	2	3	4	5	6
	Behind	Front	Above	Below	Right	Left

If both the end points are zero, then the line is visible. If the bit by bit logical intersection of the two end point codes is not zero, then the line is totally invisible. If the logical intersection is zero, then the line may be partially visible or may not be visible at all. Thus, the intersection of the line and the clipping volume has to be found out. It is simple to find end point codes for a rectangular parallelopiped clipping volume as it is an extension of 2D transformation, but for the perspective clipping volume some additional computations are required. One method is to transform the clipping volume into a conical volume.

$$X_{right} = 1$$
$$X_{left} = -1$$
$$Y_{top} = 1$$
$$Y_{bottom} = -1$$
$$Z_{behind} \text{ (or } Z_{y_{on}}) = 1$$

Now if z_{front} (Hither) = a, where 0 < a < = 1, the center of projection is at origin. Another method connects the line connecting the center of projection and center of perspective clipping volume coincident with z-axis.

The top view of clipping volume is shown in Fig. 4.5.

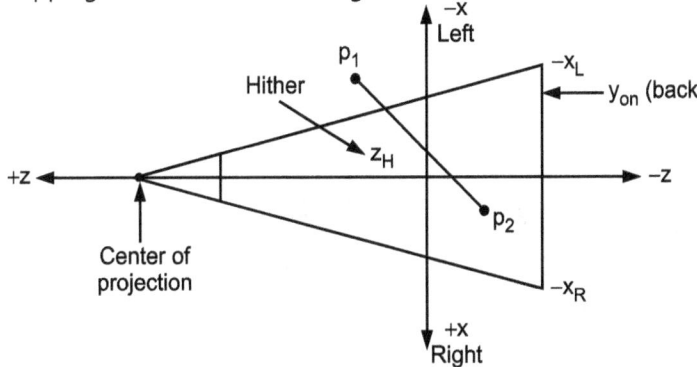

Fig. 4.5

The equation of line, $\quad x = \dfrac{z - z_{cp}}{z_y - z_{cp}}$

$\quad\quad\quad\quad\quad\quad\quad\quad = za_1 + a_2$

$\quad\quad\quad\quad a_1 = \dfrac{x_R}{z_y - z_{cp}} \quad a_2 = -a_1 \cdot z_{cp}$

The equation of line can be used to determine whether a point is inside or outside the plane.

$\therefore \quad\quad\quad\quad f_R = x - z\, a_1 - a_2$

Depending on the value of f_R for given x and z values, one can find whether the point is to the right, left as on the plane.

If $f_R > 0$ then P is to the right of the plane.

If $f_R = 0$ then P is on the plane.

If $f_R < 0$ then P is to the left of the plane.

The test functions for the position of the point is –

$$f_L = x - z\, B_1 - B_2$$

$$B_1 = \dfrac{x\, L}{z_v - z_{cp}}, \quad B_2 = -B_1\, z_{cp}$$

If $f_L > 0$ then P is to the right of the plane.

If $f_L = 0$ then P is on the plane.

If $f_L < 0$ then P is on the left of the plane.

The test function with respect to the top plane is,

$$f_r = Y - Z\; r_1 - r_2$$

$$r_1 = \frac{Y_T}{Z_y - Z_{cp}} \quad r_2 = -r, Z_{cp}$$

If $f_r > 0$ then P is above the plane.

If $f_r < 0$ then P is below the plane.

If $f_r = 0$ then P is on the plane.

Similarly, the test functions for bottom, front and back plane can be formulated.

4.3.2 Mid-Point Sub-Division Algorithm

The mid-point sub-division algorithm for 3-D clipping is as follows:

Step – 1: Find the locations of end point (end point codes) of the line segments with respect to clipping volume (using test functions in case of perspective clipping volume).

Step – 2: Check visibility of each line segment –

(a) If codes of both end points are zero then the line is completely visible. Hence, draw the line and go to Step – 4.

(b) If codes of end points are not zero and the logical ANDing of them is also non-zero the line is completely invisible, so reject the line and go to Step – 4.

(c) If codes for two end points do not satisfy the condition in 2(a) and 2(b) the line is partially visible.

Step – 3: Divide the partially visible line segments in equal parts and repeat Steps – 1 and 2 for sub-divided line segments until you get completely visible and completely invisible line segments. Draw the visible line segments and discard the invisible one.

Step – 4: Stop.

Example 4.3:

Derive the 3D primitive transformation for the following rotation. Rotate about z-axis such that x-axis passes through a point $P(x_p, y_p, 0)$ in xy plane.

Solution:

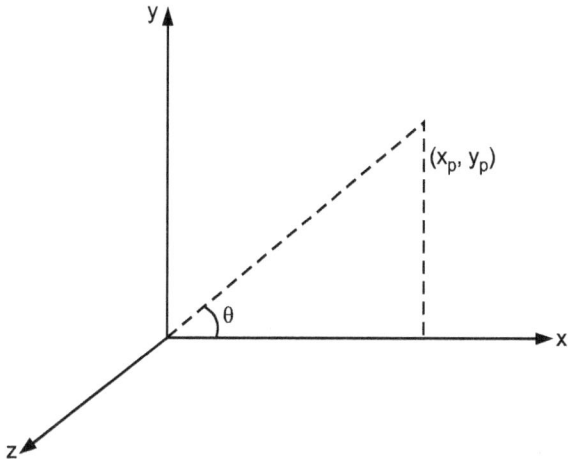

Fig. 4.6

The above Fig. 4.6 shows the three axes and the point $(x_p, y_p, 0)$ in the xy plane. To pass x-axis through a point $P(x_p, y_p, 0)$, rotate the axes in the anticlockwise direction i.e. to rotate the object in the clockwise direction.

To find, $\quad \theta = \tan^{-1} \dfrac{y_p}{x_p}$

The rotation matrix for clockwise rotation about z-axis is,

$$R_z = \begin{bmatrix} \cos(-\theta) & \sin(-\theta) & 0 & 0 \\ -\sin(-\theta) & \cos(-\theta) & 0 & 0 \\ 0 & 0 & 1 & 0 \\ 0 & 0 & 0 & 1 \end{bmatrix}$$

Substituting the value of θ we get the transformation matrix to rotate the object about z-axis such that x-axis passes through a point $P(x_p, y_p, 0)$ in xy plane.

Example 4.4:

A cube is defined by 8 vertices: A(0, 0, 0), B(2, 0, 0), C(2, 2, 0), D(0, 2, 0), E(0, 0, 2), F(0, 2, 2), G(2, 0, 2), H(2, 2, 2) perform the following transformation on the above cube.
   (i) Translation ($t_x = 2, t_y = 4, t_z = 0$).
   (ii) Scaling ($S_x = 0.5, S_y = 1, S_z = 1$).
   (iii) Reflection about planes.

Solution:

$$T = \begin{bmatrix} 1 & 0 & 0 & 0 \\ 0 & 1 & 0 & 0 \\ 0 & 0 & 1 & 0 \\ t_x & t_y & t_z & 1 \end{bmatrix}$$

$$= \begin{bmatrix} 1 & 0 & 0 & 0 \\ 0 & 1 & 0 & 0 \\ 0 & 0 & 1 & 0 \\ 2 & 4 & 0 & 1 \end{bmatrix}$$

COMPUTER GRAPHICS — WINDOWING AND CLIPPING

Now, A' = A[T]

$$= [0\ 0\ 0\ 1] \begin{bmatrix} 1 & 0 & 0 & 0 \\ 0 & 1 & 0 & 0 \\ 0 & 0 & 1 & 0 \\ 2 & 4 & 0 & 1 \end{bmatrix}$$

∴ A' = [0 0 0 1]

B' = B[T]

$$= [2\ 0\ 0\ 1] \begin{bmatrix} 1 & 0 & 0 & 0 \\ 0 & 1 & 0 & 0 \\ 0 & 0 & 1 & 0 \\ 2 & 4 & 0 & 1 \end{bmatrix}$$

∴ B' = [4 4 0 1]

C' = C[T]

$$= [2\ 2\ 0\ 1] \begin{bmatrix} 1 & 0 & 0 & 0 \\ 0 & 1 & 0 & 0 \\ 0 & 0 & 1 & 0 \\ 2 & 4 & 0 & 1 \end{bmatrix}$$

C' = [4 6 0 1]

∴ D' = D[T]

$$= [0\ 2\ 0\ 1] \begin{bmatrix} 1 & 0 & 0 & 0 \\ 0 & 1 & 0 & 0 \\ 0 & 0 & 1 & 0 \\ 2 & 4 & 0 & 1 \end{bmatrix}$$

= [2 6 0 1]

∴ E' = E[T]

$$= [0\ 0\ 2\ 1] \begin{bmatrix} 1 & 0 & 0 & 0 \\ 0 & 1 & 0 & 0 \\ 0 & 0 & 1 & 0 \\ 2 & 4 & 0 & 1 \end{bmatrix}$$

E' = [2 4 2 1]

∴ F' = F[T]

$$= [0\ 2\ 2\ 1] \begin{bmatrix} 1 & 0 & 0 & 0 \\ 0 & 1 & 0 & 0 \\ 0 & 0 & 1 & 0 \\ 2 & 4 & 0 & 1 \end{bmatrix}$$

= [2 6 2 1]

∴ G' = G[T]

$$= [2\ 0\ 2\ 1]\begin{bmatrix} 1 & 0 & 0 & 0 \\ 0 & 1 & 0 & 0 \\ 0 & 0 & 1 & 0 \\ 2 & 4 & 0 & 1 \end{bmatrix}$$

$$= [4\ 4\ 2\ 1]$$

$\therefore\qquad$ H' = H[T]

$$= [2\ 2\ 2\ 1]\begin{bmatrix} 1 & 0 & 0 & 0 \\ 0 & 1 & 0 & 0 \\ 0 & 0 & 1 & 0 \\ 2 & 4 & 0 & 1 \end{bmatrix}$$

$$= [4\ 6\ 2\ 1]$$

∴ The co-ordinates of translated cube are A'(0, 0, 0), B'(4, 4, 0), C'(4, 6, 0), D'(2, 6, 0), E'(2, 4, 2), F'(2, 6, 2), G'(4, 4, 2), H'(4, 6, 2).

(ii) Scaling transformation will be,

$$S = \begin{bmatrix} S_x & 0 & 0 & 0 \\ 0 & S_y & 0 & 0 \\ 0 & 0 & S_z & 0 \\ 0 & 0 & 0 & 1 \end{bmatrix}$$

$$S = \begin{bmatrix} 0.5 & 0 & 0 & 0 \\ 0 & 1 & 0 & 0 \\ 0 & 0 & 1 & 0 \\ 0 & 0 & 0 & 1 \end{bmatrix}$$

For.$\qquad$ A' = A[S]

$$= [0\ 0\ 0\ 1]\begin{bmatrix} 0.5 & 0 & 0 & 0 \\ 0 & 1 & 0 & 0 \\ 0 & 0 & 1 & 0 \\ 0 & 0 & 0 & 1 \end{bmatrix}$$

∴$\qquad$ A' = [0 0 0 1]
$\qquad$ B' = B[S]

$$= [2\ 0\ 0\ 1]\begin{bmatrix} 0.5 & 0 & 0 & 0 \\ 0 & 1 & 0 & 0 \\ 0 & 0 & 1 & 0 \\ 0 & 0 & 0 & 1 \end{bmatrix}$$

∴$\qquad$ B' = [1 0 0 1]
$\qquad$ C' = C[S]

$$= [2\ 2\ 0\ 1]\begin{bmatrix} 0.5 & 0 & 0 & 0 \\ 0 & 1 & 0 & 0 \\ 0 & 0 & 1 & 0 \\ 0 & 0 & 0 & 1 \end{bmatrix}$$

∴$\qquad$ C' = [1 2 0 1]

COMPUTER GRAPHICS — WINDOWING AND CLIPPING

$$D' = D[S]$$
$$= \begin{bmatrix} 0 & 2 & 0 & 1 \end{bmatrix} \begin{bmatrix} 0.5 & 0 & 0 & 0 \\ 0 & 1 & 0 & 0 \\ 0 & 0 & 1 & 0 \\ 0 & 0 & 0 & 1 \end{bmatrix}$$

$\therefore \quad D' = [0\ 2\ 0\ 1]$

$$E' = E[S]$$
$$= \begin{bmatrix} 0 & 0 & 2 & 1 \end{bmatrix} \begin{bmatrix} 0.5 & 0 & 0 & 0 \\ 0 & 1 & 0 & 0 \\ 0 & 0 & 1 & 0 \\ 0 & 0 & 0 & 1 \end{bmatrix}$$

$\therefore \quad E' = [0\ 0\ 2\ 1]$

$$F' = F[S]$$
$$= \begin{bmatrix} 0 & 2 & 2 & 1 \end{bmatrix} \begin{bmatrix} 0.5 & 0 & 0 & 0 \\ 0 & 1 & 0 & 0 \\ 0 & 0 & 1 & 0 \\ 0 & 0 & 0 & 1 \end{bmatrix}$$

$\therefore \quad F' = [0\ 2\ 2\ 1]$

$$G' = G[S]$$
$$= \begin{bmatrix} 2 & 0 & 2 & 1 \end{bmatrix} \begin{bmatrix} 0.5 & 0 & 0 & 0 \\ 0 & 1 & 0 & 0 \\ 0 & 0 & 1 & 0 \\ 0 & 0 & 0 & 1 \end{bmatrix}$$

$\therefore \quad G' = [1\ 0\ 2\ 1]$

$$H' = H[S]$$
$$= \begin{bmatrix} 2 & 2 & 2 & 1 \end{bmatrix} \begin{bmatrix} 0.5 & 0 & 0 & 0 \\ 0 & 1 & 0 & 0 \\ 0 & 0 & 1 & 0 \\ 0 & 0 & 0 & 1 \end{bmatrix}$$

$\therefore \quad H' = [1\ 2\ 2\ 1]$

∴ After scaling the coordinates of cube: A'(0, 0, 0), B'(1, 0, 0), C'(1, 2, 0), D'(0, 2, 0), E'(0, 0, 2), F'(0, 2, 2), G'(1, 0, 2), H'(1, 2, 2).

Example 4.5:
Describe the different steps involved in conversion of 2D world co-ordinate system to viewing co-ordinate transformation. Also obtain the transformation in matrix form.

Solution:
The conversion of object description from world co-ordinate to viewing transformation sequence includes following step:
   (1) Translate the view reference point to the origin of the world co-ordinate system.
   (2) Apply rotations to align x_v, y_v, z_v axes with the world co-ordinate x_w, y_w and z_w axes respectively.

The view point specified at world position (x_p, y_p, z_p) can be translated to the world co-ordinate origin with the matrix transformation.

$$T = \begin{bmatrix} 1 & 0 & 0 & 0 \\ 0 & 1 & 0 & 0 \\ 0 & 0 & 1 & 0 \\ -x_p & -y_p & -z_p & 1 \end{bmatrix}$$

$$\therefore P' = P \cdot T$$

For alignment of three axes, it is required that the three co-ordinate axis rotations depending on the direction choose for N. In general, if N is not aligned with any world co-ordinate axis, the viewing and the world co-ordinate system can be aligned with the transformation sequence R_x, R_y, R_z. That is, first rotate around the world x_w axis to bring z_v into the $x_w z_w$ plane. Then rotate around the world y_w axis to align z_w and z_v axes. Finally, rotate about the z_w axis to align the y_w and y_v axes. In case of left handed view reference system, a reflection of one of the viewing axes is also necessary.

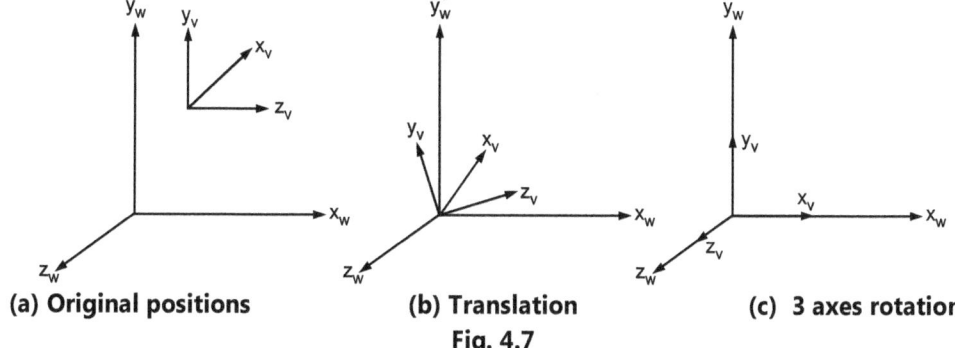

(a) Original positions (b) Translation (c) 3 axes rotation

Fig. 4.7

This is illustrated in above figure. Therefore, the composite transformation matrix is given as,

$$T_c = T \cdot R_x \cdot R_y \cdot R_z$$

There is another way to generate composite rotation matrix. A composite rotation matrix can be directly generated by calculating unit u, v, n vectors. If N and V is known the unit vectors are calculated.

$$n = \frac{N}{|N|} = (n_1, n_2, n_3)$$

$$u = \frac{V \times n}{|V \times N|} = (u_1, u_2, u_3)$$

$$v = n \times u = (v_1, v_2, v_3)$$

This method of generating composite rotation matrix automatically adjusts the direction of v so that v is perpendicular to n. The composite rotation matrix for the viewing transformation is –

$$R = \begin{bmatrix} u_1 & v_1 & n_1 & 0 \\ u_2 & v_2 & n_2 & 0 \\ u_3 & v_3 & n_3 & 0 \\ 0 & 0 & 0 & 1 \end{bmatrix}$$

This transforms u onto the world x_w axis, v onto the y_w axis and n onto the z_w axis. This matrix automatically performs the reflection necessary to transform a left-handed viewing system onto the right-handed world system.

With second method, the composite transformation matrix is –
$$T_C = T \cdot R$$

4.4 GENERALISED CLIPPING

All the clipping routines are more or less identical. They differ only in the test for determining whether a point is inside or outside and through their parameters, information about boundary is passed. These routines would be entered four times. Every time with a different boundary specified by its parameters. The routine is generalized so that it can clip along any line including horizontal and vertical boundaries. This can clip along rectangular windows parallel to the axis along the arbitrary lines i.e. window sides may be at any angles. The algorithm is a recursive language that can be used to clip along an arbitrary convex plane.

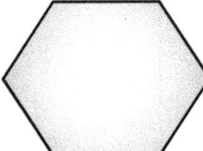

Fig. 4.8: Windows With Eight Clipping Points

4.5 INTERIOR AND EXTERIOR CLIPPING

So far we have discussed only algorithms for clipping point, line and polygon to the interior of a clipping region by eliminating everything outside the clipping region. However, it is also possible to clip a point line or polygon to the exterior of a clipping region, i.e. the point, portion of line and polygon which lie outside the clipping region. This is referred as "**exterior clipping**".

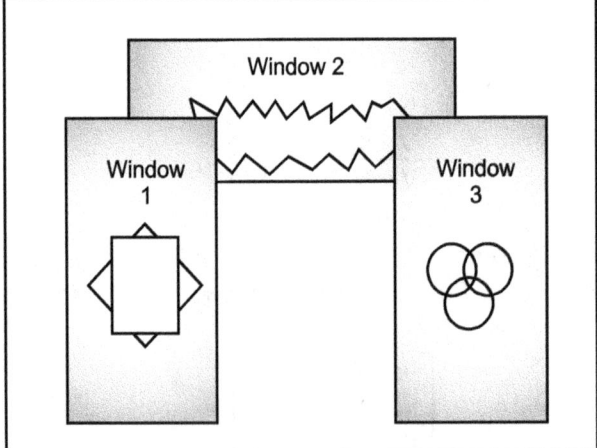

Fig. 4.9: Clipping is Multiwindow Environment

Exterior clipping is important in a multiwindow display environment, as shown in above figure 4.9. The figure shows the overlapping windows with window 1 and window 3 having priority over window 2. The objects within the window are clipped to the interior of that window. When other high-priority windows such as window 1 and/or window 3 overlap these objects, the objects are also clipped to the exterior of the overlapping windows.

4.6 POLYGON CLIPPING

A polygon is nothing but a collection of line segments. Thus, clipping a polygon can be considered as clipping each line segment in collection of line segments. But if the polygon is clipped in this way then a clipped polygon becomes one or more open polygon or discrete lines.

Since, polygon is a close contour, a clipped polygon must also be closed contour. This is due to clipping each of line segments in collection of line segments individually and generating a list of clipped line segments. The above problem can be solved. If a list of vertices is considered which defines the polygon and then starting with the first vertex and then keep on considering each vertex in list of vertices in turn and finding out whether the line segments from previous vertex to current vertex crosses window edge under consideration. Then compute the intersection and output it.

If the current vertex is visible then the output is also visible and save point as previous point for next vertex. Thus, the list of all those vertices will be generated which lies on the visible side of the window boundary. When these vertices are joined they will give a window boundary under consideration. Thus, generate an another window edge and for each window edge in turn, finally list those vertices which when joined gives clipped polygon.

This idea is used by Sutherland Hodgman's Algorithm for clipping polygon.

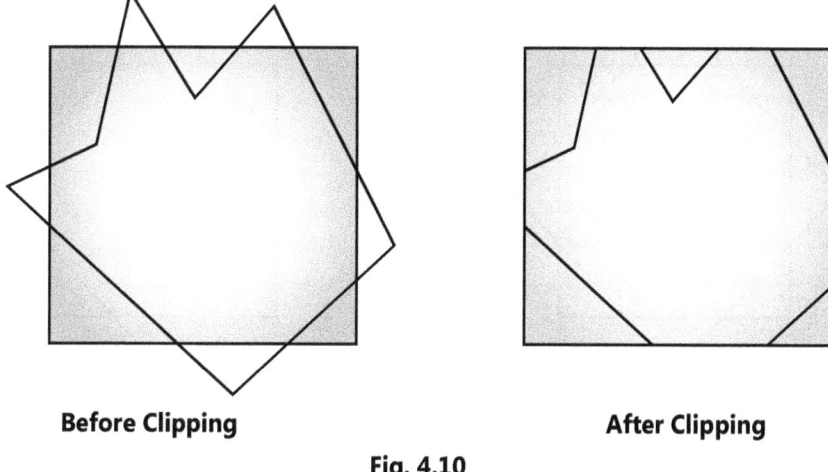

Before Clipping　　　　　　　　　　　**After Clipping**

Fig. 4.10

4.6.1 Sutherland – Hodgman's Algorithm

The Sutherland-Hodgmann's algorithm clips the original polygon against the simple window edge for obtaining intermediate polygon, by generating list of vertices. It then re-enters the procedure with intermediate polygon, which was generated in previous step and next window edge in the way, when it re-entered with last window edge it generates the list of vertices, which gives a clipped polygon.

The process of clipping against a particular window edge is as follows:
1. Consider $P_1, P_2, ..., P_n$ be the vertices of original polygon. Start with P_1 being the first point, save it as f for closing the polygon. Then save the same point P_1 as S, as a starting point. Then the visibility of P_1 is tested for next vertex. If the point lies on the visible side of window edge under consideration then, it will be written in the output list.
2. Then the second vertex P_2 is considered, since P_2 is not a first point, it must be checked whether the line from the starting point S to P_2, which is current vertex, crosses the window edge or not. If it crosses the edge under consideration, the point of intersection 'i' is computed and written down into output list. Next, the visibility of vertex P_2 is tested. If the vertex P_2 lies on visible side, it will be listed into the output list. Then, P_2 is saved as S, before going for next step.
3. The last step is to close a polygon. For closing a polygon, check whether the line SF crosses the window edge under consideration, where S denotes P_n and F denotes P_1. If it is, so then calculate the point of intersection and write it into the output list.

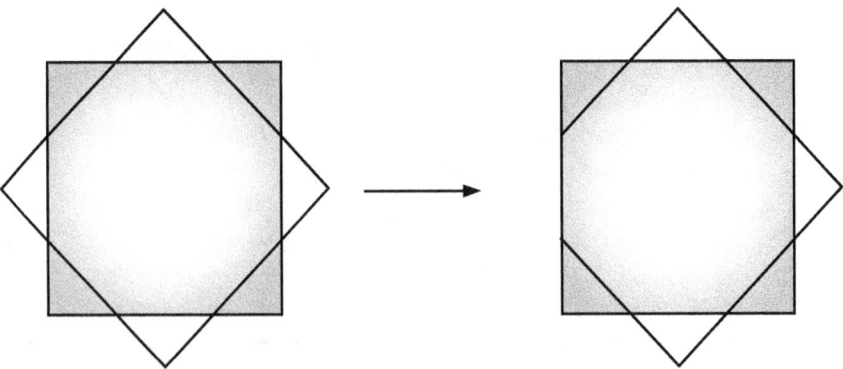

Fig. 4.11: Ist Intermediate Polygon

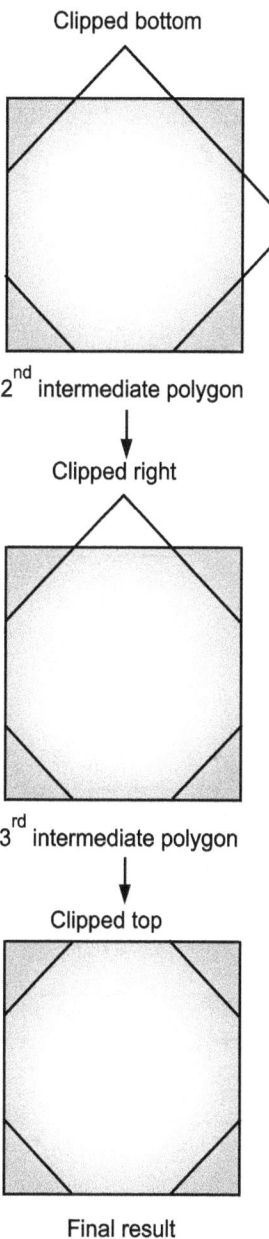

Fig. 4.12

Limitation:
1. It requires separate clipping routine, one for each boundary of the clipping window.

Flowchart for Sutherland Hodgman's Algorithm:
For Clipping Polygon:

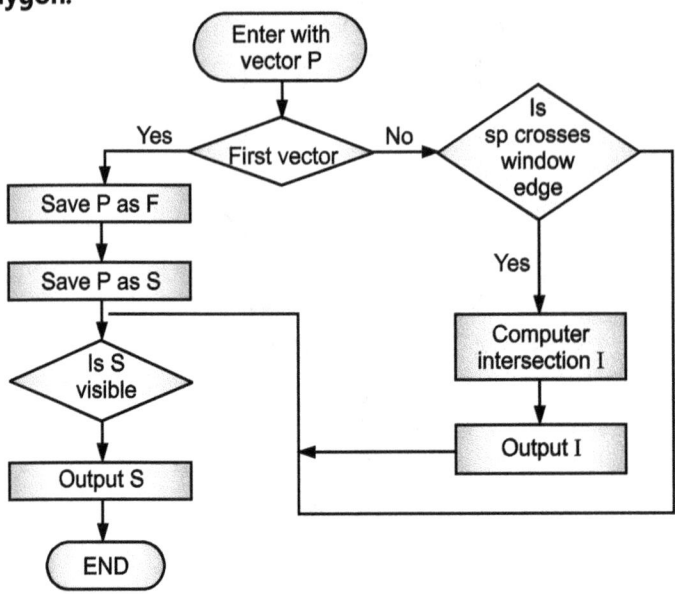

Fig. 4.13

For Closing:

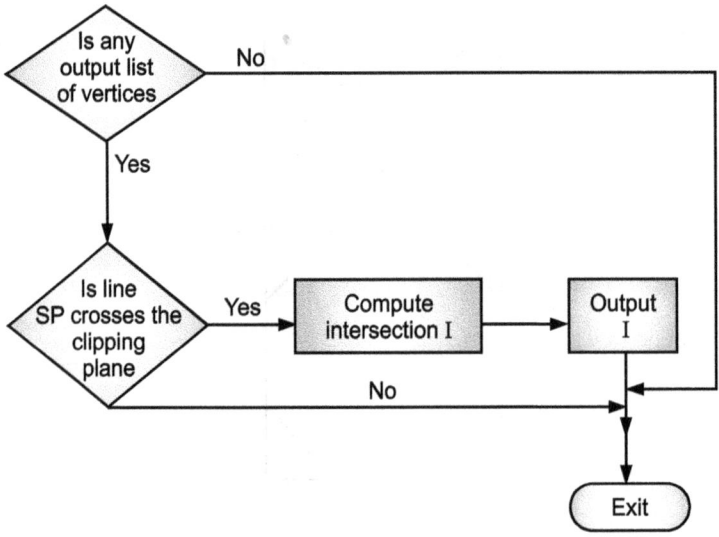

Fig. 4.14

4.7 INTRODUCTION

To obtain different views of a scene a perspective projection is developed which makes constructed object look more realistic. But for a realistic scene, only those lines and polygons are drawn which could actually would be seen, not those which would be hidden by other objects. What is hidden and what is visible depends upon the point of view of the observer. For instance, if a building is viewed from front, the front of the building is visible while the back is hidden but as seen from the rear, this situation is reversed. The contents of the building are not visible from outside as they are hidden by the buildings walls. In the projection of a three dimensional objects all parts of the objects are always displayed. This gives our drawings a transparent quality. Such figures are referred as wire frame drawings, as they look if they are wire outlines of the supposedly solid objects. Complex objects look like a confusing clutter of line segments. It is very difficult to identify which lines belong to the front of the object and which to the back. Thus, the removal of hidden portions of object is very essential in order to produce realistic looking images. This task could be assigned to the machine, then the user will be free to construct the entire model from front, back, inside and outside and still be able to see it as it will actually appear. This requires lot of parallel processing and extensive computation. There exist many solutions to the hidden surface and line problem, such as back-face detection and removal, painter's z-buffer etc.

4.8 HIDDEN SURFACE REMOVAL ALGORITHMS
4.8.1 Back Face Removal Algorithm

- Hidden-line removal is a costly process hence it is advisable to apply easy tests to simplify the problem as much as possible before undertaking a thorough analysis.
- Back-face removal is a simple test which can be performed to eliminate most of the faces which cannot be seen.
- This test identifies surfaces which face away from the viewer. The back of the object cannot be visible because bulk of the object is in the way.
- This does not completely solve the hidden-surface problem because still the front face of an object is obscured by a second object or by another part of itself. But the test can remove roughly half of the surfaces from consideration and thus simplify the problem.
- In this algorithm only polygon is considered as lines cannot obscure anything and although they might be obscured they are usually found only as edges of surfaces of an object.
- Because of this, polygons suffice for most drawings. Now, a polygon has two surfaces, a front and a black, just as a piece of paper does.
- We might picture our polygons with one side painted light and the other painted dark. But the question is "how to find which surface is light or dark"? When we are looking at the light surface, the polygon will appear to be drawn with counter clockwise pen motions and when we are looking at the dark surface the polygon will appear to be drawn with clockwise pen motions as shown below in Fig. 4.15.

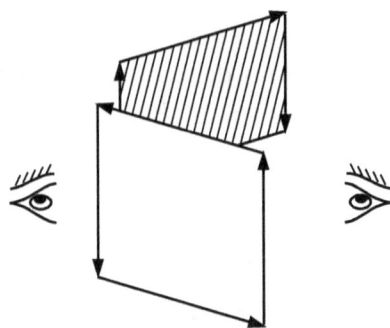

Fig. 4.15: Drawing Directions

- Let us assume that all solid objects are to be constructed out of polygons in such a way that only the light surfaces are open to the air, the dark faces meet the material inside the object.
- This means that when we look at an object face from the outside, it will appear to be drawn counter clockwise as shown in below figure Fig. 4.16.

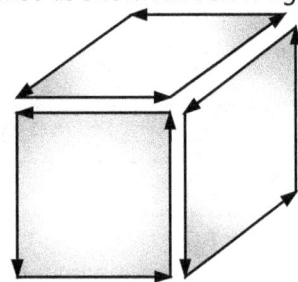

Fig. 4.16: Exterior Surfaces are Coloured Light

- If a polygon is visible, the light surface should face towards us and the dark surface should face away from us. Therefore, if the direction of the light face is pointing towards the viewer, the face is visible (a front face), otherwise the face is hidden (a back face) and should be removed.
- The direction of the light face can be identified by examining the light.

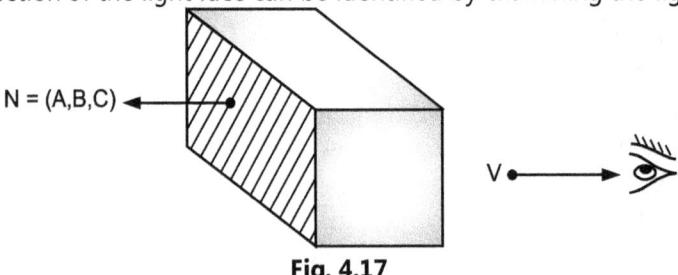

Fig. 4.17

$$N \cdot V > 0$$

where, N : Normal vector to the polygon surface with Cartesian components (A, B, C)

V : A vector in the viewing direction from the eye or camera position

We know that the dot product of two vectors gives the product of the lengths of the two vectors times the cosine of the angle between them. This cosine factor is important to us because if the vectors are in the same direction ($0 \leq \theta < \pi/2$) then the cosine is positive and the overall dot product is positive. However, if the directions are opposite ($\pi/2 < \theta \leq \pi$) then the cosine and the overall dot product is negative.

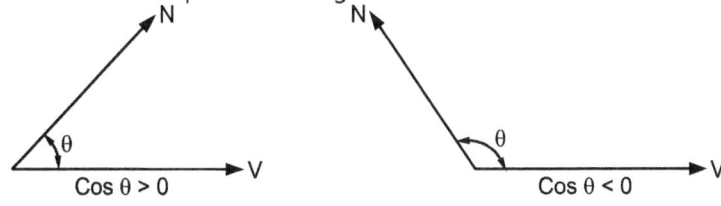

Fig. 4.18

Cosine angles between Two Vectors:

If the dot product is positive, then the polygon faces towards the viewer otherwise it faces away and should be removed.

In case, if object description has been converted to projection co-ordinates and our viewing direction is parallel to the viewing Z_V axis then $V = (0, 0, V_Z)$ and

$$V \cdot N = V_Z C$$

So that we only have to consider the sign of C, the Z component of the normal vector N. Now, if the Z component is positive then the polygon faces towards the viewer, if negative it faces away.

4.8.2 Binary Space Partition Algorithm

The Binary Space Partitioning (BSP) tree visible surface algorithm assumes that for a given viewpoint a polygon is correctly rendered if all the polygons on its side away from the viewpoint are rendered first, then the polygon itself is rendered; and finally all the polygons on the side near to the viewpoint are rendered. It is a two-part algorithm, in which, a scene is subdivide into two sections at each step with a plane that can be at any position and orientation.

The BSP tree algorithm uses one of the polygons in the scene as the separating or dividing plane. Other polygons in the scene that are entered on one side of the separating plane are placed in the appropriate half space. Polygons that intersect the separating plane are split along the separating plane and each portion is placed in the appropriate half space. Each half space is then recursively subdivided using one of the polygons in the half space as the separating lane. This subdivision continues until there is only a single polygon in each half space. The subdivided space is conveniently represented by a binary tree. This is shown in figure below. Here, for simplicity, each of the polygons and the separating plane are assumed perpendicular to paper.

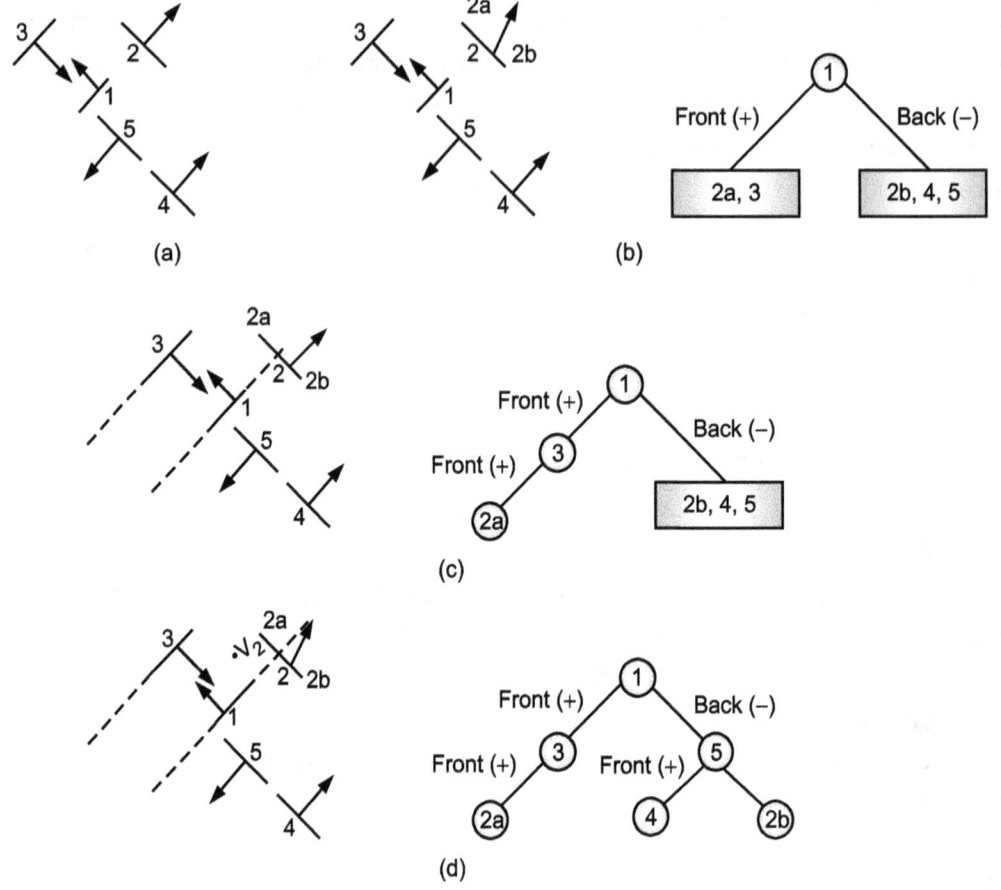

Fig. 4.19: Binary Tree

4.8.3 Z-Buffer Algorithm

This algorithm is the simplest of all hidden surface removal (HSR) algorithms. This technique is commonly used to eliminate the hidden surfaces of the object, which are to be displayed. The z-buffer algorithm is also referred as depth buffer algorithm. Mr. Edwin Catmull had developed it in the year 1975. This algorithm examines the visibility of the surface of one point at a particular time.

The Z-buffer is an extension of frame buffer idea. Z-buffer is nothing but a separate depth buffer which is used to store the Z co-ordinates or the depth of every visible pixel in the image space or video memory. Thus, two buffers are needed for the implementation of this algorithm Z-buffer (depth buffer) and a frame buffer.

Working:
The working of the algorithm is very simple. The frame buffer contains the Z-value or depth of a new pixel, which is then compared with the depth of that pixel stored in the Z-buffer. If

the comparison shows that the new pixel is infront of the pixel stored in the frame buffer, then the new pixel is written to the frame buffer and the Z-buffer is updated with the new Z-value, otherwise no action is taken.

Example:

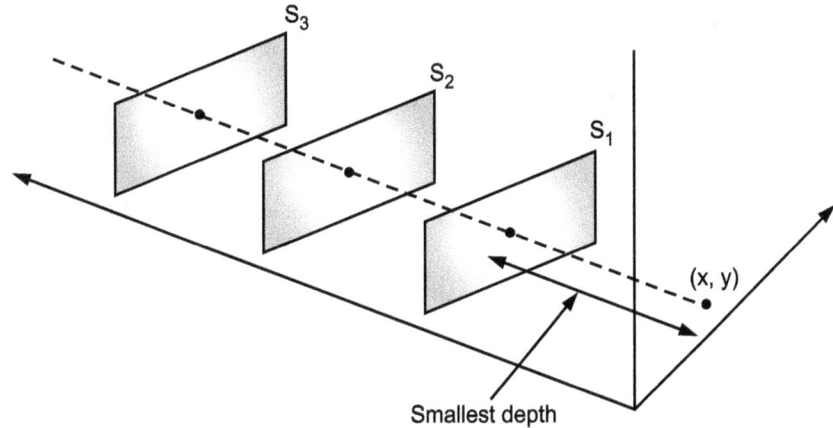

Fig. 4.20: Smallest Depth

As shown in figure 4.20 from position (x, y) surface S_1 has the smallest depth value i.e. it is the nearest surface from position (x, y) and hence it is visible at that position.

Algorithm:
Firstly, set the frame buffer to the background intensity and also set the Z-buffer to the minimum Z-value. To calculate the Z-value or depth at each (x, y) position, scan convert the each in arbitrary order. Calculate the depth Z(x, y) at that pixel. The calculated Z-value is then compared with the value previously stored in the Z-buffer at that location. If the calculated Z-value is less than the value stored in the Z-buffer i.e. Z-buffer (x, y) < Z (x, y) then replace Z-buffer (x, y) with Z(x, y) otherwise, no action is taken and next pixel is considered.

The steps for Z-buffer algorithm can be summarised as follows:
(a) Initialise the Z-buffer (depth-buffer) and frame buffer for all the co-ordinate position (x, y).
(b) For each position on each surface, compare the Z-values to previously stored values in the Z-buffer for determining visibility (i) calculate the z-value for each (x, y) position on surface (ii) If Z < depth (x, y) set depth (x, y) = Z.

If Z is not less than the value of the Z-buffer, then that point is not visible at that position. After the process has been completed for all surfaces, the Z-buffer contains the Z-values for all visible surfaces.

Advantages:
1. It is easy to implement.
2. It can be implemented in hardware to overcome the speed problem.
3. Since the algorithm processes objects one at a time, the total number of polygons in a picture can be arbitrarily large.

Disadvantages:
1. It requires an additional buffer and hence the large memory.
2. It is a time-consuming process as it requires comparison for each pixel instead of for the entire polygon.
3. The implementation of transparency and antialiasing is somewhat difficult by using Z-buffer algorithm.

4.8.4 Painter's Algorithm

This algorithm is also referred as depth sort algorithm or priority algorithm. **Newell**, who used the property of frame buffer, has developed this algorithm. The algorithm gets its name from the manner in which an oil painting is created. If he wishes, he can fill the entire canvas with the background scene. For painting the foreground object, there is no need to erase the background portion, the artist simply paints on top of them. The new paint will cover the old one so that the only newest layer of paint is visible. This is illustrated in Fig. 4.21.

  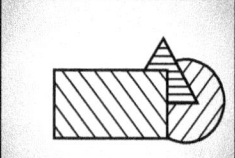

Fig. 4.21: Painter's Algorithm

In the similar manner the painter's algorithm processes polygons. More distant polygon are painted first and then the nearer polygons are painted over the more distant polygon, partially or totally obscuring them from view.

The basic idea behind this is to find the priority ordering of the polygons in order to determine which polygon is to be painted first. The hidden surface algorithm can be used by choosing the correct order to draw them and taking advantage of the properties of frame buffer.

In the hidden surface algorithm, it is possible to use image as well as the object space. The painter's algorithm or the depth sorting method is the combination of these two approaches and can perform the two basic functions given below:
1. The surfaces are sorted in order of decreasing depth.
2. Surfaces are scan converted in the order starting with the surface of greater depth.

The sorting operations are performed in object and the scan conversion of polygon surface is carried out in the image space.

Working:
- Painting of polygon surfaces onto the frame buffer, according to the depth is performed in several steps.
- In the first step, the surfaces are ordered according to the largest Z-value on the each surface. The surface having the greatest depth i.e. S is then compared with the other surfaces to determine whether there are any overlaps in depth. If there is no depth overlap occurs than the surface 'S' will be scan converted.
- The process is repeated for the other surfaces in the list until no overlaps occur, each surface is processed in the depth order and all will be scan converted.
- Suppose the depth overlap is detected at any point in the list, then some additional comparisons, are needed to determine whether any of the surface should be reordered.

- The following tests are needed to be done, for each surface overlaps. If anyone of these tests is true, no reordering is essential for that surface. The tests are listed below in order of increasing difficulty.
    (a) The bounding rectangle is the x-y plane for the two surfaces does not overlap.
    (b) Relative to the view plane, the surface 'S' is on the outside of the overlapping surface.
    (c) Relative to the view plane, the overlapping surface is on the inside of surfaces.
    (d) The projections of the two surfaces on the view plane do not overlap.
    (e) The x-extent of two surfaces does not overlap.
    (f) The y-extent of two surfaces does not overlap.

When any of the tests is found to be true for an overlapping surface, it has been clear that surface is not behind S. Then we will proceed to the next surface that overlap S. there is no need to done reordering of surfaces, if all the overlapping surfaces pass at least one of the above tests and then S can be scan converted otherwise for that overlapping surface say S, interchange surface S and S' in the sorted list. Then continue the process.

4.8.5 Warnock's Algorithm

This algorithm is based on the hypothesis of how human-eye, brain combination processes the information present in a scene. The hypothesis is that the majority of the time is spent on the areas containing large amount of information whereas for perceiving the areas containing little information, a very little time is spent.

Working:

This algorithm considers a window in the image space. It seeks to determine whether the window is empty or the contents of the window are simple enough to display. Otherwise the window is subdivided until the contents of subwindow will be simple enough to display or the size of subwindow will be at the limit of desired resolution. In the latter case, the remaining information in the window is evaluated and the result is displayed at the single intensity or colour.

The implementation of Warnock's algorithm vary in the method of subdividing the window. And also to decide the criteria whether the contents are simple enough to be displayed.

In the original Warnock's algorithm window is subdivided into four equal subwindow while in case of polygonal window the subdivision of window is decided according to the method developed by Weiler-Atherton.

The figures below illustrates the simple implementation of the algorithm. Here, a window, which is to be displayed is subdivided into four equal windows. Furthermore, a window that contains anything is always subdivided until the resolution of the display has been reached.

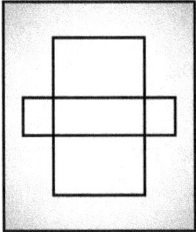

Fig. 4.22

Fig. 4.22 is composed of two simple polygon i.e. a horizontal rectangle and a vertical rectangle.

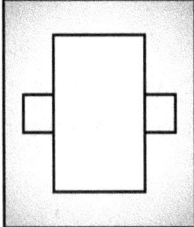

Fig. 4.23

Now, the hidden lines are removed. Hence, the figure 4.23 will be as shown. Here, the horizontal rectangle is partially hidden by vertical rectangle.

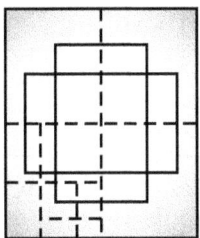

Fig. 4.24

Fig. 4.24 shows the process of subdivision for display. The subdivision process depends on the resolution. For example for 256 × 256 resolution ($2^8 = 256$) i.e. maximum of 8 subdivisions are required to reach the resolution of display.

- The subdivisions are done in a specific order such as lower left, lower right, upper left and upper right.
- The subwindows that are empty must be displayed at the back-ground intensity during the time of subdivision. It is very essential to determine whether the hidden line or hidden surface algorithm is to be applied after the detection of non-empty subdivision.
- If the hidden surface algorithm is desired, then the pixel-sized subdivision will be examined to see whether it is surrounded by any one of the polygons in the scene. If yes then all the polygons surrounding the pixel i.e. smallest subdivision are tested to identify the polygon, which is closest to the pixel location. The test must be performed at the pixel center. Then the pixel will be displayed at the intensity or colour of the closest polygon. In case, if surrounding polygon is found, it indicates that the pixel-sized window is empty and it will be displayed at the background intensity or colour.
- If the hidden line algorithm is desired then the pixel corresponding to non-empty subdivision is activated since a visible edge passes through it. Then the visible edge is displayed as a series of dots, and the empty windows are set at the background intensity.
- The process of continuous subdivision results into the generation of a tree structure for the subwindows where the display window is the root of a tree. Each node is represented by a box which contains the co-ordinates of the lower eight left corner and the length of the side of the subwidow. The subdivided windows are processed in the order a, b, c, d i.e. from left to right at a particular subdivision level in the tree, the tree structure will be as follows:

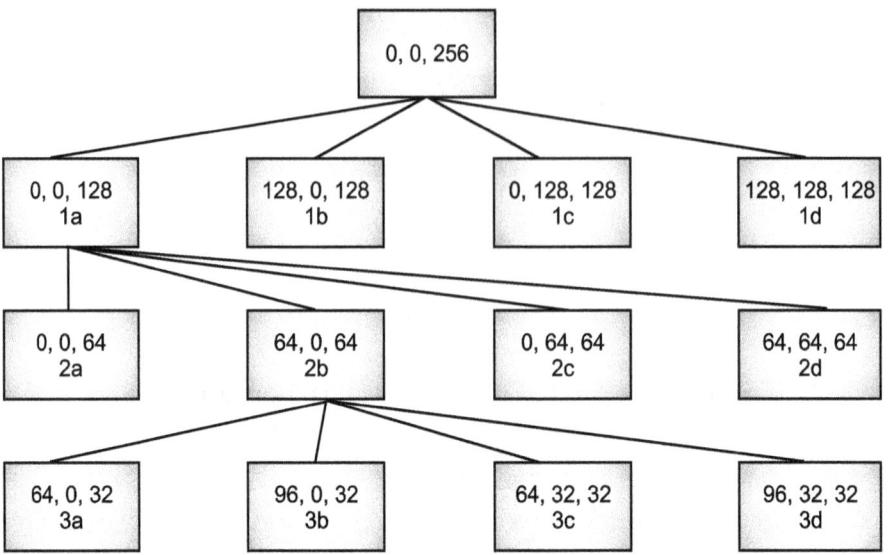

Fig. 4.25: Tree Structure

- The advantage of Warnock's algorithm is that the implementation of antialiasing can be carried out by the sub-division process to less than display pixel resolution and averaging the subpixel attributes to determine the display pixel attributes.

4.8.6 Scan-Line Algorithm

This algorithm is developed by Carpenter [CAR76]. A large amount of memory is needed for a Z-buffer because each polygon is processed independently. As each polygon is rasterized, we must be able to remember the depth of each of its pixels so that they may be compared against later polygons. A polygon may be as large as screen, so a full-screen Z-buffer is needed. But the memory requirements can be reduced by processing all of the polygons together on a scan-line by scan-line basis. This in effect is repeatedly doing a Z-buffer hidden-surface removal of a screen that is only one pixel high (a single scan line). The z-buffer only needs to hold one scan line's worth of depth information. When one scan line is done, save the result and then reinitialize the Z-buffer and move to the next scan line. Then perform the next scan line Z-buffer sort. The advantage of this algorithm is that all polygons are processed together. Instead of considering all scan lines for a polygon before moving onto the next polygon we consider all polygons for a scan line before moving onto the next scan line.

There is an another approach of scan line algorithm where Z-buffer is not required. In this approach, a scan line cuts a polygon, a line segment or span is described. These spans are then sorted for the scan lines hidden-surface removal. To order them, we need to determine the depth of the spans at a few points. The intersecting points are the span endpoints. At the x-position where a span begins, compare its depth with that of the other span active at that point to decide which is closest to the viewer. Similarly, when a span ends, which of the remaining spans active at that point could be shown. But often we can get by with even less work. Usually, each scan line looks much like its neighbours and hence can be used to simplify the calculation. If faces do not interpenetrate and the order in x of the span ends does not change from one scan line to the next then the depth ordering is the same for the two scan lines and no new sorting in Z is needed. The depth ordering is required only when the sweep through the scan lines encounters a new polygon, passes a polygon, or finds a change in the order of span end points.

4.9 HIDDEN-LINE METHOD

The hidden surface techniques such as painter's algorithm are not sufficient for calligraphic displays. On such displays we must not draw the hidden portions of lines. Thus, for each line, we must decide not only what objects lie in front of it but also how those objects hide it.

The first approach is to compare lines with objects. For each object, it considered relevant edges to see if the object hide them. The object might not hide an edge at all or might hide it entirely. It might hide an end, making the visible portion of the edge smaller or hide the middle, making two smaller visible line segments. After comparing of the line and object, the resulting visible line segments are compared in turn to the remaining objects. A segment which survives comparison to all objects are drawn.

There is no need to compare the line against all of the polygon edges in an object in order to determine whether the object hides the line. The only edges which can change whether the line is visible or not are those on the boundary where a front face meets a back face. These are called **contour edges**. The contour edges can be determined by examining the object. For a solid object, each edge has two polygons adjacent to it. If the polygons which meet at the edge are both front faces or both back faces then we have an interior edge but if one is a front face and the other a back face then it is a contour edge.

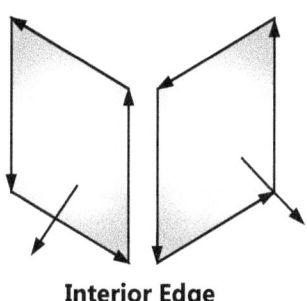   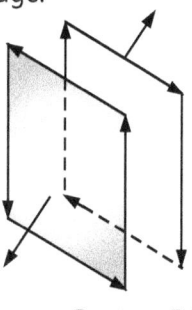

Interior Edge   **Contour Edge**

Fig. 4.26

Another approach is to compare all lines to each object. We can compare the contour edge of all objects to each line. For each intersection of a line with a contour edge, the line either passes behind an object or emerges from it. So with each such intersection, the number of faces hiding the line either increases or decreases by 1. This is referred as **quantitative invisibility**. This method find the quantitative invisibility for an initial point on a line and then follow along the connected lines to find intersection with the contour edges to maintain the quantitative invisibility. The portions of the lines with quantitative invisibility 0 are drawn.

EXERCISE

1. What is windowing and clipping? What do you mean by interior and exterior clipping?
2. Can line clipping be used for polygon clipping? Justify.
3. Explain Cohen-Sutherland Algorithm with the help of suitable example.
4. Explain the concept of generalized clipping with the help of a suitable example.
5. What is line clipping and polygon clipping?
6. Describe Sutherland-Hodgman polygon clipping algorithm? What is its limitation?
7. What is the necessity for 3D-clipping and windowing algorithm? Explain any one 3-D clipping algorithm.
8. Explain 2D mid-point subdivision algorithm for line clipping with suitable example.
9. Explain the concept of generalized clipping with the help of a suitable example.
10. Explain binary space partition algorithm for hidden surfaces.
11. Explain backface removal algorithm.
12. How does z-buffer algorithm determine which surfaces are hidden?
13. Explain the Phong model.
14. Explain the painter's algorithm in detail.
15. Why are hidden surfaces algorithm needed? How does Z buffer algorithm determine which surfaces are hidden?
16. Explain Warnocks algorithm for hidden surfaces.

UNIT V

LIGHT, COLOUR AND SHADING

5.1 LIGHT, COLOUR AND SHADING

This portion consider the shading of three dimensional objects. How to automatically set the polygon interior styles to give further realism to the image. In this chapter, we shall develop a model for the manner in which light sources illuminate objects and use this model to determine how bright each polygon face should be. We shall discuss how colours are described and how the model may be extended to coloured objects.

5.1.1 Diffused Illumination

An object illumination is an important as its surface properties computer its intensity. The object may be illuminated by light which does not come from any particular source but which comes from all directions. When such illumination is uniform from all directions, the illumination is called diffuse illumination. Usually, diffuse illumination is a background light which is reflected from walls, floors and ceiling.

Diffused Reflection:

When we assume that going up, down, right and left is of same amount then we can say that the reflections are constant over each surface of the object and they are independent of the viewing direction. Such a reflection is called diffuse reflection. In practice, when object is illuminated, some part of light energy is absorbed by the surface of the object while the rest is reflected. The ratio of the light reflected from the surface to the total incoming light to the surface is called **coefficient of reflection** or the **reflectivity**. It is denoted by R. It is closer to 1 for white surface and closer to 0 for black surface. This is because white surface reflects nearly all incident light whereas black surface absorbs most of the incident light. Reflection coefficient for gray shades is in between 0 to 1. In case of colour object reflection coefficient are various for different colour surfaces.

5.1.2 Point Source Illumination

Point source emits ray from a single point and they can approximate real world sources such as a small incandescent bulbs or candles. A point source is a direction source, whose all the rays come from the same direction, therefore, it can be used to represent the distant sun by approximating it as an infinitely distant point source.

The modeling of point sources requires additional work because their effect depends on the surface's orientation. If the surface is normal to the incident light rays, it is brightly illuminated. The surfaces turned away from the light sources are less brightly illuminated. For oblique surfaces, the illumination decreases by a factor of cos I, where I is the angle between the direction of the light and the direction normal to the surface plane. The angle is known as **angle of incidence**.

$$\cos I = N \cdot L$$

L = Vector of length one unit pointing towards the light source
N = Vector of length 1 in the direction normal to surface plane
$I_{ldiff} = K_a I_a + K_d I_l (\cos I)$
$\quad\quad = K_a I_a + K_d I_l (N - L)$
$K_a I_a$ = Intensity of light coming from visible surface
I_l = Intensity comes from point source

5.2 REFLECTION

When we illuminate a shinny surface such as polished metal or an apple with a bright light, we observe highlight or bright spot on the shinny surface. This is called as **reflection**.
Light can be reflected from an object in two ways:
  (i) Diffuse reflection
  (ii) Specular reflection

The diffuse reflection depends only upon the angle of incidence and the reflected light can be coloured, since the coefficient of reflection is involved.

Specular reflection occurs at the surface of a mirror. Light is reflected in nearly a single direction, not spread out in directions in accordance with **Lambert's law**. Plastics and many metals have a specular reflection which is independent of colour, all colours are equally reflected. For specular reflection, light comes in, strikes the surface, and bounces right back-off. The angle that the reflected beam makes with the surface normal is called the **angle of reflection** and is equal in magnitude to the angle of incidence, as shown in figure 5.1.

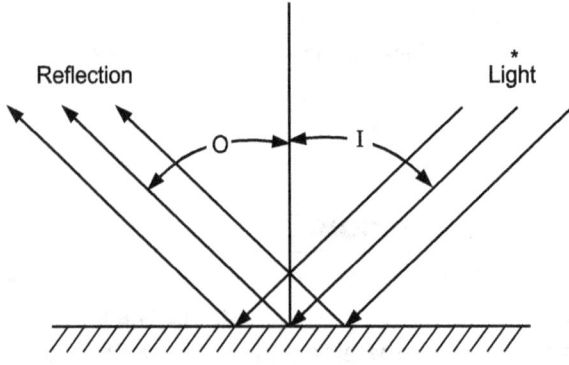

Fig. 5.1: Specular Reflection

5.3 SHADOWS

A shadowed object is one which is hidden from the light space. It is possible to use hidden surface algorithms to locate the areas where light sources produce shadows.

(I) One approach to the shadow problem is to repeat the hidden-surface calculation using the light source as the viewpoint. This second hidden-surface calculation divides the polygons into shadowed and unshadowed groups. Surfaces which are visible and which are also visible from the light source are shown with both the background illumination and the light-source illumination. Surfaces which are visible but which are hidden from the light source are displayed with only the background illumination.

(II) Another approach to the shadow problem is the use of shadow volumes. For this consider a polygon and a light source. There is a volume of space hidden from the light by the polygon. This is the polygon's shadow volume. Now, all other visible polygons can be compared to this volume. Portions which lie inside of the volume are shadowed. Their intensity calculation should not include a term from this light source. Polygons which lie outside the shadow volume are not shaded by this polygon, but might be shaded by some other polygon so they must still be checked against the other shadow volumes.

(III) Some other approaches that can be used for simplicity are assumed that all polygons are converted and then by using the generalized clipping techniques to find shadowed areas. Z-buffer techniques can also be used to simplify the sorting.

Shadow from point source of light are sharp and harsh. In the real world, we rarely find light coming from points. The sun and moon are disks, artificial light comes in a variety of shapes. Shadows from these finite shapes have softer edges.

5.4 RAY TRACING

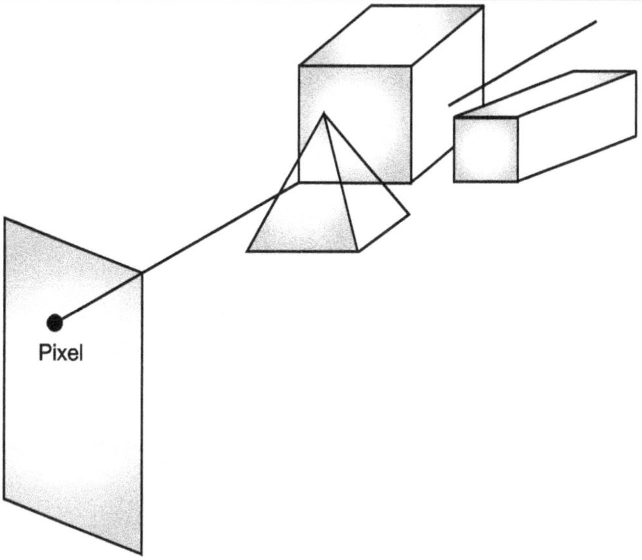

Fig. 5.2: A Ray Along the Line Sight from a Pixel Position Through a Scene

If we consider the line of sight from a pixel position on the view plane through a scene as shown in figure 5.2, we can determine which objects in the scene (if any) intersects this line. From the intersection points with different object, we can identify the visible surface as the one whose intersection point is closest to the pixel. Ray tracing is an extension of this basic idea. Here, instead of identifying for the visible surface for each pixel, we continue to bounce the ray around the picture. This is illustrated in figure 5.3.

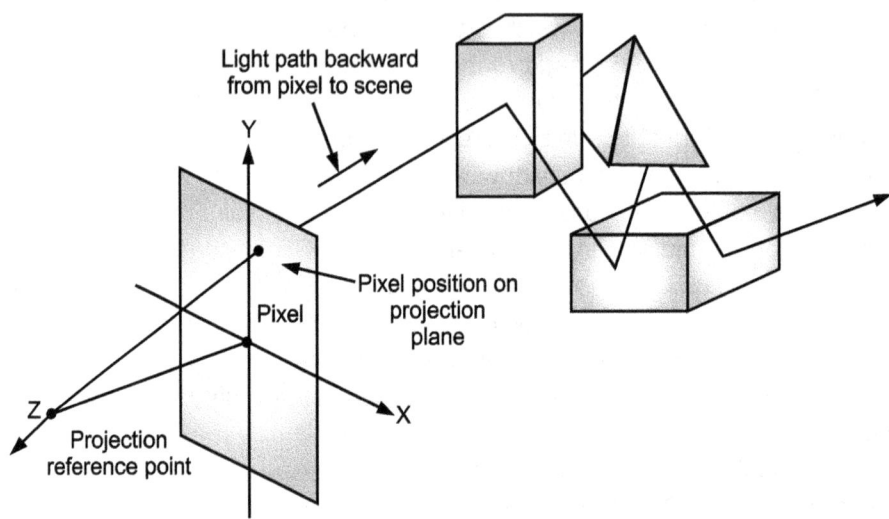

Fig. 5.3

When the ray is bouncing from one surface to another surface it contributes the intensity for that surface. This is a simple and powerful rendering technique for obtaining global reflection and transmission effects.

As shown in the figure 5.3, usually pixel positions are designated in the xy-plane and projection reference point lie on the Z-axis i.e. the pixel screen area is centered on viewing co-ordinate origin, with this co-ordinate system the contributions to a pixel is determined by tracing a light path backward from the pixel to the picture.

For each pixel ray, each surface is tested in the picture to determine if it is intersected by the ray. If surface is intersected, the distance from the pixel to the surface intersection point is calculated. The smallest calculated intersection distance identifies the visible surface along a specular path where the angle of reflection equals angle of incidence. If the surface is transparent, the ray is passed through the surface in the refraction direction. The ray reflected from the visible surface or passed through the transparent surface in the reflection direction is called **secondary ray**. The ray after reflection or refraction strikes another visible surface. This process is repeated recursively to produce the next generations of reflection and refraction paths.

5.5 COLOUR TABLE

Now-a-days, most of the display devices are capable of generating a large variety of colours. They have 8-bits of control over each of the red, green and blue channels. Therefore, they can have 256 intensity levels. With 256 intensity levels of each colour they can produce 16, 777, 216 different colours. To specify the colour of any pixel 24-bits (8-bits per colour) are required. To store 24-bit information of each colour in the frame buffer is not cost-effective. Therefore, in normal practice only few colours are specified in the tables called colour table. A colour table allows us to map between a colour index in the frame buffer and a colour specifications.

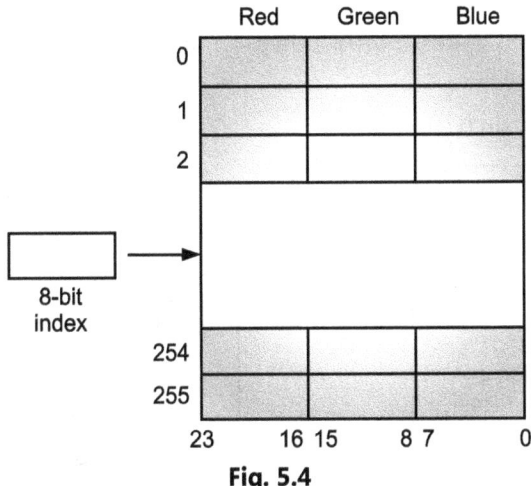

Fig. 5.4

5.6 TRANSPARENCY

A transparent surface in general may receive light from behind as well as from front i.e. it produces both reflected and transmitted light. It has a transparency coefficient T as well as values for reflectivity and specular reflection.

The coefficient of transparency depends on the thickness of the object because the transmission of light depends exponentially on the distance which the light ray must travel within the object. The expression for coefficient of transparency is given as

$$T = te^{-ad}$$

where, t is coefficient of property of material which determines how much of light is transmitted at the surface instead of reflected.

a is coefficient of property of material which tells how quickly the material absorbs or attenuates the light.

d is the distance the light must travel in the object.

The transparency and absorption coefficients can depend on colour. Some object allows us only red light while other attenuate red and blue letting only green to pass through. While dealing with coloured objects, three pair of transparency and absorption coefficients will be needed. For very clear objects, we can neglect the attenuation with distance or include it as an average value as part of (t).

When light crosses the boundary between two media it changes the direction as shown in figure. This effect is called **refraction**.

The direction of the refracted light is specified by the angle of refraction (θ_r). It is the function of the property materials called the **index of refraction (η)**. The angle of refraction (θ_r) is calculated from the angle of incidence θ_i the index of refraction η_i of the incident material and the index of refraction η_r of the refracting material according to Snell's law, given as:

$$\sin \theta_r = \frac{\eta_i}{\eta_r} \sin \theta_i$$

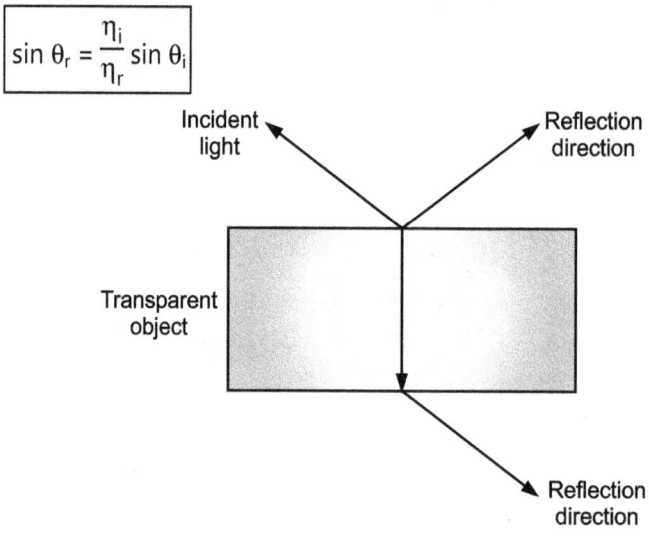

Fig. 5.5

5.7 COLOUR MODELS

5.7.1 HSV Colour Model

- The HSV colour model is user oriented. It uses colour descriptions that have a more intuitive appeal to a user.
- The colour specification in HSV model can be given by selecting a spectral colour and the amounts of white and black that are to be added to obtain different shades, tints and tones.
- This model uses three colour parameter: hue (H), saturation (S) and value (V).
- Hue distinguishes among colours such as red, green, purple and yellow.
- Saturation refers to how far colour is from a gray of equal intensity. For example, red is highly saturated whereas pink is relatively saturated. The value V indicates the level of brightness.

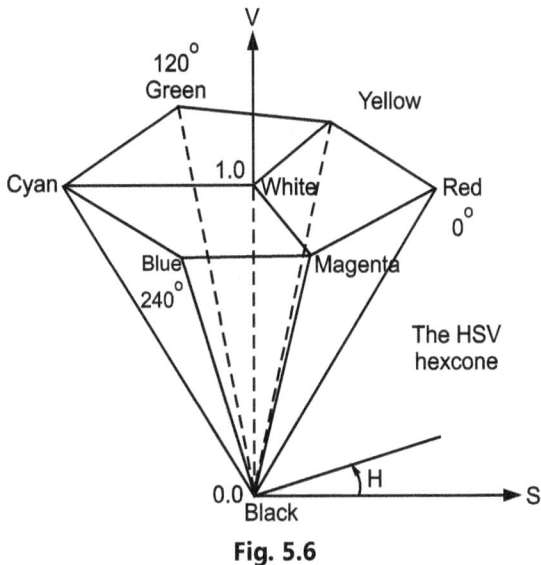

Fig. 5.6

- The model shown in Fig. 5.6 uses cylindrical co-ordinate system and the subset of the space within which, model is defined as a hexcone or six-sided pyramid.
- The top of the hexcone is derived from the RGB. If we imagine viewing the cube along the main diagonal from the white vertex to the origin (black), we see an outline of the cube that has the hexagone shape shown in Fig. 5.7.

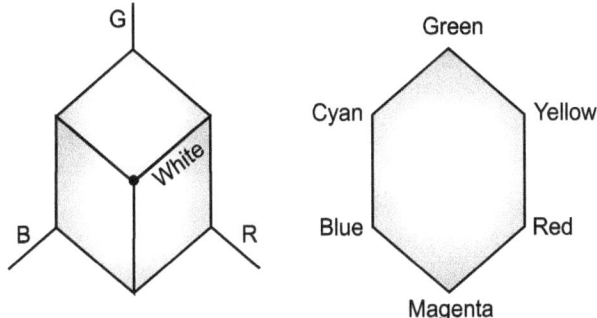

Fig. 5.7

- This boundary of cube is used as a top if hexcone and it represents various hues.
- Hue or H is measured by the angle around the vertical axis with red at 0°, green at 120° and so on as shown in the figure 5.6 of HSV hexcone.
- Complementary colours in the HSV hexcone are 180° apart saturation parameter varies from 0 to 1. Its value is the ratio ranging from 0 on the center line (X axis) to 1 on the triangular sides of the hexcone.
- The value V varies from 0 at the apex of the hexcone to 1 at the top.
- The apex represents black.

- At the top of the hexcone, colours have their maximum intensity; when V = 1 and S = 1, we have the pure hues.
- For example, pure red is at H = 0, V = 1 and S = 1, pure green is at H = 120, V = 1 and S = 1, pure blue is at H = 240, V = 1 and S = 1 and so on.
- The required colour can be obtained by adding either white or black to the pure hue.
- Black can be added to the selected hue by decreasing the setting for V while S is held constant. On the other hand, white can be added to the selected hue by decreasing S while keeping V constant. To add some black and some white we have to decrease both V and S.
- The point S = 0 and V = 1, we have white colour. The intermediate values of V for S = 0 (on the center line) are gray shades. Thus, when S = 0; the values of H is irrelevant.
- When S is not zero, H is relevant. At the apex V co-ordinate is 0. At this point the values of H and S are irrelevant.

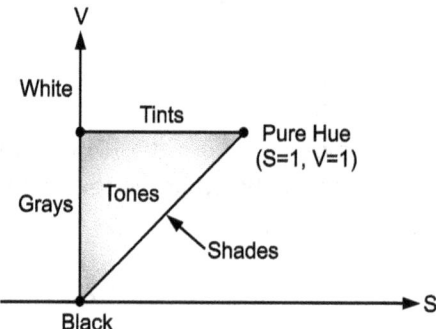

Fig. 5.8: Cross-Sectional Panel of HSV showing Tints, Tones, Shades

Fig. 5.8 shows the cross-sectional plane of the HSV hexcone. This plane represents the colour concepts associated with the term shades, tints and tones.
- As shown above, we can add to black colour to pure hue to produce different shades of the colour.
- White colour to pure hue to produce different tints of the colour.
- Both white and black colours to pure hue to produce tones of the colour.

5.7.2 HLS Colour Model

Another model based on intuitive colour parameters in the HLS colour model used by Tektronir. The three colour parameters in this model are hue (H), lightness (L) and saturation. It is represented by double hexcone as shown in figure 5.21.

The hue specifies the angle around the vertical axis of the double hexcone. In this model, H = 0 corresponds to blue. The remaining colours are specified around the perimeter of the hexcone in the same order as in the HSV model. Magneta is at 60°, red is at 120° and yellow is located at H = 180°. Again, complementary colour are 180°, apart on the double hexcone.

The vertical axis in this model represents the lightness, L. At L = 0, we have black and at L = 1, we have white. In between value of L we have gray levels. The saturation parameters S varies from 0 to 1 and it specifies relative purity of a colour.

At S = 0, we have the gray scale and at S = 1 and L = 0.5, we have maximum saturated hue. As S decreases the hue saturation decreases i.e. hue becomes less pure.

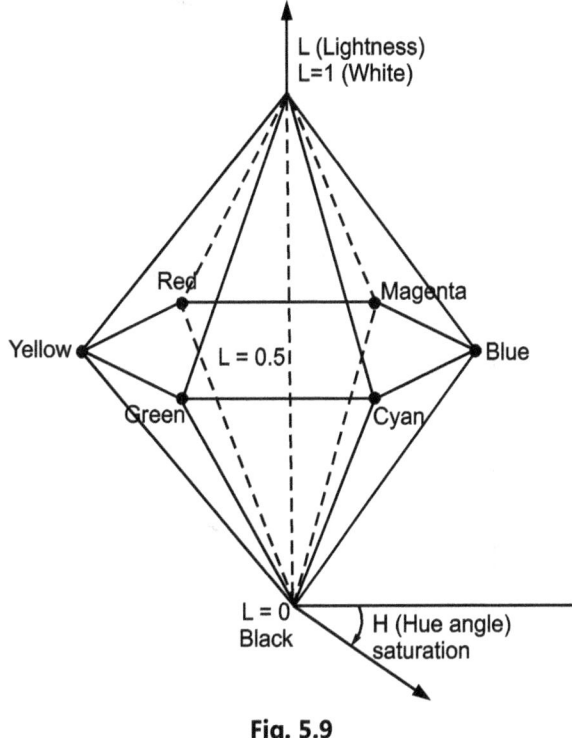

Fig. 5.9

In HLS model, a hue can be selected by selecting hue angle H, and the desired shade, tint or tone can be obtained by adjusting L and S. The colours can be made lighter by increasing L and can be made darker by decreasing L. The colour can be moved towards grays by decreasing S.

5.7.3 CMY Colour Model

In this model, cyan, magneta and yellow colours are used as a primary colour. This model is used for describing colour output to hard-copy devices. Unlike video monitor, which produce a colour pattern by combining light from the screen phosphors, hard copy devices such as plotters produce a colour picture by coating a paper with colour pigments.

The subset of the Cartesian co-ordinate system for the CMY model is the same as that for RGB except that white (full light) instead of black (no light) is at the original colours are specified by what is removed or subtracted from white light, rather than by what is added to blackness. We know that, cyan can be formed by adding green and blue light. Therefore, when white light is reflected from cyan coloured ink, the reflected light does not have red component. That is red light is absorbed as subtracted by the ink. Similalry, magneta ink subtracts the green component from incident light and yellow subtracts the blue component. Therefore, cyan, magneta and yellow are said to be complements of red, green and blue respectively.

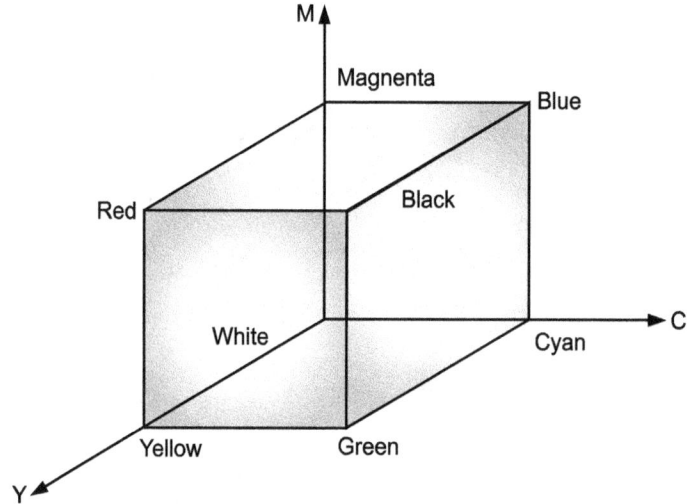

Fig. 5.10: CMY Cube

The above Fig. 5.10 shows the cube representation for CMY Model.

As shown in the figure point (1, 1, 1) represents black, because all components of the incident light are subtracted. The point (0, 0, 0), the origin represents the white light. The main diagonal represents equal amount of primary colours thus the gray colours. A combination of cyan and yellow produces green light, because the red and blue components of the incident light are absorbed. Other colour combinations are obtained by a similar subtractive process.

It is possible to get CMY representation from RGB representation as follows:

$$\begin{bmatrix} C \\ M \\ Y \end{bmatrix} = \begin{bmatrix} 1 \\ 1 \\ 1 \end{bmatrix} - \begin{bmatrix} R \\ G \\ B \end{bmatrix}$$

The unit column vector in the RGB representation for white, and the CMY representation for black. The conversion for RGB to CMY then can be given as,

$$\begin{bmatrix} R \\ G \\ B \end{bmatrix} = \begin{bmatrix} 1 \\ 1 \\ 1 \end{bmatrix} - \begin{bmatrix} C \\ M \\ Y \end{bmatrix}$$

5.7.4 RGB Colour Model

The Red-Green-Blue RGB model is generally used in computer graphics. It corresponds to Red, Green and Blue intensity settings of a colour monitor. We can represent this model with the unit cube defined on R, G and B axes. The origin represents black and the vertex with co-ordinates (1, 1, 1) is white as show as follows.

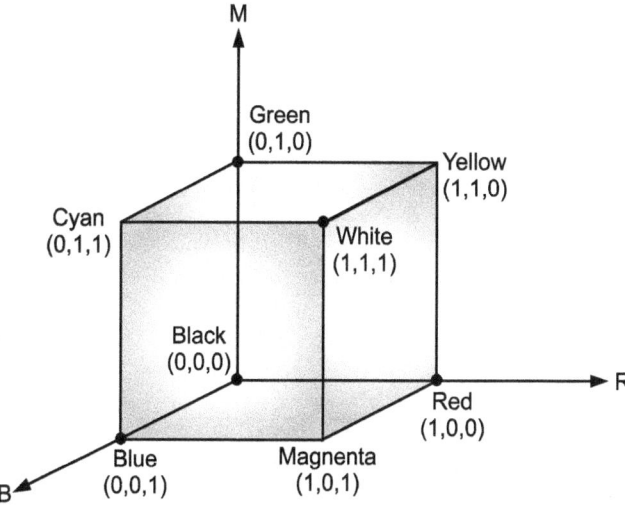

Fig. 5.11

RGB colour model is just an extension of XYZ model. Other colours are generated by adding intensities of primary colour such as Yellow (1, 1, 0) is a combination of Red and Green. Each colour is represented by a triplet (R, G, B). Chromacity co-ordinates for standard colour television i.e. NTSC standard and CIE RGB colour model are represented in tabular form.

	CIE Model	NTSC/Stand Television
R	(0.734, 0.265)	(0.670, 0.330)
G	(0.273, 0.717)	(0.210, 0.710)
B	(0.166, 0.008)	(0.140, 0.080)

5.7.5 Comparison Between RGB and HVS Model

RGB Model	HVS Model
1. In this model, the individual contribution of red, green and blue are added together to get the resultant colour.	1. This model uses three colour parameters. Hue (H), Saturation (S) and Value (V).
2. It uses Cartesian co-ordinate system.	2. It uses cylindrical co-ordinate system.
3. It is represented with the help of cube.	3. It is represented with the help of hexcone.
4. ![RGB cube diagram] Fig. 5.12	4. ![HVS hexcone diagram] Fig. 5.12

5.8 PHONG MODEL

Phong Bui-Tuong developed a popular illumination model for non-perfect reflectors. It assumes that maximum specular reflection occurs where ϕ is zero and falls off sharply as ϕ increases. This rapid fall-off is approximated by $\cos \phi$, where n is the specular reflection parameter determined by the type of surface. The values of n typically vary from 1 to several hundred, depending on the surface material. The larger values (say, 100 or more) of n are used for very shiny surface and smaller values are used for dull surfaces. For a perfect reflector, n is infinite. For rough surface, such as chalk, n would be near to 1.

5.9 SHADING

Shading is one of the major tool used to create images that are very realistic. Shaded images can create the impression that the images are real objects and not artificial ones. The advantages of using high quality shaded images are that they provide an easy, more effective and less costly way of reviewing various alternatives rather than building actual models or prototype. Once the geometric model of any object is prepared, the images are shaded and analysed to judge how the model will look like when it is finally released.

Shading models are also called as illumination models. They are used to calculate the intensity of light at a given point on the surface of object. Although the surface shading method is different. Surface shading method is referred as surface rendering method.

5.9.1 Gourand Shading

In this method, the intensity interpolation technique developed by Gourand is used, hence the name. The polygon surface is displayed by linearly interpolating intensity values across the surface. Here, intensity values for each polygon are matched with the values of adjacent polygons along the common edges. This eliminates the intensity discontinuities that can occur in flat shading.

By performing following calculations, we can display polygon surface with Gourand shading.

1. Determine the average and normal vector at each polygon vertex.
2. Apply an illumination model to easy polygon vertex to determine the vertex intensity.
3. Linearly interpolate the vertex intensities over the surface of the polygon.

We can obtain a normal vector at each polygon vertex by averaging the surface normals and all polygons sharing that vertex. This is illustrated in figure 5.13 shown below.

Fig. 5.13: Calculation of Normal Vector at Polygon Vertex, V

As such in above Fig. 5.13 there are three surface normals N_1, N_2 and N_3 for polygon sharing vertex V. Therefore, normal vector at vertex V is given as,

$$N_V = \frac{N_1 + N_2 + N_3}{|N_1 + N_2 + N_3|}$$

In general, for any vertex position V, we can obtain the unit vertex normal by equation,

$$N_V = \frac{\sum_{i=1}^{n} N_i}{\left|\sum_{i=1}^{n} N_i\right|}$$

where, n is the number of surface normals of polygons sharing that vertex.

5.9.2 Phong Shading

Phong shading also known as normal-vector interpolation shading interpolates the surface normal vector N, instead of the intensity. By performing following steps, we can display polygon surface using Phong shading:
1. Determine the average unit normal vector at each polygon vertex.
2. Linearly interpolate the vertex normals over the surface of the polygon.
3. Apply an illumination model along each scan line to determine projected pixel intensities for the surface points.

The first steps in the phong shading is same as first step in this Gourand shading. In the second step the vertex normals are linearly interpolated over the surface of the polygon. This is illustrated in Figure 5.14 as follows.

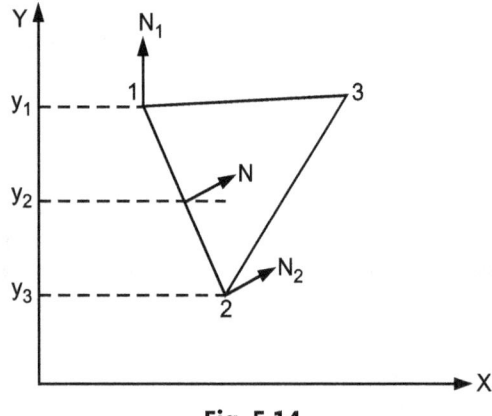

Fig. 5.14

As shown in above figure, the normal vector N for the scan line intersection point along the edge between vertices 1 and 2 can be obtained by vertically interpolating between edge end points normals:

$$N = \frac{Y - Y_2}{Y_1 - Y_2} N_1 + \frac{Y_1 - Y}{Y_1 - Y_2} N_2$$

Like, Gourand shading, here also we can use incremental method to evaluate normals between scan lines and along each individual scan line. Once the surface normals are evaluated the surface intensity at that point is determined by applying the illumination method.

5.9.3 Pseudo-C Algorithm for Gourand Shading

Gourand shading is a method for linearly interpolating a colour or shade across a polygon. It is a very simple and effective method of adding a curved feel to a polygon that would otherwise appear flat.

Firstly, calculate the gradient of shade across the line as usual:
$$\text{Gradient} = (B_s - A_s)/(B_x - A_x)$$
where,
$A_s \to$ Shade at A
$A_x \to$ x value of A

Now, calculate the exact value of the shade at C:
$$C_s = A_s + (1 - \text{frac}(A_x)) * \text{Gradient}$$

So, now you need to be able to render a trip of Gourand polygon to the screen. This involves calculating the shade of each pixel and writing it to the screen. This is a simple process, since the shade change linearly across the scan line. The process can be demonstrated by little Pseudo code.

$$\text{Shade} = C_s$$

Loop x from C_x to D_x

Plot pixel at (x, y) with colour shade.
$$\text{Shade} = \text{Shade} + \text{Gradient}$$

End of x loop.

5.10 GRAPHICAL USER INTERFACE

The graphical user interface, or "GUI", is a computer interface that uses graphic icons and controls in addition to text. The user of the computer utilizes a pointing device, like a mouse, to manipulate these icons and controls. This is considerably different from the command line interface (CLI) in which the user types a series of text commands to the computer.

A program interface that takes advantage of the computer's graphics capabilities to make the program easier to use. Well-designed graphical user interfaces can free the user from learning complex command languages. On the other hand, many users find that they work more effectively with a command-driven interface, especially if they already know the command language.

5.10.1 Features of GUI

Graphical user interfaces, such as Microsoft Windows and the one used by the Apple Macintosh, feature the following basic components:

- **pointer:** A symbol that appears on the display screen and that you move to select objects and commands. Usually, the pointer appears as a small angled arrow. Text - processing applications, however, use an I-beam pointer that is shaped like a capital I.
- **pointing device:** A device, such as a mouse or trackball, that enables you to select objects on the display screen.

- **icons:** Small pictures that represent commands, files, or windows. By moving the pointer to the icon and pressing a mouse button, you can execute a command or convert the icon into a window. You can also move the icons around the display screen as if they were real objects on your desk.
- **desktop:** The area on the display screen where icons are grouped is often referred to as the desktop because the icons are intended to represent real objects on a real desktop.
- **windows:** You can divide the screen into different areas. In each window, you can run a different program or display a different file. You can move windows around the display screen, and change their shape and size at will.
- **menus:** Most graphical user interfaces let you execute commands by selecting a choice from a menu.

The first graphical user interface was designed by Xerox Corporation's Palo Alto Research Center in the 1970s, but it was not until the 1980s and the emergence of the Apple Macintosh that graphical user interfaces became popular. One reason for their slow acceptance was the fact that they require considerable CPU power and a high-quality monitor, which until recently were prohibitively expensive.

In addition to their visual components, graphical user interfaces also make it easier to move data from one application to another. A true GUI includes standard formats for representing text and graphics. Because the formats are well-defined, different programs that run under a common GUI can share data. This makes it possible, for example, to copy a graph created by a spreadsheet program into a document created by a word processor.

Principles for Good GUI Design:
Following are some main important principles for good GUI design:
1. The user must be able to anticipate visual control's behaviour from it's visual properties.
2. The user must be able to anticipate behaviour of your program using knowledge gained from other program.
3. View every user warning and error dialog that your program generates as a an opportunity to improve your interface.
4. Provide adequate user feedback,
5. Use sound, colour, animation and multimedia clip sparingly.
6. Help users to customize and preserve their preferred work environment.
7. Design your interface so that users can do their task while being minimally aware of the interface itself.

Following figures demonstrates sample GUI screens.

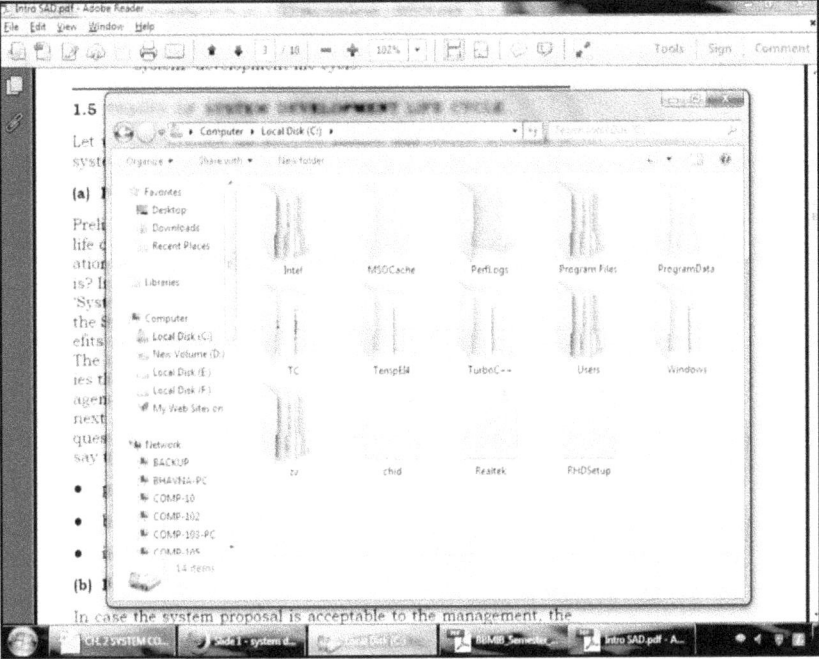

Fig. 5.15: Example screen of GUI in Windows

Fig. 5.16: Example screen of GUI in Windows

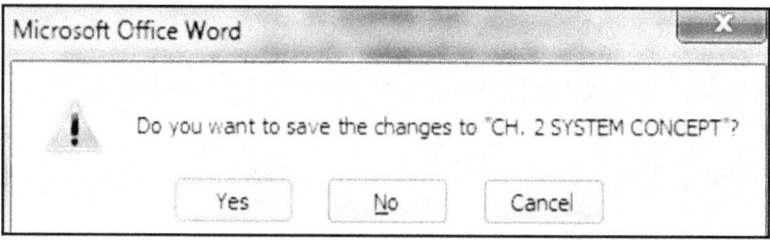

Fig. 5.17: Example Dialogue Box (GUI) of Windows

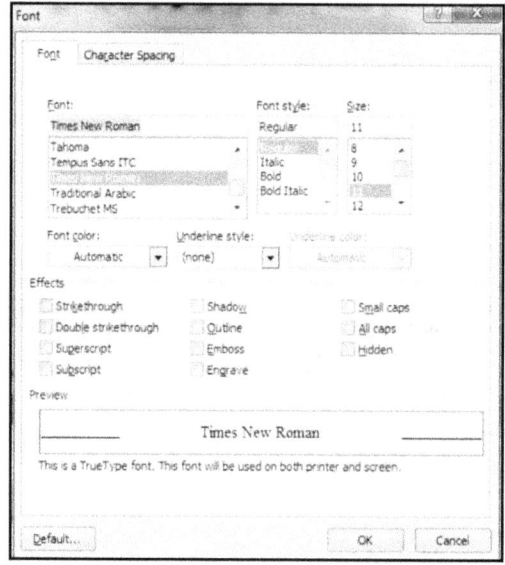

Fig. 5.18: Font Dialogue Box (GUI example)

Many DOS programs include some features of GUIs, such as menus, but are not graphics based. Such interfaces are sometimes called *graphical character-based user interfaces* to distinguish them from true GUIs

Graphical user interfaces were introduced in reaction to the steep learning curve of command line interfaces (CLI), which require commands to be typed on the keyboard. Since the commands available in command line interfaces can be numerous, complicated operations can be completed using a short sequence of words and symbols. This allows for greater efficiency and productivity once many commands are learned, but reaching this level takes some time because the command words are not easily discoverable. WIMPs ("window, icon, menu, pointing device"), on the other hand, present the user with numerous widgets that represent and can trigger some of the system's available commands.

WIMPs extensively use modes as the meaning of all keys and clicks on specific positions on the screen are redefined all the time. CLIs use modes only in the form of a current directory. Applications may also provide both interfaces, and when they do the graphical user interface is usually a WIMP wrapper around the command-line version. This is especially common with applications designed for Unix-like operating systems. The latter used to be implemented first because it allowed the developers to focus exclusively on their product's functionality without bothering about interface details such as designing icons and placing buttons.

5.11 GRAPHIC STANDARDS
5.11.1 Need for Standards

Graphics is well recognized as an effective means of communication. Some studies indicate that a graphic message is consciously recognized more than twice as fast as a text message. However, for years the use of graphics was limited to sophisticated mainframe systems because of the expense involved.

Complex graphic images require both extensive processing power and vast amounts of memory. Graphics quickly, moved into the: microcomputer environment when the size of processors and the price of memory decreased significantly.

However, this implementation of computer graphics was not widely spread because of incompatible devices and non-communicating software. Currently, graphics implementations are either written as a program for a specific device or custom installed for each graphics device.

Despite of these difficulties, graphics for use with personal computers became popular and users were in need of graphics. Certainly there is user demand for graphics, from simple menu pictorial symbols or icons, to elaborate window systems for concurrent display of data from different processes. But before personal computer graphics can really become widespread, a. standard architecture is needed for writing graphics applications and having them communicate with the huge diversity of available hardware.

From this background, it can be seen
1. Why better graphics has not been available for personal computers?
2. Why stronger efforts have not been made to standardize the production of graphics programs?

To assist in solving these problems, the American National Standards Institute (ANSI) has formed a technical committee to develop computer graphics standards.

Thus finally,

Graphics standards are provided for easy transfer of the graphics from one platform to another as there are many variations in display devices, software packages and even the graphical languages. Due to this reason the standards are developed which provides the portability.

The first standard to be accepted was the Graphical Kernel System (GKS), adopted in October 1984 and previously adopted by y the International Standards Organization. GKS defines graphics functions at the programmer level with specification of how those functions are assessed through high-level programming languages.

Other major graphics standards available are:
1. CORE
2. Programmer's Hierarchical Interactive Graphical Standard (PHIGS)
3. Initial Graphics Exchange Standard (IGES)
4. Computer Graphics Metafile Standard (CGM)
5. Virtual Device Metafile (VDM)
6. Virtual Device Interface (VDI)

Let's see these standards in short.

5.11.2 Graphical Kernel System (GKS)

The Graphical Kernel System (GKS) is a second standard also called as 2D version of CORE, it is also influenced by CORE.

The Graphical Kernel System (GKS) defines a common interface to interactive computer graphics for creating, manipulating and displaying or printing computer graphics on different types of computer graphics output devices

The Graphical Kernel System (GKS) was the first ISO standard for low-level computer graphics, introduced in 1977. GKS provides a set of drawing features for two-dimensional vector graphics suitable for charting and similar duties. The calls are designed to be portable across different programming languages, graphics devices and hardware, so that applications written to use GKS will be readily portable to many platforms and devices.

The Graphical Kernel System (GKS) is a document produced by the International Standards Organisation (ISO) which defines a common interface to interactive computer graphics for application programs. GKS has been designed by a group of experts representing the national standards institutions of most major industrialized countries. The full standard provides functional specifications for some 200 subroutines which perform graphics input and output in a device independent way. Application programs can thus move freely between different graphics devices and different host computers. For the first time, graphics programs have become genuinely portable.

However, one should point out that GKS itself is not portable. Individual GKS implementations will vary substantially as they have to support different graphics devices on different computers. Moreover, GKS is a kernel system, and thus does not include an arbitrary collection of functions to produce histograms or contour plots etc.

In order to allow particular applications to choose a graphics package with the appropriate capability, GKS has been defined to have different levels. The level structure has two dimensions, one for output (0, 1 or 2) and one for input (a, b or c). Higher levels include the capabilities of lower levels. In the United States, ANSI has defined also a level 'm', for very simple applications, which sits below output level '0'. Most implementations provide all output (level '2') and intermediate input (level 'b'). The reason input level 'c' is not usually supported is that it requires asynchronous input facilities not found in all operating systems.

The GKS functions have been defined independently from a specific programming language, and bindings to individual languages are subject to separate standard efforts which have been undertaken for all the major languages.

The Graphical Kernel System for two dimensional graphics was adopted as an ISO standard in 1985, and since that date work has been in progress to define a three dimensional superset which was accepted as an International Standard during 1988. The FORTRAN binding to GKS-3D has also been published as a Draft International Standard

The GKS functions are separated into those which pass values to GKS for control, setting or output, and those which inquire about status information. There are 8 distinct classes :
1. Control functions
2. Output attributes
3. Output primitives
4. Segment functions
5. Transformations
6. Input functions
7. Metafile functions
8. Inquiry functions

GKS-3D: A Three-Dimensional Extension to the Graphical Kernel System:
GKS-3D is nothing but a machine, language, operating system and device independent specification of a set of services for displaying and interacting with 2D and 3D pictures.

The three-dimensional Graphical Kernel System is designed to provide a basic set of 3D function with incorporating hidden-line/hidden-surface removal. Every attempt has been made to ensure full compatibility with GKS so that programs can run unmodified in the GKS-3D environment. For effective operation in a 3D environment.

The purpose of GKS-3D standards are:
1. For providing the portability of graphics application programs.
2. To assist in understanding of graphics method by application program

5.11.3 Core

CORE provides the standardized set of commands which controls the construction and display of graphics image. These commands are device independent that means "device which is used to create or display the graphics image and independent of the language in which the graphics programs were written." It provides a devices-independent viewing package that would other, more application-specific packages including modeling packages to be build on top. And hence the term "Core".

5.11.4 Programmer's Hierarchical Interactive Graphics System (PHIGS)

PHIGS - the Programmer's Hierarchical Interactive Graphics System is a programming library for 3D graphics. It is devised and maintained by the International Organisation for Standardisation (ISO), it is most commonly used on the X Window System and commonly available from several workstation venders. The PHIGS high-level graphics library contains over 400 functions ranging from simple line drawing to lighting and shading. Fully one-half of them let you determine the state of an output device or recall settings made earlier in a program. It provides to a graphics application a standard interface to display devices of any manufacturer that supports the PHIGS standard.

Before displaying a picture, the application first stores all its graphics information in the PHIGS graphics database. Thus, PHIGS is referred to as a "display list" system. The application then appears on one or more display devices and then passes the list to them. Because of its display list system structure, PHIGS is well-suited to applications that create a graphics model and then edit portions of it frequently or view it in different ways.

This basic version of PHIGS included the following major features:
- A editable hierarchical organization of graphics data called the structure store.
- A powerful logical input model in support of interaction devices.

- A workstation mechanism to allow support of multiple simultaneous input and output devices.
- 3D graphics primitives which could be specified using either 2D or 3D functions.
- Separate attributes based on primitive type.

Limitations of PHIGS:

PHIGS does not do many things necessary for photorealistic and advanced animation purposes.
- It does not do ray tracing.
- It doesn't compute shadows.
- It doesn't provide texture mapping.
- It limits the number of light sources.
- It deson't do depth cueing.

Thus, PHIGS is very appropriate for most engineering and industrial applications but may not be adequate for more advanced visualization.

5.11.5 Initial Graphics Exchange Standard (IGES)

Initial Graphics Exchange Standard has been a British standard since 1988. It is useful for exchanging data between different CAD/CAM systems. The difference between IGES (and similar standards) and CGM is that a CAD design incorporates the geometric modelling information plus information on materials, weights, costs etc. and all these are easily stored in an IGES file but not as easily in a CGM file. Like many other standards, the reality of importing IGES files does not match up to the dream and work has been done by ISO to develop STEP which has become an international standard. STEP (Standard for the exchange of product model data) includes conformance testing and it is being backed by the US government and all the major car and aerospace manufacturers and all national standards bodies.

IGES successfully met a critical need. The IGES Publication establishes information structures to be used for the digital representation and communication of product definition data. The specification is concerned with the data required to describe and communicate the essential engineering characteristics of physical objects such as manufactured products.

The Initial Graphics Exchange Specification is the U.S. national standard for the exchange of data between dissimilar CAD systems. The IGES standard, now in its sixth revision, has been expanded to include most concepts used in major CAD systems. All major and most minor non-PC-based CAD systems support some version of the IGES standard.

Applications:
1. The IGES file format can be used to transfer engineering models between Powershape and PATRAN.
2. Using IGES, a CAD user can exchange product data models in the form of circuit diagrams, wire frame, freeform surface or solid modeling representations.
3. Applications supported by IGES include traditional engineering drawings, models for analysis, and other manufacturing functions.

5.11.6 The Computer Graphics Metafile Standard (CGM)

The Computer Graphics Metafile standard was adopted by ISO in 1987 to enable transfer of pictures between various graphics packages or between different machines. For example, UNIRAS on the SUN systems could be used to create one picture and Cerel Draw on the PC could be used to create another picture. The two pictures could be combined and dressed up in GSHARP to produce another picture, which is then imported into Microsoft Word. Unfortunately, not all implementations of CGM incorporate all the variations available under the standard and so there are often difficulties in interpreting CGM files produced by different packages. Please ask for advice at the Helpdesk who will contact the Graphics Section for you.

CGM files contain snapshots, i.e. there is no information about the structure of the picture and there is no standard way of holding other data besides the picture data. This means that CAD packages often do not use CGM files to store designs or drawings for retrieval by other CAD packages. However, this standard for supporting storage of 2D graphical data has become popular and is important in the University community.

There are different requirements for the storage and retrieval of pictures. These are:
   (a) minimal file size,
   (b) ease of transfer across computer networks,
   (c) speed at which file can be generated and interpreted,
   (d) human readability of stored files.

To address these requirements, three encodings are defined in the CGM standard. These are:
- character encoding
- binary encoding
- clear text encoding

5.11.7 Virtual Device Interface (VDI)

It defines the standard way for a program to drive a graphics device. It is a standard developed by ANSI. It's main purpose is to provide a device independent way to control hardware. It is a lower level standard.

The role of the VDI is to provide device independence by creating a logical graphics device interface. Such an interface allows an application to control any graphics peripheral, regardless of individual peculiarities. For input devices, the VDI specifies the kinds of actions, such as pointing or string input, which an input device should be capable of performing. Similarly for output devices, the VDI specifies conceptual capabilities, such as the drawing of lines and polygons. The VDI developed by Graphic Software Systems provides for device independence through the following capabilities

- Device driver management.
- Co-ordinate transformation.
- Text models.
- Character I/O.
- Emulation of certain graphics primitives.
- Device inquiry.
- Error reporting.

5.11.8 Virtual Device Metafile (VDM)

It is a data format used to record pictures on disk files. A metafile is a means of permanent picture storage. It is also a graphics standard used to communicate graphical data between program or between computers. For example a graphics produced by one program may be read by other program.

5.12 ADVANTAGES OF GRAPHICS STANDARDS

Any ideal graphics software standard has a perfect device independence which allows it to operate all graphical input and output devices. Therefore advantages of such standard are as follows:
- The user can select any graphics hardware to upgrade graphics display.
- Being device independent, graphics generated based on these standards is economical for developer and user.
- Reuse of code in terms of ready routines is possible, and hence standard software packages can be used for developing other packages.
- It facilitates transport of application program from one computer to another.
- It also facilitates programmer portability.

5.13 HAZARDS OF GRAPHICS STANDARDS

Practically 100% ideal standard does not exist, and hence there are some of it's hazards, which are as follows:
- The given application may not run equally well on wide variety of devices.
- Poor definition of standard may create problems to the user.
- Standards once defined may create difficulties in accommodating new needs.
- The methods of the standard are treated as only suitable methods for solving problems, though there can be other suitable ones.

5.14 COMPUTER AIDED DESIGN

5.14.1 Computer Aided Design

Computer-aided design (CAD) is use of a wide range of computer based tools that assist engineers, architects and other design profession in their design activities. It is the main geometry authoring tool within the Product Lifecycle Management process and involves both software and sometimes special-purpose hardware. Current packages range from 2D vector base drafting systems to 3D solid and surface modellers.

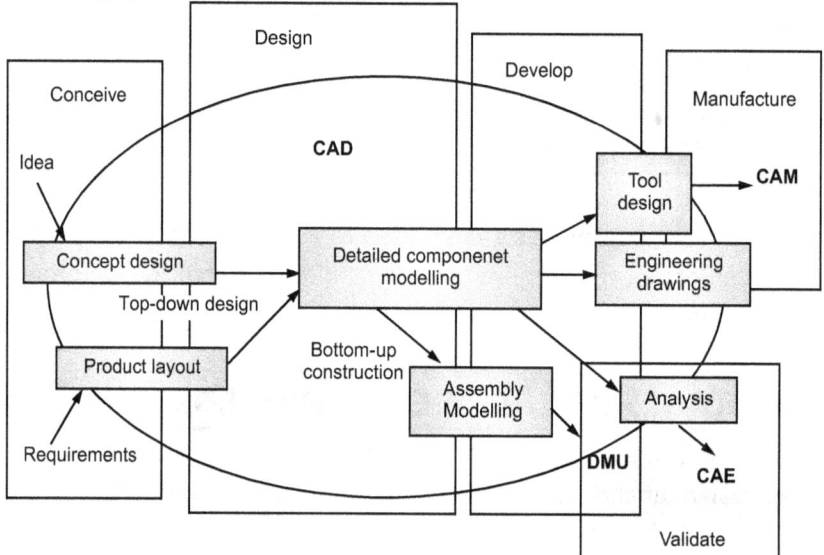

Fig. 5.19: The CAD Process

CAD is used to design, develop and optimize products, which can be goods used by end consumers or intermediate goods used in other products. CAD is also extensively used in the design of tools and machinery used in the manufacture of components, and in the drafting and design of all types of buildings, from small residential types (houses) to the largest commercial and industrial structures (hospitals and factories).

CAD is mainly used for detailed engineering of 3D models and/or 2D drawings of physical components, but it is also used throughout the engineering process from conceptual design and layout of products, through strength and dynamic analysis of assemblies to definition of manufacturing methods of components.

CAD has become an especially important technology, within the scope of Computer Aided technologies, with benefits such as lower product development costs and a greatly shortened design cycle. CAD enables designers to layout and develop work on screen, print it out and save it for future editing, saving time on their drawings.

The capabilities of modern CAD systems include (a) Wireframe geometry creation, (b) 3D parametric feature based modelling, Solid modeling, (c) Freeform surface modeling, (d) Automated design of assemblies, which are collections of parts and/or other assemblies, (e) create Engineering drawings from the solid models, (f) Reuse of design components, (g) Ease of modification of design of model and the production of multiple versions, (h) Automatic generation of standard components of the design, (i) Validation/verification of designs against specifications and design rules, (j) Simulation of designs without building a physical prototype, (k) Output of engineering documentation, such as manufacturing drawings, and Bills of Materials to reflect the BOM required to build the product, (l) Import/Export routines to exchange data with other software packages, (m) Output of design data directly to manufacturing facilities, (n) Output directly to a Rapid Prototyping or Rapid Manufacture Machine for industrial prototypes, (o) maintain libraries of parts and assemblies, (p) calculate mass properties of parts and assemblies, (q) aid visualization with shading, rotating, hidden line removal, etc, (r) Bi-directional parametric association (modification of any feature is reflected in all information relying on that feature; drawings, mass properties, assemblies, etc. and counter wise), (s) kinematics, interference and clearance checking of assemblies, (t) sheet metal, (u) hose/cable routing, (v) electrical component packaging, (x) inclusion of programming code in a model to control and relate desired attributes of the model, (y) Programmable design studies and optimization, (z) Sophisticated visual analysis routines, for draft, curvature, curvature continuity...

Originally software for CAD systems were developed with computer language such as Fortran, but with the advancement of object-oriented programming methods this has radically changed. Typical modern parametric feature based modeler and freeform surface systems are built around a number of key C programming language modules with their own APIs.

Today most CAD computer workstations are Windows based PCs; some CAD systems also run on hardware running with one of the Unix operating systems and a few with Linux. Some CAD systems such as NX provide multiplatform support including Windows, LINUX, UNIX and Mac OSX.

CAD of Jet Engine

CAD and Rapid Prototyping

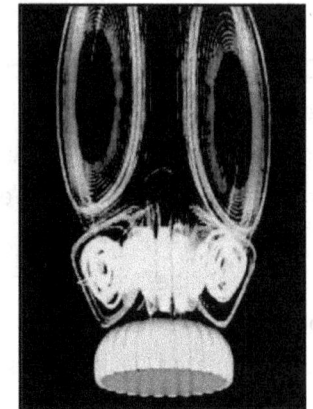
Parachute Modeling and Simulation

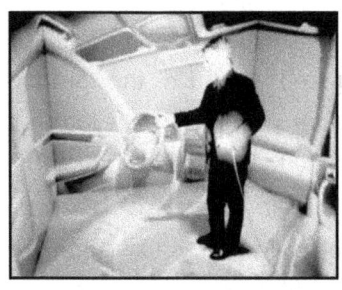
Virtual 3-D interiors (Virtual Environment)

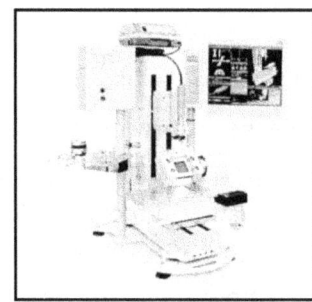
CAM (jewelry industry)

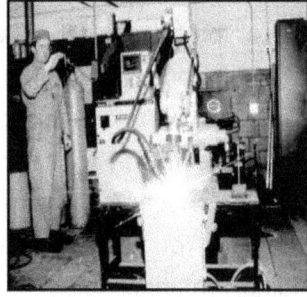
CAM

CAD design

CAM

CAD robot

Fig. 5.20

Generally no special hardware is required with the exception of a high end OpenGL based Graphics card; however for complex product design, machines with high speed (and possibly multiple) CPUs and large amounts of RAM are recommended. The human-machine interface is generally via a computer mouse but can also be via a pen and digitizing graphics tablet. Manipulation of the view of the model on the screen is also sometimes done with the use of a spacemouse/SpaceBall. Some systems also support stereoscopic glasses for viewing the 3D model.

5.14.2 Computer Aided Manufacturing

Since the age of the Industrial Revolution, the manufacturing process has undergone many dramatic changes. One of the most dramatic of these changes is the introduction of Computer Aided Manufacturing (CAM), a system of using computer technology to assist the manufacturing process.

Through the use of CAM, a factory can become highly automated, through systems such as real-time control and robotics. A CAM system usually seeks to control the production process through varying degrees of automation. Because each of the many manufacturing processes in a CAM system is computer controlled, a high degree of precision can be achieved that is not possible with a human interface. The CAM system, for example, sets the toolpath and executes precision machine operations based on the imported design. Some CAM systems bring in additional automation by also keeping track of materials and automating the ordering process, as well as tasks such as tool replacement.

Computer Aided Manufacturing is commonly linked to Computer Aided Design (CAD) systems. The resulting integrated CAD/CAM system then takes the computer generated design, and feeds it directly into the manufacturing system; the design is then converted into multiple computer-controlled processes, such as drilling or turning.

Another advantage of Computer Aided Manufacturing is that it can be used to facilitate mass customization: the process of creating small batches of products that are custom designed to suit each particular client. Without CAM, and the CAD process that precedes it, customization would be a time-consuming, manual and costly process. However, CAD software allows for easy customization and rapid design changes: the automatic controls of the CAM system make it possible to adjust the machinery automatically for each different order.

Robotic arms and machines are commonly used in factories, but these do still require human workers. The nature of those workers' jobs change however. The repetitive tasks are delegated to machines; the human workers' job descriptions then move more towards set-up, quality control, using CAD systems to create the initial designs, and machine maintenance.

5.14.3 Entertainment

One of the main goals of todays special effects producers and animators is to create images with highest levels of photorealism. Volume graphics is the key technology to provide full immersion in upcoming virtual worlds e.g. movies or computer games. Real world phenomena can be realized best with true physics based models and volume graphics is the tool to generate, visualize and even feel these models! Movies like Star Wars Episode I, Titanic and The Fifth Element already started employing true physics based effects.

Fig. 5.21: Entertainment Games

5.14.4 Medical Content Creation

Medical content creation has become more and more important in entertainment and education in the last years. For instance, virtual anatomical atlas on CD-ROM and DVD have been build on the base of the NIH Visible Human Project data set and different kind of simulation and training software were build up using volume rendering techniques. Volume Graphics' products like the VGStudio software are dedicated to the used in the field of medical content creation. VGStudio provides powerful tools to manipulate and edit volume data. An easy to use keyframer tool allows to generate animations, e.g. flights through any kind of volume data. In addition VGStudio provides highest image quality and unsurpassed performance already on a PC!

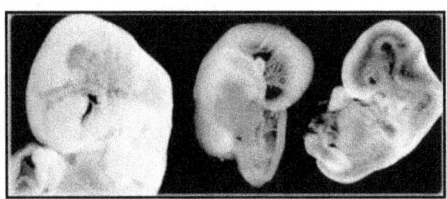

Fig. 5.22: Images of a fetus rendered by a V.G. Studio MAX user

5.14.5 Advertisement

Voxel data can be used to visualize the most fascinating and complex facts in the world. The visualization of the human body and medical content creation is an example. Voxel data sets like CT or MRI scans or the exciting Visible Human data show all the finest details up to the gross structures of the human anatomy. Images rendered by Volume Graphics 3D graphics software are already used for US TV productions as well as for advertising. Volume Graphics cooperates with companies specialized on Video and TV productions as well as with advertising agencies.

Fig. 5.23: Neutron Radiography of a car engine

5.14.6 Visualization

Visualization is any technique for creating images, diagrams, or animations to communicate a message. Visualization through visual imagery has been an effective way to communicate both abstract and concrete ideas since the dawn of man.

Visualization today has ever-expanding applications in science, engineering Product visualization, all forms of education, interactive multimedia, medicine etc. Typical of a visualization application is the field of computer graphics. The invention of computer graphics may be the most important development in visualization. The development of animation also helped advance visualization.

Visualization of how a car deforms in an asymmetrical crash using finite element analysis   **Computer aided Learning**

Fig. 5.24

Visualization is the process of representing data as descriptive images and, subsequently, interacting with these images in order to gain additional insight into the data. Traditionally, computer graphics has provided a powerful mechanism for creating and manipulating these representations. Graphics and visualization research addresses the problem of converting data into compelling and revealing images that suit users' needs. Research includes developing new representations of 3D geometry, choosing appropriate graphical realizations of data, strategies for collaborative visualization in a networked environment using three dimensional data, and designing software systems that support a full range of display formats ranging from PDAs to immersive multi-display visualization environments.

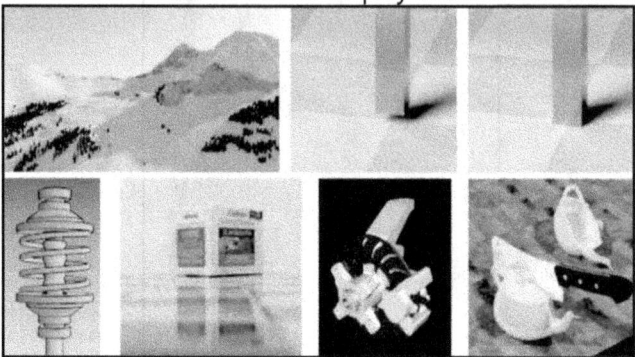

Fig. 5.25

EXERCISE

1. Explain HSV and HLS colour models.
2. Explain the Phong model.
3. Compare RGB and HVS model.
4. Explain CMY colour model.
5. Compare Gouand and Phong's method of shading.
6. Write a short note on Ray Tracing.
7. Describe:
   (i) Diffused illumination
   (ii) Point source illumination
8. Define:
   (i) Reflection, (ii) Shadows, (iii) Ray tracing, (iv) Colour tables
9. Write short notes on:
   (i) Ray tracing, (ii) Transparency
10. Compare RGB and CMY colour models.
11. Write short notes on following (any one):
    (i) Diffused illumination; (ii) Color models; (iii) Transparency; (iv) Shading algorithms.
12. Explain HSV and CMY colour model.
13. What is surface rendering? Explain Gourand method of shading.

***

www.ingramcontent.com/pod-product-compliance
Lightning Source LLC
Chambersburg PA
CBHW080242170426
43192CB00014BA/2540